# PRAISE FOR *LIVING LIFE IN THE ZONE*

"How do you balance your life; how do you stay *in the zone*? You stay strong in your Christian beliefs and make it the focal point of your life. I highly recommend *Living Life in the Zone* to you; you won't be sorry. Don't miss it!"

— **Lee Corso**
Analyst, ESPN *College GameDay*

"One of my most rewarding experiences in recent years has been sharing my Christian testimony at In The Zone events. In my profession, sports often conflicts with Sunday church attendance. But fellow believers in the world of sports will testify with me that when we submit to Christ's desire for a very personal 24/7 relationship, we receive a supernatural blessing that enables us to successfully navigate the conflicts of the professional world, family, and the Great Commission. *Living Life in the Zone* is an uplifiting instrument that inspires me to know we are not alone and life can be a mission accomplished!"

— **Chris Mortensen**
ESPN Sports

"As I travel across America, I have observed that most men—when totally honest—admit they are tired, lonely, and angry. The causes of those feelings are known to everyone; just look at today's headlines and around your neighborhood. In *Living Life in the Zone*, Joe and Kyle present practical, biblical wisdom for any man who wants to deepen his relationships with his most important teammates: his wife, his children, his friends, and his coworkers. Take this forty-day journey and watch how your life takes on new purpose and brings you truly great victories."

—

"We keep score in all our games—not just in sports but also in life: our bank accounts, our net worth, the square footage in our homes, the Boone and Crockett number of the last deer we killed, and the points scored in backyard basketball. As men, keeping score is what we do. But how are we scoring with the most important game of all—life? Like all games, it will end someday, and there *will* be a score, and God is keeping it. *Living Life in the Zone* is a practical and challenging book that helps us to see the scoreboard much clearer and make sure that when the final gun sounds, we end up winning. And I mean winning at what matters: marriage, raising kids, knowing God. In the time it takes to listen to the sports recap each day, you can spend a life-changing forty days knowing how to keep a score that really counts. On to the zone!"

— **Mike Huckabee**
FOX News

"Finally, here's a men's book that takes information and presents it in such a way that it can be transformational. *Living Life in the Zone* is a must-read for any man who is serious about his relationships with God and walking His talk in his life. Kudos to Joe and Kyle."

— **Rod Cooper, PhD**
Distinguished Fellow,
Gordon-Conwell Theological
Seminary

"Our society's definition and God's definition of *manhood* are often miles apart. I love how Kyle and Joe use sports to bring forth the truth of the Word of God. The challenges of *true* manhood are clearly addressed in a way that sports fans can relate. God calls man to have faith and integrity, show sacrifice and leadership, and carry a strong legacy. *Living Life in the Zone* carefully illustrates these points."

— **Allan Houston**
Coach and former NBA All-Star,
New York Knicks

"Today's fast-paced, sports-centric culture not only fails to show us a path to authentic manhood, but it doesn't deliver the essential tools we need to get there either. *Living Life in the Zone* offers both a compelling direction for us men and a glimpse into the real power source that strengthens us along the way."

— **Danny Wuerffel**
Former Heisman Trophy winner
and NFL quarterback

"Every one of us wants to succeed in life. We want to experience a life that surpasses expectation. But far too often we end up sacrificing one aspect of our lives in order to succeed in another. In this book, Kyle Rote Jr. and Joe Pettigrew give men an inside look at the lives of some of the most successful sports and business personalities around. And they reveal the secrets these men have to experiencing a full life, not just an aspect of it. No matter what stage of life you find yourself in, *Living Life in the Zone* will give you the perspectives you need to get the most out of everything you do."

— **Ed Young**
Fellowship Church senior
pastor and author, *Outrageous,
Contagious Joy*

"*Living Life in the Zone* is a practical and fun read. I am a big sports fan and really enjoyed the way Joe and Kyle weaved in some extremely interesting stories about well-known athletes, teams, and coaches with take-away biblical truths that challenge me to be a better follower of Christ."

— **Tim Wildmon**
President, American Family
Association/American Family
Radio

"*Living Life in the Zone* applies spiritual truths to the dilemma of balancing career and family in today's culture. Joe Pettigrew and Kyle Rote Jr. draw on athletic metaphors to illustrate the importance of doing things God's way, rather than our way. The book is very readable and full of practical insights."

— **Tom Osborne**
Legendary coach,
University of Nebraska

"Joe and Kyle take you farther than the locker room and the playing field. They allow you to go on a journey with your own heart to ask yourself questions every man wants to ask but is afraid no one has the answers. But God's Word does have the answers, and this book talks to you man-to-man about the four most important issues of your life: balance, fatherhood, marriage, and work. Can't wait to pass it on to my sons!"

— **Ken Whitten**
Senior pastor,
Idlewild Baptist Church

"*Living Life in the Zone* has hit me right in the middle of my heart, soul, and mind. It's mandatory reading for every man out there searching for answers to life's toughest questions."

— **Pat Williams**
Executive vice-president,
Orlando Magic

# LIVING LIFE IN THE ZONE

# LIVING LIFE IN THE ZONE

## A 40-DAY SPIRITUAL GAME PLAN FOR MEN

# KYLE ROTE JR.

# DR. JOE PETTIGREW

**THOMAS NELSON**
*Since 1798*

NASHVILLE DALLAS MEXICO CITY RIO DE JANEIRO

Published in Nashville, Tennessee, by Thomas Nelson. Thomas Nelson is a registered trademark of Thomas Nelson, Inc.

Thomas Nelson, Inc. titles may be purchased in bulk for educational, business, fund-raising, or sales promotional use. For information, please e-mail SpecialMarkets@ThomasNelson.com.

Unless otherwise noted, Scripture quotations are taken from the New King James Version®. © 1982 by Thomas Nelson, Inc. Used by permission. All rights reserved.

Scripture quotations marked NIV are from the Holy Bible: New International Version®. © 1973, 1978, 1984 by International Bible Society. Used by permission of Zondervan Publishing House. All rights reserved.

Scripture quotations marked KJV are from the Holy Bible, King James Version.

Scripture quotations marked ESV are from the English Standard Version. © 2001 by Crossway Bibles, a division of Good News Publishers.

### Library of Congress Cataloging-in-Publication Data

Pettigrew, Joe, 1954–
    Living life in the zone : a 40-day spiritual game plan for men / Joe Pettigrew, Kyle Rote, Jr.
      p. cm.
    ISBN 978-0-8499-4652-3 (pbk.)
    1. Christian men—Religious life. 2. Sports—Religious aspects—Christianity. I. Rote, Kyle, 1950– II. Title.
BV4528.2.P5 2009
248.8'42—dc22                              2009040832

*Printed in the United States of America*

09 10 11 12 13 RRD 6 5 4 3 2 1

*This book is dedicated to the loves of our lives:*
*Trudy Pettigrew and Mary Lynne Rote*
*Trudy, married to Joe for thirty-five years*
*Mary Lynne, married to Kyle for thirty-eight years*
*Other than Jesus Christ, the greatest gifts God has*
*given to us*

# CONTENTS

# FINDING THE ZONE IN YOUR RELATIONSHIPS WITH YOUR FRIENDS

# FINDING THE ZONE IN YOUR RELATIONSHIPS AT WORK

## FINDING THE ZONE AS YOU LOOK TO THE FUTURE

# ACKNOWLEDGMENTS

We would like to thank the following individuals for their help in making *Living Life in the Zone* a reality. Their support is very much appreciated.

| | |
|---|---|
| Ken Birdsong | Teb Bondurant |
| Dr. Rodney Cooper | Mike Gottfried |
| Lori Hill | Phil Lutey |
| Ashley McBroom | Jere McGuffee |
| Carol Oates | Larry Payton |
| Michael Pence | Samantha Pence |
| Tara Pettigrew | Tyler Pettigrew |
| Trudy Pettigrew | Mary Lynne Rote |
| Danny Sartin | Steve Smith |
| Chuck Tilley | Duke and Clara Waddell |
| Tommy West | Kem Wilson Jr. |

Les Steckel and the committed staff
of the Fellowship of Christian Athletes

Rick Caldwell and the godly staff of Men's Fraternity

Jimmy Sexton and the talented staff
of Athletic Resource Management

# PREGAME HUDDLE

The purpose of In The Zone Ministries is to glorify God by empowering men with the skills and the mind-set to live their lives "In The Zone" and enjoy the abundant life that Jesus Christ promised to His followers. This concept of living life to the fullest is only possible if a man has a personal relationship with Christ—and has a compelling desire to live in obedience to God.

For those of you who are using this book as the focus of a men's group, Bible Study, or church-wide teaching series, we encourage you to use the questions at the end of each chapter to move from the theoretical and passive to putting your faith into action. For those of you who are using this book as a private devotional, we encourage you to use the questions at the end of each chapter to create a personal action plan for your own use.

Admittedly, we are fellow strugglers in this life. However, we have found that God's Word taken in its proper context speaks to every core issue a man can face. And when God speaks, He doesn't stutter. In addition, we recognize that many men tend to compartmentalize their lives—so we have chosen to focus on what our research has told us are the most stressful compartments—faith, fatherhood, marriage, work, and friendships. We readily acknowledge there are many more areas of concern, but we also know that the lordship of Jesus Christ reigns over every single one.

We want you to be equipped to have maximum impact—not only for your sake but more importantly for the kingdom's sake. Living life to the fullest with a clear purpose is living life In The Zone—God's zone.

As promised by Scripture, we will inevitably have trials, tribulations, disappointments, and failures. But living In The Zone means the God who promises to never leave us nor forsake us will use these experiences to both glorify Himself and mold us into the men He created us to be. May this be your experience as it continues to be ours.

Each day's reading is divided into seven categories that are intended to help you with your quest to live life In The Zone. They are:

- Thought of the Day—A short idea to ponder
- The Coach's Corner—Discovering the relevance of God's Word in your life
- The Game Plan—What the Word of God has to say about today's topic
- Playmakers—Real-life examples of real men in the real world
- Time Out—Questions for personal reflection
- Today's Assignment—Action items for today
- Home-Field Advantage—Praises and concerns you want to bring before God

Let's get started. God desires for you to live life In The Zone.

—JOE AND KYLE

# WHY A FORTY-DAY STUDY—JUST FOR MEN?

God considers forty days a spiritually significant period of time. As men we are creatures of habit, and we often find ourselves in a rut where we do the same things over and over. There are certain areas of our lives in which we are willing to get out of our comfort zone, and yet other places where we would just as well be left alone. Throughout the Bible, God uses forty days as a significant period of time in which to accomplish His purposes. We have provided here a brief look at many of those instances in the Bible in which forty days is used. It is our prayer that God will utilize this forty-day study to change your life forever. And while a period of forty days may not appear magical to you, it seems to be a time frame that God has used several times to change the world.

## INSTANCES IN THE BIBLE WHERE GOD MADE MAJOR CHANGES AND TRANSFORMATIONS AFTER THE PERIOD OF FORTY DAYS

- It rained for forty days and forty nights when God wanted to cleanse the world and start over (Genesis 7:12).
- Noah waited another forty days after it rained before he opened a window in the ark (Genesis 8:6).
- Moses was on the mountain with God for forty days—twice (Exodus 24:18; 34:28–29).
- Moses' face shone after the forty days on the mountain (Exodus 34:29).
- It took the spies forty days to search out the Promised Land and bring back fruit (Numbers 13:25).
- Goliath challenged the Israelites for forty days before being killed by David (1 Samuel 17:16).
- Elijah, strengthened by one angelic meal, spent forty days walking to Mount Horeb, where the Lord passed by, and he heard the voice of God (1 Kings 19:8).
- Jonah warned the city of Nineveh that they had forty days until God would overthrow the city. The people repented in those forty days, and God spared the city (Jonah 3:4, 10).
- Jesus fasted for forty days in the wilderness (Matthew 4:2).
- Jesus was tempted by Satan for forty days (Matthew 4:1–2).
- Jesus was seen on earth for forty days after His resurrection (Acts 1:3).

So let's get started today by praying that God will use the next forty days to change your life forever.

# HOW DO YOU KNOW WHEN YOU ARE "LIVING LIFE IN THE ZONE"?

*Therefore do not worry, saying, "What shall we eat?" or "What shall we drink?" or "What shall we wear?" For after all these things the Gentiles seek. For your heavenly Father knows that you need all these things. But seek first the kingdom of God and His righteousness, and all these things shall be added to you. Therefore do not worry about tomorrow, for tomorrow will worry about its own things. Sufficient for the day is its own trouble.*

—MATTHEW 6:31–34

1

## Day 1

# With God

## Going to Him First

---

### Thought of the Day

*God desires to be your first responder,
not your last resort.*

---

### The Coach's Corner

When things are going well in our lives, we sometimes believe it's of our own doing, when in actuality it's really God working through us. At times, we become bigheaded and prideful and assume we don't need God because everything is just fine. And after we have unsuccessfully tried to solve our problems, fix the situation, or change the outcome, *then* we think of going to God. But then it hits us! Bad luck strikes in our lives, and we realize that our well-being is totally outside of our control. We realize that we are not in control of our own lives or our own destiny, as we had originally thought. God uses these experiences to draw us closer to Him or at least back to Him. However, when things are going great with our marriage, our kids, our friends, and our work, it's hard to acknowledge that we are not in ultimate control.

> ## TRUE HAPPINESS IS FOUND ONLY IN JESUS AND HIS WORD. WE ARE TO BE A PART OF THE FALLEN WORLD BUT NOT CONTROLLED BY IT.

The bright lights and culture of New York's Madison Avenue work desperately to define who we are and what we need to be happy in this life. If we buy into the hype, then clearly all we need in order to be successful is to stay in a Holiday Inn Express; and all we need to become irresistible to women is to buy AXE cologne. They convince us that a pill or a five-minute workout will have us looking like the ripped guys on TV, and that if we purchase our wife something skimpy from Victoria Secret then . . . well, that doesn't work either. So we find ourselves searching for happiness. It seems as though life should be ideal since we purchased all the right things, joined the right Web sites, and found the perfect job. But you know as well as we do that true happiness is found only in Jesus and His Word. We are to be a part of the fallen world but not controlled by it.

What makes us want to try to fix all of our problems on our own, without asking God for help? What makes us think that we have the answers to all of life's troubles? What makes us feel that the world is expecting us to be totally self-sufficient if we are real men? Certainly these aren't God's ideas. He wants to help you think through your problems, help design a resolution to them, and work to bring about a solution that will glorify Him. God wants to be the first one you think about, not the last one you go to after you have exhausted all other avenues.

## The Game Plan

God desires an intimate relationship with you. That relationship is of greater value than anything you alone can create. God wants you to go to Him first. He wants you to know:

- Nothing can separate you from His love—Romans 8:38–39: "For I am persuaded that neither death nor life, nor angels nor principalities nor powers, nor things present nor things to come, nor height nor depth, nor any other created thing, shall be able to separate us from the love of God which is in Christ Jesus our Lord."
- He stands ready to meet you at your points of need—Matthew 7:7–8: "Ask, and it will be given to you; seek, and you will find; knock, and it will be opened to you. For everyone who asks receives, and he who seeks finds, and to him who knocks it will be opened."
- Every gift from Him is a good gift—Luke 11:13: "If you then, being evil, know how to give good gifts to your children, how much more will your heavenly Father give the Holy Spirit to those who ask Him!"
- He created you to be part of His team and part of His game plan—John 15:16: "You did not choose Me, but I chose you and appointed you that you should go and bear fruit, and that your fruit should remain, that whatever you ask the Father in My name He may give you."

## Playmakers

Few coaches in the world have captured the hearts of men more completely than Coach Tony Dungy. Although he loved football, Coach Dungy was one of those coaches who knew there were more important things in his future than just coaching ball. He always knew that football was part of his life's mission but not the only reason God placed him on this earth. Coach Dungy recently decided to step down from the game he loved so much and began the transition from Super Bowl–winning coach to spending more time and effort as a father, husband, and builder of young men. "We just felt this was the right time," Dungy said. "Don't shed any tears for me. I got to live a dream most men don't ever get to live."[1]

When Coach Dungy left the Indianapolis Colts, he departed as one of the most respected and beloved coaches in the history of the game. His accomplishments included 148 career wins, ten consecutive playoff appearances, and having the distinction of being the first African American coach ever to win the Super Bowl. Dungy's professional career began when he was a standout player for the Super Bowl champion Pittsburgh Steelers and ended two years after he guided his team to their first championship. Tony was often observed as a strong-willed man who was a master of keeping his emotions in check and holding his composure. He has faced his share of difficult trials in his thirty-one-year NFL career, including one that was very close to his heart.

Perhaps as men, we can most identify with Coach Dungy, not just through his unbelievable football successes but through the terrible tragedy that he and his family faced in their personal lives with the death of their teenage son. Just a few days before Christmas in 2005, Tony and his wife, Lauren, received the phone call that all parents pray never comes. It was an emergency phone call from the Tampa Police Department letting them know that their son James had been found unresponsive in his Tampa apartment. Later that day police confirmed James had taken his own life in an apparent suicide. Those around Tony described a man who immediately turned his grief over to his first responder—God. Tony was fortunate already to have in place a network of Christian men he could call upon in his time of need. Since dealing with his tragedy, Tony has been transparent and open about the pain he and Lauren encountered and the many life lessons they have learned from their son's suicide.

When Tony speaks, he humbly describes how two special people have received the gift of sight from his son's donated corneas. He has taken the opportunity to counsel numerous young people across the country who seem to be wrestling with issues similar to those that claimed the life of his son. At a recent prayer breakfast in Detroit, Tony shared his innermost thoughts on his son's death and how he relied on God in the midst of his pain. "If God had talked to me before James's death and said that his death would have helped these people, it would have saved them and healed their sins, but I would have to take your son, I would have said no; I can't do that. But God had the same choice two thousand years ago with His Son, Jesus Christ, and it paved the way for you and me to have eternal life. That is the benefit you can get if you accept Jesus into your heart today as your Savior."[2] We often look at many successful men like Tony Dungy and simply assume that they have the perfect life. As a key player on a Super Bowl–winning team, as a coach of a Super Bowl–winning team, as a man earning millions of dollars, as a man with a loving family, and as a man with a celebrity status known throughout the world, what else could anyone possibly want?

Tony spoke of the biggest regret in his life, and it was not losing a game or failing to get a number one draft pick that he wanted. His main regret in life was that he did not hug his son James when he saw him for the last time during the Thanksgiving holidays in 2005. When unforeseen things happen in your life, who do you turn to? For many of us we turn first to ourselves to solve our problems, then to friends, then to our family—and often last, to God. As men we try to fix our problems, solve all the messy situations, or untangle the messes before we bother God with our problems. When we can't seem to make it better, then we start looking for help. God wants you to think of Him first.

## WHEN UNFORESEEN THINGS HAPPEN IN YOUR LIFE, WHO DO YOU TURN TO?

During a recent private conversation with Tony we spoke not only of the In The Zone conferences but also about our common interest in influencing men. Tony's passion for using both the good and the bad in life to glorify God is an example all of us can follow. When things go wrong, He wants to be your first responder—not your last resort. When things go wrong, find a place where you can have a conversation with your Father and ask for His help. Why does God allow pain in our lives? Coach Dungy often responds to that question, "Because you are loved by God and the pain allows you to head back to your Father"[3]— your first responder, your best friend.

## TIME OUT

1. What problem are you grappling with today that you need to turn over to God?
2. Ask your wife who she sees as your first responder when you are in trouble.
3. Describe a time in your life when your relationship with God has been more about Him pursuing you than you pursuing Him.

## TODAY'S ASSIGNMENT

Identify the most pressing problem you are dealing with and give it to God. Ask Him to glorify Himself and mature you in the midst of this crisis.

---

## HOME-FIELD ADVANTAGE

### *Praises and concerns you want to bring before God*

_____

_____

_____

_____

---

# DAY 2

# WITH YOURSELF

## HAVING SOME ALONE TIME WITH GOD

## THOUGHT OF THE DAY

*Make time to be alone with God regularly.*

## THE COACH'S CORNER

You have probably heard that you need some time alone with God every day. However, your busy schedule seems never to allow you to slow down, and your quiet time often gets pushed back, postponed, or simply forgotten. It seems impossible to hear God speak to us in the midst of all the noise and clutter that surrounds us. Yet, some very busy men have committed to carve out a small section of time each day and set it aside for silence, study, meditation, and prayer. But this may mean silencing your cell phone, turning off your computer, stopping all interruptions, taking your phone off the hook, and/or simply closing your door. It sometimes requires that you go off alone to a quiet place where you can listen and talk to God. Surely you recall that Jesus regularly carved out alone time to be with His Father. He often retreated to the mountains or local hillside simply to be away from the large crowds where He could talk and listen to God. This alone time is often difficult in today's busy culture, but you make time for what is truly important to you. Some men have found that special time early in the morning before work, others allocate their lunch time for the meeting, others find time while at work to carve out their alone time, and still others find time prior to going to bed. Your time alone with God can help provide structure to your daily routine, placing God in a prominent position where He will not get squeezed out.

Sometimes men report that their quiet time turns out to be frustrating. You have so much to do, so many pressures, and not enough time to deal with it all. When you finally have some alone time, you often let the world creep in and your mind starts to fade. You begin thinking about all the many things you have to do, what everyone needs from you today, and what you are missing out on during this time. Many times you even find yourself daydreaming about stuff that isn't even important. Disruptions and distractions are the most common tactics Satan uses to take our mind off of God. Satan hates for us to spend quiet time alone with God.

> YOUR TIME ALONE WITH GOD CAN HELP
> PROVIDE STRUCTURE TO YOUR DAILY ROUTINE,
> PLACING GOD IN A PROMINENT POSITION
> WHERE HE WILL NOT GET SQUEEZED OUT.

Quiet time is more than just clearing out our day to make an appointment with God. It's more like a sit-down visit with your closest friend and confidant. It's especially important for those of us who have made our lives so busy we would even make God Himself get an appointment to talk to us! Good relationships need priority time; they can't survive as just another item on the agenda. Worse yet, most relationships die if time is not specifically set aside for them. Won't you decide today to create a daily time to spend with God? He has been waiting.

## THE GAME PLAN

God desires to spend alone time with you. Jesus valued time alone with God—and you will find it extremely important as well. God wants you to know:

- Never pray to impress others—Matthew 6:5–8: "And when you pray, you shall not be like the hypocrites. For they love to pray standing in the synagogues and on the corners of the streets, that they may be seen by men. Assuredly, I say to you, they have their reward. But you, when you pray, go into your room, and when you have shut your door, pray to your Father who is in the secret place; and your Father who sees in secret will reward you openly. And when you pray, do not use vain repetitions as the heathen do. For they think that they will be heard for their many words. Therefore do not be like them. For your Father knows the things you have need of before you ask Him."
- Your love for Him should encompass every aspect of your person—Matthew 22:37–38: "Jesus said to him, 'You shall love the LORD your God with all your heart, with all your soul, and with all your mind.' This is the first and great commandment."

- You must find a special time and place to be alone with Him—Mark 1:35: "Now in the morning, having risen a long while before daylight, He went out and departed to a solitary place; and there He prayed."
- Praying to Him doesn't have to be complicated—Luke 11:2–4: "So He said to them, 'When you pray, say: Our Father in heaven, hallowed be Your name. Your kingdom come. Your will be done on earth as it is in heaven. Give us day by day our daily bread. And forgive us our sins, for we also forgive everyone who is indebted to us. And do not lead us into temptation, but deliver us from the evil one.'"

## PLAYMAKERS

Quiet time in today's busy world can often seem unattainable. The main question you have to answer is whether you are willing to pay the price to secure the necessary time alone with God. To make this happen, you have to carve out a slot in your day, and you simply can't permit routine interruptions. You might say, "It won't work," "I have a demanding boss," "I have a crisis to deal with," "I have important phone calls to make," "I have demanding customers," "I have kids and they have problems," or "My wife is driving me crazy" . . . we are all in the same boat in regard to finding this precious time. Many times we find it hard to comprehend that the most important and successful men in the world have only twenty-four hours in their day just as we do.

Yet many very successful men manage to set aside a portion of their day, every day, to communicate with God without worry of interruption. These men are the ones who often appear to be the most content because they have found quiet time alone with their Father.

One of the most widely recognized and admired sports person-alities in the world today is James Brown (more commonly known as "J. B."). J. B., currently the host of *The NFL Today* on CBS, was also the host of the number one *Fox NFL Sunday* for many years, a prime-time play-by-play announcer for NCAA Basketball, and a correspondent for HBO's *Real Sports*. He is sometimes jokingly referred to as the "Hardest Working Man in Sports." He is probably best known for his upbeat personality, distinctive voice, and vast knowledge of the game of football.

> **THE MOST IMPORTANT AND SUCCESSFUL MEN IN THE WORLD HAVE ONLY TWENTY-FOUR HOURS IN THEIR DAY JUST AS WE DO.**

J. B. is also a committed Christian man who loves to share his faith with others. He is one of only a few national sports com-mentators who never back down from sharing with people about who he is and what he believes. His faith is apparent not only when he is being interviewed but also by his involvement in numerous activities designed to build the kingdom of God. J. B. is seen weekly by millions; however, most people are surprised to learn that he was not a big-time college or pro football player. Instead, he was a successful collegiate basketball standout at Harvard University and was drafted by the NBA's Atlanta Hawks. While you can see J. B. almost any weekend when national sports are on TV, many say he is best recognized for his time as the long-time host of *Fox NFL Sunday*, featuring Terry Bradshaw, Howie Long, and Jimmy Johnson.

J. B. was recently quoted on the Christian Broadcasting Network as saying, "Everything that I do revolves around Jesus Christ being Lord and Savior of my life."[1] Someone once inquired as to how he handles his celebrity status. He said, "I'm humbled by it and pray that I'll never get to the point where I think I'm so much better than anyone else. Terry and I talk about this a lot."[2] There is a lesson that J. B. thinks of often that can be found in Psalm 75:5–6: "'Do not lift up your horn on high; do not speak with a stiff neck.' For exaltation comes neither from the east nor from the west nor from the south." J. B. lives his life according to what he believes.

One of the least understood aspects of J. B.'s longevity and star power is that he spends time Sunday morning praying before going live to the world with his NFL show. He says he turns over his total performance to God. Quiet time for J. B. is essential to doing his best. J. B. says, "I have a little routine, but it's not a mindless routine. It is important. I will call to have prayer with my wife and my mother while I'm on the road. Too many times I've embarked upon a broadcast without having been prayed up. It's amazing how 'the little things' so easily beset us."[3] He prays God will keep watch over his tongue and allow him only to say things that please Him. J. B. insists having his time alone with God is essential for him to be the man God has called him to be.

## BE QUIET, BE STILL, AND LET GOD SPEAK TO YOU.

No matter what your job, you can find ways of creating time to be alone. If you think of all the time you spend unproductively (i.e., watching *SportsCenter* replays or another *Seinfeld* classic), you realize *you can* find the time. Many men, once alone, don't know what to do, so they decide to read the entire Bible until the Old Testament book of Numbers brings their efforts to a grinding stop. It is always a good idea to have an insightful devotional or a structured tool such as *Walk Thru the Bible*, the *Upper Room*

devotionals, or *Our Daily Bread* to bring clarity and enlighten-
ment to the Scriptures. Many men have chosen a proven classic
like *My Utmost for His Highest* to enhance their quiet time. Most
importantly, be quiet, be still, and let God speak to you. Having
material available that can get you in the right mood to meet
your Father can be extremely valuable. The length of time you
spend will increase, but that is not the focus. You don't have to
worry about doing all the talking; it is amazing what we can learn
when we listen to God.

## TIME OUT

1. What time each day could you commit to spend
   consistently with the Lord?
2. How can you help protect your spouse's quiet time from
   the day-to-day grind of life?
3. Where is your favorite place to meet God?

## TODAY'S ASSIGNMENT

Identify a time and place where you can have a consistent quiet
time with God. Don't get discouraged when you don't maintain
your plan perfectly. Keep trying. Start today with a commitment to
yourself. Ask God to remind you if you forget. Don't let Satan steal
your lifeblood of abiding with God.

## HOME-FIELD ADVANTAGE

*Praises and concerns you want to bring before God*

_____

_____

_____

_____

_____

# Day 3

## WITH YOUR WIFE

### A LIFETIME OF SACRIFICE

### THE COACH'S CORNER

Dr. James Dobson, founder of Focus on the Family, was asked, "Why are men so insensitive to women's needs today?" He answered, "I question whether men have really changed all that much. I doubt if men ever responded as women preferred. Did the farmer of a century ago come in from the fields to say, 'Tell me how it went with you today'? No. He was as oblivious to his wife's nature then just as husbands are today."[1] Several years ago Dr. Dobson wanted to discuss ways of using the platform of sports to further the kingdom. He extended an invitation and we sat down in his studio at Focus on the Family to tape a show that discussed ways of intersecting faith and sports. It became obvious that Dr. Dobson was a sports fan but that he also understood the irony that some men seem to be more interested in their favorite sports team's daily activities than they do the daily concerns of their wife. As we all know, sports is an area that men have heightened sensitivity to—seemingly twenty-four hours a day; however, only a foolish man concerns himself more with his favorite sports team than the heart issues of his wife.

Many of you are struggling with ways to show your wife just how much you really love her. You may have been married for several years, and your marriage just may have gotten a little rusty. When we hear scriptures stating how much we are supposed to love our wives, it often makes us feel guilty or insignificant. Included here are a few simple tips on how to improve your relationship with your wife, whether you have been married for fifty years or five months:

- Your wife desires to be touched and held all throughout the day, not just at bed time. While sex is often on your radar, she desires more subtle interaction. How do you say goodbye to your wife in the morning? How do you greet her in the evening? Do you communicate with her during the day?
- With the constant barrage of beautiful women on TV, on the Internet, and in magazines and newspapers, your wife wants to be assured she is still the one for you. She wants to know you are still attracted to her, since she often sees herself as always falling short of those she is compared with in the media.
- Your wife craves alone time with you (not family time ... alone time with you). Many times that time comes in the form of her downloading the many problems of the day, the unbelievable imperfections of the children (or you),

and her enormous wish list for herself and the family. You have heard it before; she really wants someone to listen empathetically to her, not solve her problems.

- Your wife desires to know that all is OK in her world and in the world of her family. She is concerned about the financial stresses on the family as well as the emotional stresses. Her deepest desire is to feel secure and safe.

- Your wife desires that you become the spiritual leader of the family. She wants someone who will live up to the biblical model of a real man. She wants a man who is grounded in his faith, not just in his work. She wants a man who places God first, his wife second, his children third, and his work further down the list.

To love your wife as Christ loves the church is an overwhelming charge for us and the command that many men feel is impossible to accomplish. Jesus' love for His church had no strings attached to it. He sacrificed everything He had for the one thing He loved. His love for His church was not based upon whether or not the church loved Him back.

**ONLY A FOOLISH MAN CONCERNS HIMSELF MORE WITH HIS FAVORITE SPORTS TEAM THAN THE HEART ISSUES OF HIS WIFE.**

We must constantly ask God to help us be more creative in ways of showing our wives how much we love them. This may result in a change in every aspect of our lives. If you have a ministry that is eating up a lot of your time and keeping you away from your wife, she may wonder if your ministry is more important to you than she is. We must not sacrifice our wives for our ministries. God established marriage first; it was man who came up with what we call *ministry* today. God commands us to love our wives, to serve Him, and give ourselves wholly to Him. We are often too busy doing other things we believe to be more important than this important command for all of us: "Love your wives, just as Christ also loved the church" (Ephesians 5:25).

## THE GAME PLAN

The Bible tells you to place your wife above all of your earthly possessions. God wants you to:

- Love your wife, but make sure your love of God is still the top priority in your life—Luke 14:25–27: "Now great multitudes went with Him. And He turned and said to them, 'If anyone comes to Me and does not hate his father and mother, wife and children, brothers and sisters, yes, and his own life also, he cannot be My disciple. And whoever does not bear his cross and come after Me cannot be My disciple.'"

- Sacrifice yourself to help make your wife holy, pure, and blameless—Ephesians 5:25–27: "Husbands, love your wives, just as Christ also loved the church and gave Himself for her, that He might sanctify and cleanse her with the washing of water by the word, that He might present her to Himself a glorious church, not having spot or wrinkle or any such thing, but that she should be holy and without blemish."

- Live with your wife in an understanding way—Ephesians 5:33: "Nevertheless let each one of you in particular so love his own wife as himself, and let the wife see that she respects her husband."

- Celebrate and appreciate the ways in which your wife is a Proverbs 31 woman—Proverbs 31:26: "She opens her mouth with wisdom, and on her tongue is the law of kindness."

## PLAYMAKERS

It has now been many years since the wife of the greatest basketball coach in the history of the game passed away. Most articles written about the legendary Coach John Wooden center around his winning records and his unique ability of coaching some of the best college players ever to play the game of basketball. We know him as the renowned coach of the UCLA Bruins and because of his tremendous on- and off-the-court success in the 1950s, 60s, 70s, and 80s. His Bruin teams once won eighty-eight games in a row. They won an unprecedented seven NCAA national championships back to back and a total of ten national championships before he was finished. The national news media would often focus in on the legendary coach during the games as he sat quietly on the bench, usually clinging to a rolled-up program. Coach Wooden always appeared to be calm, cool, and collected. He was never known as one of those out-of-control stalking coaches who marched up and down the sidelines while screaming at the officials. Much has been written about how he dealt with superstars such as Kareem Abdul Jabbar (Lew Alcindor), but it was the day the team's rebel and star center Bill Walton informed the coach that he was going to grow a beard that became a defining moment for Coach Wooden and the entire team. Bill was well aware that facial hair was a violation of his coach's neatness code. Walton was the star of the team, if they in fact had a star. Walton believed that the team couldn't win without him, and ironically so did everyone else. Coach Wooden pondered the situation for a while and then told Bill he respected his decision and let him know the team would miss him very much. Walton, stunned by the coach's response, was the first person at practice the next day, and, yes, he was cleanly shaven.

Coach Wooden's poise and charisma taught us that, while big-time college athletics might be extremely stressful, they weren't life or death. There were things more important to Coach Wooden than basketball and winning, and one of those was his wife of fifty-three years, Nellie. Visit Coach Wooden in his modest one-bedroom Los Angeles condo, only a short drive from the UCLA campus, and you will see a home dedicated somewhat to UCLA basketball but mostly to his wife. The many awards and the numerous pictures of their children and grandchildren are just the way she left them when she died. The hundreds of prestigious awards and framed pictures of the coach with many of the most influential people in the world are where she placed them years ago. Coach Wooden openly confesses that he hasn't replaced or moved a single item in the house. Even though some things might be outdated, he is satisfied to remember his home as it was when Nellie was the head coach in charge.

It was a pleasure for me (Joe) to visit with Coach Wooden in his home. To sit in his den and listen to the stories from one of the world's greatest coaches was an honor. During our visit with Coach Wooden, he received a call from someone Coach addressed as just "Billy." We later learned that the identity of "Billy" was the famed Bill Walton. Coach Wooden indicated that many of his players call and check in on him on a regular basis. When he talks about his family, faith, and career it seems as though he sees himself as just a regular guy. Yet, when you listen to the coach talk about his wife, you realize there was something magical about their relationship. If you were to spend just one evening with the coach, you would notice immediately that he is still passionately in love with Nellie. He always sleeps on the same side of the bed that he has slept on for over fifty years, never sleeping on her side. Your eyes would focus on the tattered box on Nellie's side of the bed, as it contains what appears to be letters neatly placed inside. Looking more closely, you see the letters are from Coach Wooden written to Nellie over many years. He writes her a note on the twenty-first day of every month and has done so for more than 250 consecutive months. When he discusses the handwritten notes, he only shares that he tells her things like, "It's been twenty-four years, nine months, and ten days since you were released from your pain and taken to heaven. But you are with me always."[2] He writes to her about their children and their grandchildren, what they are doing, and what he has been doing. He is a man who treated his wife in a very special way.

## IF GOD WERE TO ASK YOU IF YOU LOVED YOUR WIFE THE WAY YOU ASSUME HE LOVES THE CHURCH, WHAT WOULD YOU SAY?

After reading this, you may have the feeling that you aren't treating your wife in a manner consistent with God's Word. She may receive your attention only after you have dealt with other stressful areas in your life. You may be feeling enormous pressure at work (businesses are closing every day); you may be feeling pressure at home (men are losing their jobs every day); and you may be feeling pressure in your marriage (women are leaving their husbands every day). When you first got married you couldn't keep your hands off your wife, and now life is just too busy. If God were to ask you if you loved your wife the way you assume He loves the church, what would you say?

## TIME OUT

1. What impresses you most about the respect Coach Wooden shows for his wife?
2. What are some ways you can show honor to your wife?
3. Of all the numbers attached to Coach Wooden's life, what impresses you the most?

## TODAY'S ASSIGNMENT

What is something you could do (not buy) for your wife today that she wouldn't expect but would express your love for her? How about a letter?

---

### HOME-FIELD ADVANTAGE

*Praises and concerns you want to bring before God*

_____

_____

_____

---

## DAY 4

# WITH YOUR CHILDREN

## TALKING THE TALK—WALKING THE WALK

### THOUGHT OF THE DAY

*As men we often talk the talk, but God is interested in us walking the walk, especially for our children.*

### THE COACH'S CORNER

You need to ask yourself, "Am I truly a godly dad?" In spite of your demanding schedule, do you try to always set the right example for your children? We know our children learn more from watching us than by simply listening to us. Therefore, we must constantly be mindful of what we say and do; our actions should not contradict our words. When the phone rings, many fathers have caught themselves asking their child to tell the caller they aren't home. Others are guilty of treating their wives in a manner that is not acceptable to God. And still others spend more time on their own hobbies and careers than they do with their children. Our children tend to embrace the saying, "What we see is who you are."

## WE TELL OUR CHILDREN WHAT OUR PRIORITIES ARE BY THE WAY WE UTILIZE OUR TIME.

There might have been many times over the years when you have realized that your actions did not exemplify the lessons you hoped your children would learn. Some men choose to play golf on Sunday morning instead of going to church, others go into the office on Sunday morning, and yet others sit back and allow strangers to teach valuable lessons to their children. We tell our children what our priorities are by the way we utilize our time. The Bible is very specific regarding when we should teach our children about Him. We are to teach our children about God every chance we get—morning, noon, and night. We are not to leave it up to the church to teach our children; it is our responsibility to provide them constantly with both an example of godly living and teachings from His Word. It has been said that although Eve took the first bite out of the apple, it was Adam who God came looking for.

The road to spiritual leadership is not automatic. Samuel Logan Brendle, a respected leader in the Salvation Army, wrote:

> It is not won by promotion, but by many prayers and tears. It is attained by confessions of sin, and much heart searching and humbling before God; by self-surrender, a courageous sacrifice of every idol, a bold, deathless, uncompromising and uncomplaining embracing of the cross, and by an eternal, unfaltering looking unto Jesus crucified. It is not gained by seeking great things for ourselves, but . . . by counting those things that are gain to us as loss for Christ. This is a great price, but it must be

unflinchingly paid by him who would not be merely a nominal but a real spiritual leader of men, a leader whose power is both recognized and felt in heaven, on earth and in hell.[1]

## THE GAME PLAN

The Bible wants us to be honest and upfront with our families when things are difficult. God wants you to know:

- Your children will be blessed if you live a godly life— Proverbs 20:7: "The righteous man walks in his integrity; his children are blessed after him."
- Every father should proclaim his experiences with God's faithfulness—Isaiah 38:19: "The living, the living man, he shall praise You, as I do this day; the father shall make known Your truth to the children."
- Your job is to pass God's teachings on to your kids and their kids—Joel 1:3: "Tell your children about it, let your children tell their children, and their children another generation."
- As fathers we must encourage our children—1 Thessalonians 2:11–12: "As you know how we exhorted, and comforted, and charged every one of you, as a father does his own children, that you would walk worthy of God who calls you into His own kingdom and glory."

## PLAYMAKERS

There are many of us who would welcome professional athletes striving to be more outstanding role models for our children who many times look up to them. We would enjoy watching a professional game with our children and not worrying about if they can read the lips of players and coaches on the sidelines. We want to watch ESPN without having to hear the stories about a player beating up his wife, players driving while intoxicated, players shooting and fighting in nightclubs, or coaches violating NCAA rules. When the superstars engage in unsportsmanlike behavior and unlawful activities, it sends a negative message to many children who believe their idols can do no wrong. Some athletes disagree with the thought that they are called to be positive role models for children today. Their argument is that they are being paid large sums of money to win, not to act nice and be a role model for somebody else's kid. However, in every NFL, NBA, and Major League Baseball contract, players are required to sign and live up to a morals clause. Sadly, each year a few athletes choose not to follow these guidelines and thus jeopardize their careers in professional sports, sending negative messages to millions of young fans.

Few professional athletes have more name recognition than "Sir" Charles Barkley, one of the NBA's former superstars. There are only four players in NBA history who have compiled twenty thousand points, ten thousand rebounds, and four thousand assists: Kareem Abdul-Jabbar, Wilt Chamberlain, Karl Malone, and Charles Barkley—a most impressive group. There is no argument that he belongs among the world's elite basketball professional athletes. Charles was a perennial All-Star and All-NBA selection during his career, and his pinnacle may have been winning the NBA Most Valuable Player award in 1993. However, when the conversation turns to the personal antics of Barkley today, many people think first of the entertaining, sometimes outrageous commentary on life that he proudly provides. He is known as a big talker who enjoys interacting with fans, sometimes making them his friends and sometimes not. He was intensely criticized at the midpoint of his career, when it was reported that he spit at a child sitting at courtside. He explained after the game that he had meant to spit on a certain fan who had been taunting him, and that he just missed.

Charles may also be known to many for his Nike sports commercial that sparked a great deal of controversy both in and out of the NBA. In the commercial spot, Charles emphatically warned those listening, "I am not a role model . . . parents should be role models—not me. I'm a professional basketball player. I am paid to wreak havoc on the basketball court. Parents should be role models!"[2] His bold statement to the world created instant controversy from fans and some NBA players as well. His public announcement drew criticism from a number of NBA players, including MVP David Robinson of the San Antonio Spurs. David felt Barkley should step up and be accountable as a positive role model to kids today. He indicated that Barkley, as a big-time sports celebrity and public figure, was a role model whether he liked it or not; it was simply a matter of what role he would set. Was he going to be a good role model or a bad one? It was interesting that Dennis Rodman, one of the NBA's so-called bad boys, was silent on the matter, leaving many to assume that he agreed with Sir Charles.

Professional athletes always seem to be in the news for their off-the-court/field problems. We have seen the nation's headlines full of players who are acting as anything but positive role models. Sometimes we have to wonder why these guys don't get it! They are treated as kings, are acclaimed by fans, and have bank accounts that would make most red-blooded males jealous. Why would these men do anything that would risk their profitable and influential positions in our world or in their sport? Sadly, there are few days that go by when we don't read of a professional athlete being arrested or investigated for something.

**ALLAN'S FATHER TOOK HIS SPIRITUAL LEADERSHIP ROLE SERIOUSLY—AND ALLAN WAS BLESSED BY HIS FATHER'S EXAMPLE.**

Former NBA All-Star Allan Houston, speaking to a large gathering of men at a recent In The Zone conference, proudly said his father "lived the Bible more than any other man I know." Allan went on to discuss the pressures on professional athletes today and their critical need for a positive role model. It's clear that Allan's father took his spiritual leadership role seriously—and Allan was blessed by his father's example. We are called to be the spiritual leader of our family.

Les Payne, a Pulitzer Prize–winning reporter and columnist for *Newsday* reported that when Charles Barkley was arrested in Scottsdale for a DUI on New Year's Day 2008, Barkley's alibi was that he was "going around the corner to have sex with a woman who'd performed quite well, thank you, the previous week." According to Payne, Barkley also offered to tattoo the policeman's name on his rear end if he'd let him off the hook. Not surprisingly, the officer refused the role model's offer.[3]

Even the images of the many great athletes who are trying to be model citizens and positive role models are being damaged by the irresponsible guys of professional athletics. The concerns surrounding the public image of professional athletes have become so grave that the commissioners of the four major sports (National Basketball Association, National Football League, National Hockey League, and Major League Baseball) and the NCAA met to establish the Citizenship Through Sports Alliance. Their focus was to demand good citizenship from all participating athletes. NBA commissioner David Stern said, "You mimic behavior, good and bad, and what you see on televised games. Athletes need to accept that they are role models!"[4]

## TIME OUT

1. If you were a pro athlete, what one lifestyle temptation would be most difficult for you?

2. What would your spouse say is your most obvious disconnect between your walk and your talk as it applies to your children?
3. What occasion do you most regret when you failed to walk the talk?

## TODAY'S ASSIGNMENT

Identify a situation when you have not set a godly example for one of your children, and decide today to apologize to them for your failure.

---

## HOME-FIELD ADVANTAGE

*Praises and concerns you want to bring before God*

_____

_____

_____

_____

---

## DAY 5

# WITH YOUR FRIENDS

## DEVELOPING REAL FRIENDSHIPS

### THOUGHT OF THE DAY

*Every man deserves to have a true godly friend.*

### THE COACH'S CORNER

Whom you associate with will have a profound impact on your life, and that impact will either be positive or negative—never neutral. The Bible provides clear instruction to us regarding our association with the right kind of friends who will influence us in a spiritual way. As Christians we should pursue friendships with those who are considered to be wise men. God's Word teaches us that wise men are focused on the ultimate prize—Jesus Christ. You should not depend on men who are lazy, men who are ultra critical (always finding fault), men who are always defeated, or men who bring you down.

On the other hand, you also know those who are beneficial friends. These men are those who are there for you but may not always tell you what you want to hear. They will not judge you unrighteously or condemn you, no matter how much trouble you have gotten yourself into. They understand (though may not be able to completely relate to) where you stand. They can see the other side of most situations and provide you with godly advice. If you do get off track, they will lovingly guide you back in the right direction—God's direction—provided your spirit is teachable.

> **WHOM YOU ASSOCIATE WITH WILL HAVE A PROFOUND IMPACT ON YOUR LIFE, AND THAT IMPACT WILL EITHER BE POSITIVE OR NEGATIVE—NEVER NEUTRAL.**

We accelerate the development of godly habits by making friends with men who are grounded in their faith, and it helps us when we spend time with them. However, the opposite can also be true because if your friends are not walking in the faith and do not strive to follow Christ, they will have a negative influence on you. God's Word clearly says that evil, ungodly friends will corrupt you. Many of us have already learned this the hard way. Some of us have had friends who led us down the wrong path. We have had friends who influenced us to do the wrong things. And we always found ways to defend our relationship with them:

- "But he is one of my closest buddies."
- "I really do like them! They make me laugh and take my mind off my problems!"
- "They understand me. I have known them forever."

As a Christian man your main focus is God—not yourself, not your friends. Does your Bible say, "And you shall love your friends with all your heart, with all your soul, with all your mind, and with all your strength"? No, I don't think so!

**WE ACCELERATE THE DEVELOPMENT OF GODLY HABITS BY MAKING FRIENDS WITH MEN WHO ARE GROUNDED IN THEIR FAITH.**

You have a clear idea of the type of men with whom you should surround yourself. Finding true biblical friends can take time, and may become frustrating. Our goal is not to obtain as many friends as possible but rather to acquire friendships of true quality and value. The friend you are looking for will respect you regardless of your actions (good, bad, or indifferent)—because the essence of grace is undeserved favor. He is the friend who is free of critical thinking, is generous with his love, and holds within his spirit a depth of biblical understanding. His face shines with acceptance and is not darkened by condemnation and faultfinding. He lives the Word of God. His words (which are often God's words) and walk are in perfect alignment. He has a reverential fear that drives him to his knees in humbleness and holy adoration before God's throne.

Most men don't have a true confidant. Most of us don't have a friend with whom we share our innermost secrets. Yet the truth is, two God-fearing men working together can surely do more than one.

## THE GAME PLAN

The Bible wants you to have true friends who bring out the best in you. God wants you to know:

- We are called to love everyone—John 15:12–13, 17: "This is My commandment, that you love one another as I have loved you. Greater love has no one than this, than to lay down one's life for his friends . . . These things I command you, that you love one another."
- A biblical friend will help you fight life's most difficult challenges—Proverbs 17:17: "A friend loves at all times, and a brother is born for adversity."
- Your close friends should be chosen very carefully— Ecclesiastes 4:9–10: "Two are better than one, because they have a good reward for their labor. For if they fall, one will lift up his companion. But woe to him who is alone when he falls, for he has no one to help him up."
- The best friendships result when both men become more faithful, obedient, and useful to God—Proverbs 27:17: "As iron sharpens iron, so a man sharpens the countenance of his friend."

## PLAYMAKERS

Many of us have met some of our most treasured friends while playing sports, participating in the band, or in a church group. There is something about working side by side with someone for days on end that tends to create a lasting bond between you. This sense of togetherness builds when two men are going through the same type of agony and stress together. There are countless stories of men who became close friends while serving in the military, playing sports or being involved in an activity in which they counted on each other. After such events, these men frequently stay friends for life. But when these friendships result in the saving of a life, it becomes more profound and important. In recent years the media has given some attention to a true feel-good story between two old teammates and good friends, both of whom played for the NFL's Dallas Cowboys—Everson Walls and Ron Springs.

It all started in northern Louisiana at Grambling State University where a young player named Everson Walls was a superstar on the football field. Everson led the nation in interceptions, but when he came out of college, NFL teams shunned him because they thought he was too slow to compete at the next level. So unlike most collegiate star athletes, he wasn't drafted. It didn't matter! He was signed by the Dallas Cowboys and played thirteen seasons, leading the NFL in interceptions for three of those seasons. His eight years in Dallas were filled with accolades and tremendous accomplishments. In his rookie year, he broke the Cowboys' single-season record for interceptions with eleven. He was later named to the Pro Bowl team four times. What is most impressive about Everson, however, just might be what he has done since leaving professional football.

Everson's friend was Ron Springs, who played at Ohio State University for three years under the legendary head coach Woody Hayes. Ron led the Buckeyes in both rushing and receiving as a junior. He was drafted by the Cowboys and played eight years in the NFL, six with the Cowboys and two with the Tampa Bay Buccaneers. Ron scored twenty-eight career touchdowns and ran for more than 2,500 yards during his NFL career.

During Walls's first training camp with the Cowboys, he and Springs became fast friends, and their friendship grew during the four years they played together. While they didn't see each other regularly after their retirement, they seemed to have a kindred spirit. Recently, both men shared more than football, more than friendship . . . they shared life. Everson found out his friend was physically in bad shape due to diabetes and was in desperate need of a kidney transplant. He also learned Ron's adult son was the only direct donor for him. Springs had suffered from diabetes for over sixteen years and had been on the national waiting list for a transplant since 2004. His diabetes had led to the amputation of his right foot and two toes on his left foot. In addition, the former Dallas Cowboy running back's disease had caused his hands to curl into knots. The once-famed running back was confined to a wheelchair.

Everson decided to give his lifelong friend and former team-mate one of his kidneys. This act has shone a bright light on the sometimes-dim world of professional athletes. Those who know him well acknowledge Everson certainly didn't do this to be hailed as a hero. He simply wanted to help a friend. Perhaps, however, he should be hailed as a hero. Everson not only gave the gift of life to his longtime teammate, he also saved the promising NFL career of another young man.

### DO YOU HAVE A FRIEND FOR WHOM YOU WOULD BE WILLING TO LAY DOWN YOUR LIFE?

Shawn Springs, Ron Springs's son, followed his dad to Ohio State as a standout and currently plays for the NFL's New England Patriots as a defensive back. Shawn, as the only biological match, was planning on donating his kidney to his dad in order to save his life, but to do so would end his NFL career. More than merely saving the life of a dear friend, the former NFL defensive back shattered the old stereotype of the self-absorbed athlete. His unbridled determination and work ethic earned him a storied NFL career. Everson was more than just a great football player; he was a great man and a devoted friend. Everson Walls simply wouldn't let Shawn end his NFL career nor let his friend Ron lose his life. No greater love has a man, "than to lay down one's life for his friends" (John 15:13). Do you have a friend for whom you would be willing to lay down your life?

## Time Out

1. Outside your family, who would be your closest friends?
2. Who would your wife say is the friend who helps you become more faithful to God?
3. Which friend of yours is the best role model for your children? Why?

## Today's Assignment

Call a friend today, and tell him how much you appreciate him and what his friendship means to you.

---

## Home-Field Advantage

*Praises and concerns you want to bring before God*

_____

_____

_____

_____

_____

---

# DAY 6

# AT WORK

## WOULD YOUR COWORKERS BE SURPRISED THAT YOU ARE A CHRISTIAN?

## THE COACH'S CORNER

Because work is so important to men, relationships in the work-place are often very important. Some less-desirable jobs can be enjoyable and interesting because of your fellow workers. On the other hand, a perfect job can be a miserable situation if you are surrounded by difficult people. For Christian men, our work is a calling from God. You were put in your current position for a reason; however, it may not be clear to you now. God didn't just put you in your position to provide you with an income. He wants you to represent Him in all your relationships, including relationships with your coworkers. As a believer, you will have many opportunities to show how God is working in your life. You may not be called to be an evangelist at work but rather a man who always seems to work with the right heart, a man who treats others the way he wants to be treated, a man who doesn't cheat or steal, and a man who is compassionate and fair to others.

Being Christlike in the workplace is often difficult. If your coworkers know you are a Christian, they are always watching to see what you do in specific situations, especially when things are going downhill. When something goes badly for you and you were not at fault, they look to see what you do. When you are passed over for a promotion that you deserved, they wait for your response. When they know you are a big hunter and the first day of deer season arrives, they wonder if you will call in sick. They listen to see if you are someone with whom they can share a secret, and they notice if you are someone who will refuse to listen to an inappropriate joke.

## FOR CHRISTIAN MEN, OUR WORK IS A CALLING FROM GOD.

While we may know how to conduct ourselves at work, it is often difficult to make the transition from Sunday morning to Monday morning. The lessons are so clear on Sunday, but the realities are so hard on Monday. When we are surrounded by our friends on Sunday, the world seems so black and white; it is relatively easy to distinguish right from wrong. But when we return to the workplace, we realize that the real world has many shades of gray. By the time we reach the middle of the week, it becomes easier to simply blend into the culture. We resist it. We feel guilty about it, and we may even try to refocus on our desire to be more Christlike. While it is exceedingly difficult to act consistently the way we know we should, it is important that we identify obstacles that stand in our way. We must ask ourselves, *If I am the only glimpse of Jesus my coworkers will see today, will they be more likely to want to meet Him*?

CBS Sports's Spencer Tillman interviewed FedEx Services president Mike Glenn at an In The Zone conference in Mississippi several months ago. Mike is considered by many to be a marketing genius in the fast-paced corporate world of mass advertising. Mike was influential in the creation of many winning FedEx Super Bowl ads, the PGA's FedEx Cup, as well as the FedEx's entrance into NASCAR with Joe Gibbs. Mike challenged a large group of men to "not put your faith in the drawer when you get to the office. I know it is hard . . . but if you do this God will use you."[1] He cautioned men not to be afraid to stand up for their beliefs no matter where they find themselves. God puts us in specific places and expects us not to be ashamed of Him.

## THE GAME PLAN

God wants you to be His feet in the world . . . even at work! God wants you to know:

- God created it all—including your workplace—and He claims authority over it—Psalm 89:11: "The heavens are Yours, the earth also is Yours; the world and all its fullness, You have founded them."
- Whatever your job, do it in such an excellent and joyful way that it demands an explanation—Matthew 5:14–16: "You are the light of the world. A city that is set on a hill cannot be hidden. Nor do they light a lamp and put it under a basket, but on a lampstand, and it gives light to all who are in the house. Let your light so shine

before men, that they may see your good works and glorify your Father in heaven."

- You must proclaim Christ to others so that they can be in fellowship with Him and experience complete joy—1 John 1:3–4: "That which we have seen and heard we declare to you, that you also may have fellowship with us; and truly our fellowship is with the Father and with His Son Jesus Christ. And these things we write to you that your joy may be full."

- Especially in suffering, don't be ashamed of Christ because He can still be communicated powerfully through you—2 Timothy 1:12: "For this reason I also suffer these things; nevertheless I am not ashamed, for I know whom I have believed and am persuaded that He is able to keep what I have committed to Him until that Day."

## PLAYMAKERS

While interviewing a number of players involved in the Atlanta Braves spring training camp, we sat down with John Smoltz to find out how difficult it is to be the feet and hands of Jesus in today's sports world. John indicated that he feels that every move he makes is being observed and evaluated by someone, and when they know you are a believer they seem to look to see if you walk the walk not just talk the talk. There are many professional baseball players who are committed Christians like John, but probably no one has shared his faith as publically on the national stage as Orel Hershiser has.

At the peak of his successful career in the late 1980s, Orel Hershiser was the pitching ace of a stacked Los Angeles Dodger rotation. He was unbelievable on the mound, one year stringing together fifty-nine consecutive scoreless innings while also winning the Cy Young Award as the National League's best pitcher. At the pinnacle of his career he underwent major reconstructive shoulder surgery, forcing him to miss an entire year—and most believed he was finished. No one could say whether or not the man who had been called "Bulldog" was ever going to pitch again. With much effort and rehabilitation, Orel toughed it out, winning 106 more games—a testament to his competitiveness and love for the game of baseball. After surgery he modified his style by adding several new pitches to his arsenal, including a slider, a two-seam fastball, and an excellent pickoff move.

Earlier in his career with the Dodgers, when he began to struggle on the mound, manager Tommy Lasorda called him into his office to attempt to pump up his young megastar. No one knows what was said behind closed doors, but whatever Lasorda said to him in the "Sermon on the Mound," as the pep talk later become known, seemed to have worked. After pitching five consecutive shutouts, the sinker-baller broke former Dodger Don Drysdale's record streak by one out (giving him fifty-nine scoreless innings) with a ten-inning scoreless, no-decision effort in his final start of the season at San Diego.

Hershiser was a three-time National League All-Star, pitching eighteen years in the major leagues for Los Angeles, Cleveland, San Francisco, and the New York Mets. In 1988, he was named World Series Most Valuable Player, Associated Press Athlete of the Year, and *Sports Illustrated* Sportsman of the Year. Few pitchers since Orel have finished a season the way he finished his remarkable 1988 campaign.

**THE EYES THAT MATTERED MOST TO HIM BELONGED TO THE ONE TO WHOM HE SANG PRAISE—GOD.**

Hershiser was known to be generous in working in the community as well as being as being a confidant and close friend to all in his clubhouse. One of his favorite things to say was that "you don't have to be a wimp to be a Christian." Hershiser attributed his love for God as the motivating factor and source of all his strength while playing in the major leagues. Baseball fans always watched as he often calmed himself down on the mound by singing Christian hymns, in an attempt to drown out all the noise in the opposing stadiums. At one point during the final game of the World Series, television cameras focused in on him singing to himself between pitches. The night after winning the World Series, Orel Hershiser appeared on *The Tonight Show* with Johnny Carson. The show was taped in Los Angeles, so the audience that night was dominated by avid Dodger fans. During his informal interview, Johnny said, "I read something in the paper that when you get a little distressed and you want a little control, you sing to yourself."[2] He then asked Orel what he was singing during the decisive final game of the World Series. In response, Orel Hershiser stood tall and began singing the Doxology—the song he had sung the night before:

> *Praise God, from Whom all blessings flow;*
> *Praise Him, all creatures here below;*
> *Praise Him above, ye heavenly host;*
> *Praise Father, Son, and Holy Ghost.*

Hershiser would never smoke or drink and steered clear of swearing during his career. Due to programs such as *The Tonight Show*, Orel earned the respect of a nation for his faith in Jesus as well as for his celebrated skills as a baseball superstar. His faith gave him peace, even as he stood on the mound of a clinching World Series game in front of thousands in person and millions on TV. He knew that every young boy who was awake was watching him.

But the eyes that mattered most to him belonged to the One to whom he sang praise—God.

## TIME OUT

1. Would most people you work with know you are a Christian?
2. Which, if any, of your coworkers would your wife suggest as potential partners in ministry for you?
3. What is the most difficult part of your job in regard to living out who you are as a man of God?

## TODAY'S ASSIGNMENT

Ask your friends to pray for you to have a godly impact on your coworkers.

---

## HOME-FIELD ADVANTAGE

*Praises and concerns you want to bring before God*

_____

_____

_____

---

## DAY 7

# REGARDING YOUR FUTURE

## LIVING ABOVE IT ALL—OR SIMPLY GOING WITH THE FLOW

### THOUGHT OF THE DAY

*God has a detailed plan for your life—now and forever.*

### THE COACH'S CORNER

It is sometimes hard to believe that God has a plan for your life. With all of the deadlines, ballgames, bills to pay, and honey-do's to knock out, it is refreshing to know there is an ultimate plan. Many times at work we are involved in long-range planning projects. We focus significant attention on where the business will be and how to get there. However, often we don't focus on where we will be or what we will be doing. We frequently just go with the flow. But isn't it exciting to know Christ has a unique plan for our lives? God has given each of us unique talents and a unique personality. We are called to find ways of using these gifts for His glory.

Some of you may have a hard time believing God has a plan for your future. Many believe that because we have free will, we, rather than God, control our own destiny. God is not limited to our time frame, though we often wish He were. He created time; He is not subject to it. Although we have many decisions to make, God already knows what we will choose. Just because He knows what our future choices will be doesn't mean these choices are not made freely: we are ultimately responsible for our own actions and decisions. The Bible says God wants good for you and not bad (Jeremiah 29:11). So when bad things happen we sit back and wonder, "What's up with this?" Oftentimes, though, the things we consider to be bad turn out to be God-sent. He wants us to faithfully trust that He can redeem the time to glorify Himself and mature us so that we conform more closely to the image of Christ. His ultimate plan is for us to meet Him in heaven.

**GOD DESIRES THAT WE LIVE OUR LIVES IN SUCH A WAY THAT OTHERS WILL WANT TO HAVE SOME OF WHAT WE HAVE.**

If you could look into the future, what would you see? What would your family look like? Where will you be working? When we think of the future, we are sometimes concerned, frightened, and worried. We see so much anger and meanness in the world today that it is easy to want to buckle down and live only in the moment. God wants us to improve the world. He has big plans for you, but you must die to your current life. He wants us not to conform to the world but to be set apart from it. God's clear direction for us as we look to the future is that we should go and make disciples of others. God desires that we live our lives in such a way that others will want to have some of what we have. They will desire a future that is full of promise, is rewarding, and honors God.

## THE GAME PLAN

The Bible says God has a plan for your life. God wants you to know:

- God desires for every man to have an abundant life—John 10:10: "The thief does not come except to steal, and to kill, and to destroy. I have come that they may have life, and that they may have it more abundantly."
- You were called by Jesus to be "spice" to the world—Matthew 5:13: "You are the salt of the earth; but if the salt loses its flavor, how shall it be seasoned? It is then good for nothing but to be thrown out and trampled underfoot by men."
- You are called to make disciples, and God promises to be with you in the process—Matthew 28:19–20: "Go therefore and make disciples of all the nations, baptizing them in the name of the Father and of the Son and of the Holy Spirit, teaching them to observe all things that I have commanded you; and lo, I am with you always, even to the end of the age."
- If we are doing the will of the Father, we are part of the family of God—Matthew 12:50: "For whoever does the will of My Father in heaven is my brother and sister and mother."

## PLAYMAKERS

We all have dreams. Some dreams come true while others often do not. For most of us, not having all our dreams come true has certainly been a good thing. What if we all married who we dreamed we would marry? Just imagine if we all grew up to be what we wanted to be when we were children. The world would be full of firemen, policemen, racecar drivers, doctors, and cowboys.

While many people seem to have life all planned out, others seem to simply take whatever life gives them as it passes by. A number of professional athletes have had successful careers after they retired or quit playing professional sports. However, studies have shown that most professional athletes are unprepared for life after the game. Less than half of professional athletes have a college degree, and even fewer have a trade skill that will allow them to start their own business. While superstar players can occasionally land endorsement contracts or television commentator jobs, the rank and file often find themselves with the challenge of creating a new identity once their career and stardom are over. Stories abound of players stung by divorce and failed business ventures. A survey of former NFL players found that in their first year out of the game, 27 percent experienced financial problems, and 18 percent reported severe emotional problems. Almost all said they felt depressed once they were off the gridiron.[1]

> **WHILE MANY PEOPLE SEEM TO HAVE LIFE ALL PLANNED OUT, OTHERS SEEM TO SIMPLY TAKE WHATEVER LIFE GIVES THEM AS IT PASSES BY.**

Among those professionals who were smart enough to create a personal long-term strategic plan, there was one NFL athlete who was never worried about life after football. A star quarterback for the Dallas Cowboys for nearly a decade, Roger Staubach endeared himself to fans of "America's team" with his last-minute game-winning plays that led Dallas to two Super Bowl victories and four National Football Conference (NFC) championships. He grew up outside of

Cincinnati, Ohio, the son of a hardworking salesman. He believed that playing football just might be his only opportunity to go to college. A few years after being admitted to the United States Naval Academy, Staubach excelled and was awarded the prized Heisman Trophy during his junior year. He was only the fourth college junior to win the coveted award given to America's most outstanding college football player. Navy's head coach Wayne Hardin called Roger "the greatest quarterback Navy ever had."[2] With the Heisman Trophy neatly tucked away and a successful season at the Academy, Roger would normally have been one of the top picks in the 1964 NFL draft. However, Roger needed to complete his required naval service of four years before he would be allowed to play in the NFL.

Due to what would be a long absence from the game while serving his country, many teams were extremely skeptical and thought he would lose his touch during his years away from football. Disappointingly, Roger was not selected until the tenth round of the draft. Staubach continued his navy career for another five years before joining his team in 1969 as a twenty-seven-year-old rookie. "I never thought we would see this Heisman Trophy winner in a Cowboys' uniform," remarked the Cowboy's head coach Tom Landry.[3] The wait was worth it as over the next several years Roger's quickness, his missile for an arm, and his extensive knowledge of the game placed him in the NFL Pro Bowl . . . six times. Roger's God-given talents also allowed him to earn the league MVP award, a spot in the Cowboys' illustrious Ring of Honor, and an induction into the Pro Football Hall of Fame in 1985.

With the success that he had on the football field both in college and in the National Football League, Roger probably didn't need to worry about life after football; however, he did. During his seasonal time off from professional football, he worked and studied to be a real estate salesman, and he eventually ascended to the position of assistant vice president for the Henry S. Miller Realty

Company located in Dallas. While still playing for the Cowboys, he utilized the Dallas-based commercial real estate firm to learn the ropes of commercial real estate and founded The Staubach Company upon his retirement. Under his leadership, The Staubach Company has grown to over 1,400 employees with locations in more than sixty cities throughout America.

As a happily married man and father, Roger often thought of his need to support his young family of five children when his career with the Cowboys was over. A career in the commercial real estate industry in the off-season gave Roger just the flexibility he needed, and he discovered he loved his work in the new industry and was very good at it. He often humorously joked that his real estate mentor, Henry S. Miller, resembled his football mentor, Tom Landry, in two ways. One, "they had the same haircut (bald)," and two, "they wouldn't ever benefit themselves at the expense of someone else."[4] Roger appeared to create a seamless transition from the NFL world to the competitive world of business. His transition away from football also worked not only because of his unwavering character but also because he made acquiring a vocational skill a priority early in his football career. Roger Staubach realized God gave him multiple talents, and he celebrated his giftedness in more than one vocation.

When Roger and I (Kyle) trained together for the *ABC–TV SuperStars* competition at the Cooper Clinic in Dallas in the mid-1970s, I realized the multiple athletic talents he had. We all know Roger for his football prowess, but he was a great baseball and basketball talent as well.

Roger's impact in the military, college, NFL, corporate, and Christian arenas is still being felt. "During FCA's fifty-three-year history of ministering to athletes and coaches, a number of extraordinary individuals have been used mightily by God to influence others in their communities and the nation to have a personal belief in and commitment to Jesus Christ as their Savior and Lord," says Fellowship of Christian Athletes president Les Steckel. "Roger Staubach is one of those people."[5]

## TIME OUT

1. What gifts do you believe God will use in your future to honor Him?
2. What is your spouse's biggest concern regarding your family and the future?
3. Is it difficult to believe that God truly has a plan for your life?

## TODAY'S ASSIGNMENT

If you needed to make a change today that would impact your future in a positive way for the kingdom, what would it be?

## HOME-FIELD ADVANTAGE

*Praises and concerns you want to bring before God*

_____

_____

_____

_____

# FINDING THE ZONE IN YOUR RELATIONSHIP WITH YOUR WIFE

*Husbands, love your wives, just as Christ also loved the church and gave Himself for her, that He might sanctify and cleanse her with the washing of water by the word, that He might present her to Himself a glorious church, not having spot or wrinkle or any such thing, but that she should be holy and without blemish.*

—EPHESIANS 5:25–27

# GOING AGAINST THE TREND

## STAYING FAITHFUL IN AN UNFAITHFUL GENERATION

### THOUGHT OF THE DAY

*Staying faithful requires constant thought, action, and prayer, as well as the willingness to flee temptation.*

### THE COACH'S CORNER

Whatever happened to *I Love Lucy*, *Ozzie and Harriett*, *The Cosby Show*, or Tim "the Tool Man Taylor" from *Home Improvement*? We now turn on the TV and see *The Bachelor*, *Desperate Housewives*, *Army Wives*, *Sex in the City*, *Housewives of Orange County*, *America's Next Top Model*, and *Dirty Sexy Money*. It seems that everywhere we look our generation is trying to sell sex or at least plant the seed that casual sex for singles or being unfaithful is an acceptable behavior. While the times have certainly changed, God's Word is applicable to every generation. The Bible is full of examples of the dangers and the destruction of marital unfaithfulness. Although times are tough for many businesses today, the sex and pornography industry seems to be growing even faster than the national debt! Everywhere you look, there is temptation to be unfaithful to your standards, to your wife, and also to your family.

We all have memories of our dating days. The never-ending quiet evenings spent talking for long hours about nothing, the childlike kidding and joking, the insignificant trips that were so exciting. Love was really all we wanted or needed. How to please our girlfriend was the focus of hours of thought. She looked at you as if you were the smartest, sexiest, and strongest man she had ever met. Marriage soon followed, and she quickly learned just how different you were from her dad. The trips got more elaborate and the gifts more expensive. The quest for things became essential, and it was closely followed by bills—lots and lots of bills. The long, quiet talks became budget sessions, and slowly the romance began to break down. The introduction of children made for such a happy yet stressful time. But the time the children took from both of you slowly lulled your relationship to sleep. Now between work and children you are so tired that you tend to put your marriage on hold. Your wife surely knows you love her, but there are simply too many things to deal with to worry about focusing on recharging the marriage. What does God have to say about the importance of keeping your marriage strong?

**WHILE THE TIMES HAVE CERTAINLY CHANGED, GOD'S WORD IS APPLICABLE TO EVERY GENERATION.**

Although we know our world is full of temptations, what are we to do on a daily basis to keep focused on our marriage? Many men refuse to go to lunch with a female coworker without being accompanied by a male. An executive from Federal Express noted that he never goes on a business trip with a female associate without his wife going along. The famed evangelist Billy Graham would never ride in a car alone with a woman unless it was his mother, his wife, or his daughter. When asked why he was emphatic about not getting into a car with another woman, his answer was simple: "I don't want to give anyone something to talk about, and I don't want to be put in a place of temptation."[1]

## THE GAME PLAN

The Bible says that God desires for you to stay faithful. God wants you to know:

- God will protect the covenant of marriage—Hebrews 13:4: "Marriage is honorable among all, and the bed undefiled; but fornicators and adulterers God will judge."
- No one should separate those whom God has put together—Matthew 19:6: "So then, they are no longer two but one flesh. Therefore what God has joined together, let not man separate."
- God is the source of all faithfulness—2 Thessalonians 3:3: "But the Lord is faithful, who will establish you and guard you from the evil one."
- God encourages us to get married—Proverbs 18:22: "He who finds a wife finds a good thing, and obtains favor from the LORD."

## PLAYMAKERS

Being faithful to your wife in today's world requires vigilance and determination with a protective covering and wisdom from the Holy Spirit. The embarrassing examples we have seen in recent years from powerful political men alone have been disappointing to say the least. Among those who received the most media attention were:

1. Bill Clinton (president of the United States): an affair with a White House intern
2. John Edwards (candidate for presidency): cheating on cancer-stricken wife
3. David Vitter (senator from Louisiana): sex with a prostitute
4. Eliot Spitzer (governor of New York): sex with a high-priced prostitute
5. Mark Foley (congressman from Florida): solicited sex from underage male pages
6. John Ensign (senator from Nevada): affair with campaign aide married to his friend
7. Mark Sanford (governor of South Carolina): disappears and leaves his children on Father's Day to see his mistress

**BEING FAITHFUL TO YOUR WIFE IN TODAY'S WORLD REQUIRES VIGILANCE AND DETERMINATION WITH A PROTECTIVE COVERING AND WISDOM FROM THE HOLY SPIRIT.**

South Carolina's governor Mark Sanford may have been on his way to being one of the leading presidential candidates in 2012, but now his political career is likely finished—enter the power of being unfaithful! Mark Sanford, who went missing for several days (including Father's Day 2009), was found to have lied to his family, his staff, and the public concerning where he had been. However, after being seen in Atlanta returning to the country, he came clean and admitted he was having an affair with a close friend in Argentina. His longtime wife, Jenny Sanford, simply addressed reporters by saying that if the media would like to better understand what makes the governor tick, she has several copies of her husband's autobiography, *The Trust Committed to Me*.

The governor of South Carolina, who has identified himself on many occasions over the years as an evangelical Christian, seems to have fallen . . . and fallen hard. The fact that he was married for more than twenty years is most significant, but choosing to spend Father's Day in the company of the other woman instead of his own family is something many fathers today will never completely understand. He had been in Argentina with his mistress instead of vacationing at the beach in the Carolinas with his wife and four sons.

According to *USA Today*, "The bottom line is this: I have been unfaithful to my wife," the governor said. "The relationship started with casual e-mail back and forth, but then recently over this last year developed into something much more than that . . . I hurt my wife, I hurt my boys . . . I hurt a lot of different folks . . . and all I can say is that I apologize. It began very innocently," the governor said of his affair with a woman whom he had known for eight years. "Our 'remarkable friendship' during the past year 'sparked' into something else," he said.[2]

Temptation, especially sexual temptation, is a strong force in the lives of men today, just as it has been since the beginning of time. There are ways we can guard ourselves against being unfaithful to our wives, but this may be an extremely hard battle for many. The first step is to recognize the lies Satan plants in our minds that always propel us toward temptation—lies such as, "It's OK, everybody does it" or "It's OK as long as no one gets hurt" or "Times have changed since Jesus made up the rule about loving only one woman." Here are several other falsehoods Satan uses to lead men down the path toward adultery, and the truths that eventually set men free:

- Satan wants you to believe: What I think about doesn't matter as long as I don't act on it.
- God wants you to know: Our thoughts often become our actions.
- Satan wants you to believe: I would be happier with someone else.
- God wants you to know: Only Jesus can ever fully make you happy.
- Satan wants you to believe: Life is passing me by; I deserve something more exciting.
- God wants you to know: You have already received more than you deserve.
- Satan wants you to believe: When others pay attention to me, they think I'm special.
- God wants you to know: People often use flattery to get what they want.
- Satan wants you to believe: I can get away with an affair.
- God wants you to know: God will expose your sin.

## TIME OUT

1. Have you had a time when you felt tempted to cheat on your wife and family?
2. Are there places you visit, shows you watch, or Internet sites you visit that tempt you?

3. Is something going on in your life right now that you know is wrong but you are having a hard time dealing with?

## TODAY'S ASSIGNMENT

Repentance is where powerlessness ends and forgiveness begins. If you are currently involved in a tempting relationship, today is the day to end it. Find the things in your life that are tempting you, and find a way of removing yourself from the temptation. Ask God to help you get out of the destructive maze; He knows how to help.

---

## HOME-FIELD ADVANTAGE

*Praises and concerns you want to bring before God*

_____

_____

_____

_____

---

# LOVING AN IMPERFECT WOMAN

## REKINDLING YOUR MARRIAGE

### THOUGHT OF THE DAY

*No one is married to a perfect woman: learn to celebrate the uniqueness God put into your wife.*

### THE COACH'S CORNER

She does things that irritate you, things that outright frustrate you, and she doesn't always do things the way your mother did. While you love your wife, you have discovered she has a number of small imperfections that you did not discover prior to saying, "I do." While living with an imperfect woman can surely be difficult, your wife is probably a saint to put up with you. There are many reasons a marriage can begin to slowly die. God made your wife just the way He wanted her to be. Her imperfections help refine us and make us more holy. God uses her to smooth out your rough edges and help to make you more like Him. One of the fatal faults for most husbands is that we fail to continue dating and pursuing our wives after we marry them. Going to fancy restaurants, taking romantic walks, or driving aimlessly for hours in the car (wasting gas) just doesn't seem as important after we have *won the prize*. If we were to look at why we don't continue dating our wives, most of us would have similar excuses:

- "I am worn out." You work hard all day, and when the weekend finally arrives you really just want to stay in and watch the ballgame or play with the kids. The idea of grooming yourself or dressing up on your day off is not appealing.
- "I have too much to do." With little free time between work, "honey do's," and the children, you never seem to have time to do what you want or need to do. You feel there will never be an end to the tasks around the home that need to be done.
- "I really don't want to argue." You don't want to discuss money, hear that your kids are growing up to be imperfect, discuss what needs to be fixed around the house, and talk about what the "Joneses" just purchased. Often a night out turns into a staff meeting, not a romantic evening.
- "We have kids." Now this is a good one. There are things that must be done in order for you to be a quality father, and having a date would take quality time away from your kids. You certainly don't want them to grow up without developing the skills necessary to play in the NBA!
- "We're broke." A night out can be somewhat expensive, and there never seems to be enough money. Your wife's

tastes have probably changed since you were dating. Back then, pizza would do; now it seems only "chick" food is on the menu.

- "I just don't want to go." It can seem like a waste of time. She knows you love her; you don't have to prove it again, right?

A date night once a week can be a marriage saver. Ground rules can usually be helpful as well. We have included a list of possible subjects for discussion; however, you are encouraged to develop your own list as well:

- We will not talk about the kids, in-laws, bills, or next week's to-do list.
- We will not talk about all the things we don't have time to do or how we can't afford this night out.
- We will not discuss any subject that may lead to a disagreement.
- We will talk about ways God is working in our lives and in our marriage.
- We will talk about, and plan, the things we may do together in the future.
- We will talk about ways we can be a blessing to the neighborhood, the kid's schools, or our church.

## THE GAME PLAN

The Bible says that God expects you to treat your wife and His daughter special. God wants you to:

- Live with your wife in a spirit of patience and under-standing—1 Peter 3:7: "Husbands, likewise, dwell with them with understanding, giving honor to the wife, as to the weaker vessel, and as being heirs together of the grace of life, that your prayers may not be hindered."

- Be the leader of your home—1 Timothy 3:12: "Let deacons be the husbands of one wife, ruling their children and their own houses well."
- Celebrate your marriage to your wife as Christ celebrates His marriage to His wife, the church—Isaiah 62:5: "For as a young man marries a virgin, so shall your sons marry you; and as the bridegroom rejoices over the bride, so shall your God rejoice over you."
- Celebrate with your wife the joy of physical union—Proverbs 5:18: "Let your fountain be blessed, and rejoice with the wife of your youth."

## PLAYMAKERS

Bobby and Ann Bowden are as close to college football royalty as it gets. Few college coaches whom we have had the pleasure of knowing have done more for combining faith and football than Bobby Bowden. As the renowned head football coach of Florida State University, Bowden has solidified his place among the greatest college football coaches of all time. But as with most successful men, he didn't start out on top, and he had some help. In fact, Coach Bowden worked his way up through the college football ranks, shouldering many of the same pressures the rest of us face—marriage, work, kids, money, and so on.

From the beginning, Bobby Bowden's biggest teammate and fan has been his wife, Ann. The two married at a young age—Bobby, nineteen, and Ann, sixteen—sneaking across the Georgia border in Bobby Bowden Sr.'s car to tie the knot. Ann recalls, "He and I have been together just about every day of our lives since I was fifteen . . . We started going together when we were kids, and he's still a big kid, going off with his friends to play games . . ."[1]

Life didn't slow down for Bobby and Ann. If anything it began to speed up. After graduating from high school, the couple went on to Howard College, now Samford University, in Birmingham, Alabama. With two kids in tow already, they were motivated and eager to begin their college experiences. Ann was head cheerleader, and Bobby became the football team's star quarterback. They each somehow found time to serve as president of their respective fraternity and sorority. Day by day, they were learning to balance it all—faith, family, marriage, and responsibilities.

Together Ann and Bobby raised six kids. This required a great deal of compromise and unwavering commitment to one another. They were in for the long haul. "There was no divorce in either one of our families," said Anne. "No matter how tough things got—no matter if I locked him out of the house a couple of nights because he was spending more time with his buddies talking football than paying attention to me and the kids—we never considered divorce." They became a team at home, each falling into certain roles. "I realized we were working for the same thing," said Ann. Bobby would spend the day coaching and return home to begin his shift of caring for their growing family and helping Ann. "I tell him even now, you sit up there in that fancy football office overlooking the stadium, the king of your domain. But I'm still the head coach of this house."[2]

Bowden received his first head coaching position at his alma mater, Howard College. After a few years, he moved his family to Tallahassee to become an assistant coach for Florida State University, working alongside Bill Peterson, Bill Parcells, and Joe Gibbs. In 1965, Bowden joined the West Virginia University football program as assistant coach, soon becoming the head coach. Shortly thereafter, Bobby Bowden was offered the head coaching position at FSU. The family, especially Ann, was not eager to leave West Virginia. In the end, they decided returning to Tallahassee would be a good short-term move for the family. Coach Bowden rejoined FSU as head coach in 1976 with a starting salary of only $37,500. Little did they know, Bowden would become a legendary coach there and would still be coaching the Seminoles thirty-three years later.

> **"HAPPINESS IS NOT MONEY, AND IT'S NOT FAME, AND IT'S NOT POWER. HAPPINESS IS A GOOD WIFE, A GOOD FAMILY, AND GOOD HEALTH."**
>
> **—BOBBY BOWDEN**

The Bowdens have become permanent fixtures in Tallahassee. Ann Bowden has become as much a part of the FSU family as her husband. It is even rumored she recommended placing spears on the football helmets. She took on a leadership role all her own, including founding the Extra Points Club. They still reside in the house they bought in 1976 even though many times over the years, Ann tried to negotiate a move to a larger home—the couple did eventually decide to expand their home. Bobby once said, "All that say the University Center at Florida State is the largest brick construction project in the history of the southeast . . . well, when my house is finished, the UC is going to drop to number two."[3]

As the royal family of college football, football is life for the Bowdens. Coach Bowden seems happiest when he is on the field coaching. Three of the couple's six children have also gone on to follow in his footsteps, becoming well-known, successful college football coaches. In spite of his love for the game and his great success, football is not what matters most to Bobby Bowden, who said, "Happiness is not money, and it's not fame, and it's not power. Those are nice, but they only last a finger snap. Happiness is a good wife, a good family, and good health."[4] Someone once asked Ann how she thought her husband had changed over the years. Ann remarked, "His belt has grown a few notches, and his hair a little grayer; there's a small bald spot on the back of his head. But inside, he is still the man I married sixty years ago, well, almost, with a few changes. He's a little more tolerant and understanding and has the same will and determination and competitiveness."[5]

Despite the many highs and lows, the Bowdens have held strong for more than sixty years. The ESPN College Football Awards recognized Coach Bowden in 2009 with the NCFAA Contributions to College Football Award for "exceptional contributions to college football and a lifetime of achievement and integrity." Ann Bowden introduced Bobby by saying, "He has had to sacrifice much of his time with his family. They said something to me about me sacrificing a lot. Actually, I think it's the coaches that sacrifice a lot with families and what their children go through as they grow up and the activities that they have. He has never faltered in his faith. You know faith is what brings you through, faith and family. And we have had the honor of having a great family and a great faith. I have watched him grow stronger through the years."[6] Apparently the feeling is mutual as Coach Bowden said of his wife, "All of the success that our family has had and my success is because of Ann's drive. She is the inspiration behind us. She took care of the home front even when I was there. There was no doubt who ran the home front."[7]

## TIME OUT

1. Remember the last time you truly worked hard at making your marriage more interesting and fun. What did you do?
2. What would your wife identify as the single thing most missing from your marriage?

3. Identify a couple you know who seems to have a marriage that is alive and well, with aspects you would like to replicate. What do you admire most about them?

## TODAY'S ASSIGNMENT

Call your spouse and ask her out on a date. Let her get excited about when and where. Pull out your calendar or Outlook, and identify two dates that you can schedule with your wife over the next thirty days. On the way home today, stop and pick up something for your wife that will be unexpected.

---

## HOME-FIELD ADVANTAGE
*Praises and concerns you want to bring before God*

_____

_____

_____

_____

_____

---

## Day 10

# Improving Your Sex Life

### God Invented Sex—It's OK to Enjoy It

---

## Thought of the Day

*God encourages you to fully enjoy the physical intimacy that only sex can provide.*

## The Coach's Corner

Many of you have been married for many years, and finally, you no longer blush bright red when the word *sex* is mentioned out loud— it's more of a faint pink tinge. For most of us growing up, sex wasn't talked about very much, if at all. Not at home, not with family, and certainly not in church! The very mention of the word would have turned ears to scarlet and had the deacons popping antacid pills. But God created sex not only for procreation but also for the pleasure of the husband and wife. You may want to read Song of Solomon in your Bible; you would be shocked at how forthcoming the Word is.

Every year the youth group discussed abstinence, but little could actually be learned from such generic conversation. Most guys would, of course, act as if they were experts on the subject. A few might have been, but most were clueless. For most men, there were no father-son talks about sex. The school didn't desire to touch it, and the church wouldn't get close to the subject; consequently, men were left to fend for themselves. Therefore, we have grown up in a generation where *sex* is a bad word. God created sex, and He made it for a very special purpose.

> **GOD CREATED SEX NOT ONLY JUST FOR PROCREATION BUT ALSO FOR THE PLEASURE OF THE HUSBAND AND WIFE.**

Have you heard a good sermon lately on "How to Have a More Satisfying Sex Life"? We never cease to be amazed at all the books and CDs available regarding how to improve your sex life, most written by women. It seems if we could just read the right book and *get it* then everyone would be more satisfied. For most men, this subject is not easy to talk about: we would agree that most of us think about sex often; we just don't discuss it. The idea that men think about sex every few seconds, like the claim that we use only a small percentage of our brains, is often repeated but has been found to be untrue unless you are single (or you are married with no children, or you are under the age forty-five, or . . . ). It has been said that over half of today's men think about sex every day or several times a day, fewer think about it a few times a week and still fewer think about it less than once per month. So now that we have discovered that we are not perpetually sex-starved monsters, what does this mean for us?

Although sex is a subject the world has made dirty, God is not shocked by the passion of our sexual desire or by its fulfillment. For married men to enjoy the excitement and pleasure of sex seems to fit with His original nature and plan. A study of the major factors in the failure of Christian marriages today ranked "failed sexual expectations or unmet needs" as one of the most important causes of divorce. Experts say that these unmet needs most often refer to those unmet needs in the bedroom.[1] Where does a Christian man talk about sex? With whom?

## THE GAME PLAN

The Bible says that God encourages sexual fulfillment in married couples. God wants you to know:

- He provides comfort for you through marital sex—Genesis 24:67: "Then Isaac brought her into his mother Sarah's tent; and he took Rebekah and she became his wife, and he loved her. So Isaac was comforted after his mother's death."
- He encourages you to recognize how the desire for marital love drives you—Genesis 29:20: "So Jacob served seven years for Rachel, and they seemed only a few days to him because of the love he had for her."
- How valuable and how vulnerable your passion for sex is—Song of Solomon 8:7–9: "Many waters cannot quench love, nor can the floods drown it. If a man would give for love all the wealth of his house, it would be utterly despised. We have a little sister, and she has no breasts. What shall we do for our sister in the day when she is spoken for? If she is a wall, we will build upon her a battlement of silver; and if she is a door, we will enclose her with boards of cedar."

- The enjoyment in sexual fulfillment with your wife, but don't worship it—Ecclesiastes 9:9: "Live joyfully with the wife whom you love all the days of your vain life which He has given you under the sun, all your days of vanity; for that is your portion in life, and in the labor which you perform under the sun."

## PLAYMAKERS

After the engagement and then the wedding, one of the most difficult things for any young couple to adjust to is the fact that sex is suddenly . . . OK! All the years of abstinence and silence on the forbidden topic, all the years of feeling guilty for even asking questions, all the years of wondering and dreaming, all the years of thinking about sex as a four-letter word, suddenly just goes away. Sex is now not only expected and allowed, but—gasp!—it's a part of God's ultimate plan! Suddenly, we have two young people who have tried their hardest to remain pure, and now they may be facing some challenges they never expected. Because the mind-set that *sex is bad* has been forced into most young men's minds for as long as they can remember, it becomes hard to relate to your wife physically. This often creates tension between you and your new wife. If sexual frequency doesn't match what the world or TV says is normal, your wife sometimes experiences a false sense of guilt in her head, and you develop insecurity. The entire situation is misread, and you assume something is wrong with both of you. It can even escalate into a young couple thinking they are not appealing to each other. And what God has purposed for good between a husband and wife becomes distorted.

In a 1975 interview with Phyllis George on the old CBS *NFL Today Show*, NFL Hall of Fame quarterback Roger Staubach was asked about his image as a "clean-cut family man," compared to the other famous NFL quarterback of the day, Joe Namath, and his image as a playboy. This type of conversation is still alive today as often quarterbacks are basically labeled as being either a Joe Namath–type or a Roger Staubach–type.

Namath was known as a real authentic playboy, likely to be seen at a nightclub with beautiful women. Staubach was known as a straight-laced type, married to his childhood sweetheart and, by modern standards of celebrity, barely a sex symbol at all. Mr. Namath once owned a nightclub called Bachelors III, a playground for the excesses of single men pursuing sexual conquest. Roger Staubach, the clean-cut former naval officer who quarterbacked the Dallas Cowboys in the 1970s, once said, "I enjoy sex as much as Joe Namath, only I do it with one girl."[2]

The monogamous love life of the Staubach–type seems to mirror the lives of most of us regular guys today. The single life lived by NFL superstars like Tom Brady and Tony Romo, who spent the weekend before the 2008 playoffs in Mexico with celebrity Jessica Simpson, is really fantasyland for most of us. "More Americans are like the Roger Staubachs of the world than the Joe Montanas of the world," said Richard Deitsch, an editor for *Sports Illustrated*. "They are more likely to marry their college girlfriends than they are to marry someone famous like Carrie Underwood or Jessica Simpson."[3]

Sex is everywhere we look today. Movies, television shows, sit-coms, novels, Web sites, advertisements, commercials . . . even the so-called *family* channels on TV promote sex in disguise. Characters in almost all shows sleep together before they're married, and the entire industry seems to promote casual sex. These shows are often humorous on a superficial level but fail to show the emotional and often physical consequences of such choices. This is obviously an extremely dangerous situation, not only for our youth but also for us as well. How can we say we are trying to guard our spouses from temptation when we are allowing such trash into our homes? How can we protect our eyes and ears when it seems sex is plastered all over, even in our homes? Are we supposed to never see movies? Never turn on the television set? Never pick up a novel? Never venture outside of our houses? Well, that certainly is an option but not a real comfortable or realistic option for most men.

**HOW CAN WE SAY WE ARE TRYING TO GUARD OUR SPOUSES FROM TEMPTATION WHEN WE ARE ALLOWING SUCH TRASH INTO OUR HOMES?**

Just maybe a real-life example will help us to stay focused on what we have committed to as husbands. We know A. C. Green to be a real role model. A. C. was a sixteen-year NBA workhorse who played power forward on three Los Angeles Lakers title teams, as well as playing with Phoenix, Dallas, and the Miami Heat. He holds the record for the most consecutive NBA games played at 1,192. In the NBA, his name became synonymous with consistency both athletically and sexually. During a visit with A. C. in Memphis several years ago, I (Kyle) was impressed with how bold he was in giving God the glory for his self-control. He preached and lived abstinence in his personal life until he married his wife, Veronique, in 2002. He could have been the inspiration for the movie *The 40-Year-Old Virgin*. There were many jokes on talk shows when he got married because not many professional athletes wait until they're almost forty years old to have their first sexual experience. He was consistently faithful on and off the court. He has led a movement by example and by encouraging kids to remain abstinent. It's been an effective tool coming from a professional athlete with a charismatic personality. His example was not ignored by adults either. Green was inducted into the World Sports Humanitarian Hall of Fame in 2001 and the Oregon Sports Hall of Fame in 2003 and was also recognized by the U.S. House of Representatives.

## TIME OUT

1. On a scale of 1 to 10, how would you classify your sex life with your spouse?
2. Ask your wife the same question as well.
3. Is there anything you can do that could strengthen your sex life with your spouse? If so, what?

## TODAY'S ASSIGNMENT

Consider something spontaneous: i.e., coming home early just to talk, leaving work in the middle of the day, or renting a hotel room for a night. Choose a new habit today that will make you more attractive to your wife.

## HOME-FIELD ADVANTAGE

*Praises and concerns you want to bring before God*

_____

_____

_____

_____

# BUILDING UP YOUR SPOUSE

## CREATING YOUR REAL DREAM TEAM

## THOUGHT OF THE DAY

*Celebrate your wife's strengths and affirm her in her role as your partner for life.*

## THE COACH'S CORNER

The term *dream team* is used often in sports; however, it can also be used when referring to other situations such as a husband and wife team at home. What makes a team a real dream team in sports? We want to see people who work well together, a team that is focused on the same outcome, a team that knows the strengths and weaknesses of every member, and a team with individual members who can be counted on when it's crunch time. God's Word provides a great concept of how a real dream team can work in our marriage. Proverbs 31 is an excellent scripture to study as you determine what your job is in working with your wife to create your team. We can certainly assume these types of skills can also work in our marriage. When we refer to a dream team we also think of a team that is emotionally close, when one team member just seems to know what another player will do prior to them doing it. A family dream team can actually be a real possibility.

When we begin to think it's time to get married, we really don't focus too much on finding a wife who complements us. We are usually looking for a girl we find attractive, a real soul mate, and someone we feel shares the same general perspective toward life. Many times your mothers probably told you that opposites attract. And while you bought into that crazy idea, it was only after you married someone who was your opposite that you realized that just maybe you shouldn't have listened to your mother on this one. But this subject usually doesn't even come up until you have been married for several months and realize that your new wife is driving you crazy.

## A FAMILY DREAM TEAM CAN ACTUALLY BE A REAL POSSIBILITY.

Your wife has strengths that are extremely valuable to God, whether or not they seem valuable to you. Since these personality traits were created by God especially for your wife, your role is to affirm where she is really gifted. Often what you see in your wife as weaknesses are really her strengths that have been taken to an extreme. For instance, if she is a very giving and sharing person, that strength taken to an extreme might turn her into someone whom you complain is always giving her time to everyone but you—then you feel left out.

Many times we find it more convenient to mention the things we don't like about our wives than to recognize and celebrate the special gifts God has given to them. We frequently become aware of the things we'd like to modify in them rather than applaud the things we should cherish. Too often we are quick to focus on their flaws, instead of building them up with our actions and our heartfelt words.

Countless research studies show that the most successful way to change a person's performance is to reward her positively when her behavior is positive. Yet a lot of married men grapple with being critics and not encouragers. Belittling hardly ever brings positive change, yet sorrowfully, some men keep trying over and over and over. Instead of affirming, complimenting, and building up their wives, they often fall into the trap of putting down their wives—worst of all, putting them down in front of their friends. That may be one of the most foolish mistakes men can make.

## YOUR WIFE HAS STRENGTHS THAT ARE EXTREMELY VALUABLE TO GOD, WHETHER OR NOT THEY SEEM VALUABLE TO YOU.

On the other hand, only one thing is better than a private compliment to your wife, and that is when you brag on her to others when she is listening. This practice is proven to boost her confidence as a wife, mother, and team member. Think of all the dream teams that have existed over the years and what different personalities the coaches had to work with. Creating your dream team with only two should be a cinch.

## THE GAME PLAN

The Bible says that God expects you to build up your wife. God wants you to know:

- You are to set an example in obedience to God—1 Kings 9:4–5: "Now if you walk before Me as your father David walked, in integrity of heart and in uprightness, to do according to all that I have commanded you, and if you keep My statutes and My judgments, then I will establish the throne of your kingdom over Israel forever, as I promised David your father, saying, 'You shall not fail to have a man on the throne of Israel.'"

- When you sacrificially love your wife, you are acting in your own self-interest—Ephesians 5:28–30: "So husbands ought to love their own wives as their own bodies; he who loves his wife loves himself. For no one ever hated his own flesh, but nourishes and cherishes it, just as the Lord does the church. For we are members of His body, of His flesh and of His bones."

- You can team up with your wife to teach your children a godly lifestyle—Deuteronomy 6:7: "You shall teach them diligently to your children, and shall talk of them when you sit in your house, when you walk by the way, when you lie down, and when you rise up."

- You can team up with your wife by setting boundaries for your children that both of you will enforce—Proverbs 22:6: "Train up a child in the way he should go, and when he is old he will not depart from it."

## PLAYMAKERS

We all know Coach Mike Holmgren, who helped lead the San Francisco 49ers, Green Bay Packers, and Seattle Seahawks to the Super Bowl. He is widely regarded as one of the best coaches in the NFL. In his thirty-eight years of coaching thus far, he is credited with helping to develop many of the NFL's star quarterbacks, including Brett Favre, Joe Montana, Steve Young, and Matt Hasselbeck.

But there is much more to Mike Holmgren than football. He grew up in San Francisco with a close-knit family, playing football and attending First Covenant Church. The first thing you should know about Coach Holmgren is that he is a man of faith, believing quiet time with God is crucial. Second, the coach is a family man, married to his wife, Kathy, for over thirty-five years. They have four daughters together, and Mike jokes, "Having daughters is pretty good. I get to make a lot of decisions at work; I make none at home."[1]

We can all imagine the immense pressure an NFL head football coach must be under. Coach Holmgren has also had his share of personal difficulties, including the devastating news that his wife had cancer. Despite these extreme pressures and his tremendous success, Coach Holmgren knows what matters most. "My priorities in life are faith, family, and football—in that order ... but I will not risk losing my marriage or my family for my career. If pro football ever begins to undermine what matters most in life, then I'll go back to coaching high school. It's that simple!"[2]

In January 2006, head coach Mike Holmgren was preparing the Seattle Seahawks to face the Pittsburgh Steelers in Super Bowl XL. Many football fans raised an eyebrow when it was announced that the coach's wife, Kathy, would not be present in the stands of Ford Field in Detroit for the big game. Kathy Holmgren, who always had a passion for mission work, was recruited for a mission trip by their daughter Calla, a doctor specializing in obstetrics and gynecology. Northwest Medical Teams, a non-profit relief organization, and Covenant Church (the home church of the Holmgrens') organized the trip to bring supplies, medicines, and aid to people in the Congo. This would not be Kathy's first trip to the Congo; she had served as a missionary nurse more than thirty years earlier. In fact, she said, "I became a nurse to become a medical missionary.

So right after nursing school, I decided to go to the Congo."[3] So on game day, Kathy found herself half a world away on an aid mission trip to the Congo to care for war survivors.

**"I WILL NOT RISK LOSING MY MARRIAGE OR MY FAMILY FOR MY CAREER."**

**—MIKE HOLMGREN**

You may think Coach Holmgren would have objected, wanting his family with him for the big game. Quite the contrary, not only was the trip planned prior to the Seahawks making it to the Super Bowl, the trip was actually a Christmas present from Mike to his wife. The coach explained, "It gives me great joy that she will go. This is who she is. While at times she is 'Mike Holmgren's wife' she is also very much her own woman, and I've always loved that about her."[4]

This is a couple who has figured out how to be together and yet appreciate one another as separate people. As Kathy once shared with *Packer Plus*, "The older I've gotten, I realize that each one of us, we have to find our own life. If he's happy in what he does, that makes for a better partner for me. And he feels the same way about me. So he's really very nice about giving me opportunities to enrich myself and to really do the kinds of things that I like to do. It's real important for each one of us to have our own life, so that I don't depend on him for my happiness. I have to be happy on my own. But we really do like to spend time together, so it's not like we lead separate lives. Whenever we can be together, we would opt for that because we really like each other."[5]

**THE BEST RELATIONSHIPS DEMAND FLEXIBILITY AND A LITTLE GIVE-AND-TAKE.**

Many people have described Mike and Kathy's marriage as a dream team. They have kept their faith, marriage, and family first. The Holmgrens have found a way to support one another's passions, strengths, and goals, no matter the distance or location. Coach Holmgren didn't dwell on the fact that Kathy would miss the big game (the biggest game!) but instead celebrated the opportunity she had to pursue her passion. And Kathy was rooting for her man from across the world, filled with nervous energy for her husband's big game. The best relationships demand flexibility and a little give-and-take.

## TIME OUT

1. What tasks do you know that your wife hates that you can take off of her plate?
2. Ask your wife to help you identify how you can best create a real dream team at home.
3. Identify things you both dislike to do in your home, and then determine how to share the responsibilities to still get the job done.

## TODAY'S ASSIGNMENT

Find an opportunity several times this week to brag on your wife in front of your friends and your children. In addition, consider doing something unusual to lessen her burden, for example: hire someone to watch the kids for a couple of hours, hire a maid for one day, bring home dinner—do something that will really surprise your team mate and make her feel special.

## HOME-FIELD ADVANTAGE

*Praises and concerns you want to bring before God*

_____

_____

_____

_____

_____

# DON'T LOOK FOR TROUBLE

## FAULTFINDING IS NOT A SPORT

### THOUGHT OF THE DAY

*Don't set yourself up for disappointment; two imperfect people can never have a perfect marriage.*

### THE COACH'S CORNER

To a certain extent, many of us are cheap. Have you ever taken parts from two broken-down machines and tried to miraculously put them together and make one machine that worked? A friend once told of a time when he took the old but working motor off of one lawnmower and put it on the frame of another old lawnmower that needed a motor. After hours of sweating, he finally figured out how this new combination mower could work, but it was still not running very smoothly. Sometimes that is the way it is with our marriage: we bring together two imperfect people and are disappointed when we don't have a perfect marriage. God knows how hard it is to make a marriage work. He uses the imperfections in each of us to constantly remind us that the true source of joy and satisfaction is not in our spouses but only in Him.

It's easy to find fault in our wives—far too easy for the majority of us. Many times, the imperfections are easier to see than all the positive things they do for the family. Think about it—if your neighbor just painted his home and missed a spot, what's the first thing you see? If a family member cooked your dinner and used too much seasoning, what's the first thing you notice when you put the food into your mouth? If you see the missed spot on the wall, aren't you doing your friend a favor by pointing it out? And if the food tastes terrible, doesn't she expect total honesty out of you? Your answer will reveal how long you have been married!

> **GOD USES THE IMPERFECTIONS IN EACH OF US TO CONSTANTLY REMIND US THAT THE TRUE SOURCE OF JOY AND SATISFACTION IS NOT IN OUR SPOUSES BUT ONLY IN HIM.**

Many of us carry this unique capacity to identify the faults of others to an extreme. We feel we need to inform our spouses about every blunder we find in every situation—it can really become like a game. We sometimes try to justify our comments by saying that we are simply trying to help them out by identifying what we see as inadequacies and problems. And yet, when we try to help by pointing these errors out, for some unknown reason, they get upset. Honesty is the best policy, isn't it?

When our children proudly present to us a piece of artwork they created at school, does it matter if the car is taller than the house? Are we being looked to for support or validation? What purpose would it serve to mention what we see when the artwork has already been completed, and they are so proud? We rarely realize the extent of the damage that can be done by just one poorly chosen word of criticism, and so we must reflect on the effect of the criticism before we identify the problems. When we find fault in something our spouses have done, we are usually adding a negative element to our relationships. If our wives know that we are going to find error with everything they do, they will hesitate to share with us anymore unless they are actually seeking criticism.

> **WE RARELY REALIZE THE EXTENT OF THE DAMAGE THAT CAN BE DONE BY JUST ONE POORLY CHOSEN WORD OF CRITICISM.**

The dominant response to consistent criticism will ultimately cause the other person's personality to go silent or close up. This is why it is so important for abundant praise to far outweigh criticism. Especially when it comes to your wife, make sure there is plenty more affirmation than there is criticism. If you truly enjoy keeping score, otherwise known as masochism, you better try multiple affirmations for each criticism.

## THE GAME PLAN

The Bible says that God doesn't focus all of His attention on what you do wrong, so neither should you. God wants you to:

- Love unconditionally without getting bitter about your disappointments—Proverbs 18:22: "He who finds a wife finds a good thing, and obtains favor from the LORD."

- Let Him be the sole judge of others; that includes your wife—James 4:12: "There is one Lawgiver, who is able to save and to destroy. Who are you to judge another?"
- Let Him be the sole determiner of how your wife should be given rewards—1 Corinthians 4:5: "Therefore judge nothing before the time, until the Lord comes, who will both bring to light the hidden things of darkness and reveal the counsels of the hearts. Then each one's praise will come from God."
- Be an example, not a stumbling block to your wife and don't allow a stumbling block in your home—Romans 14:13: "Therefore let us not judge one another anymore, but rather resolve this, not to put a stumbling block or a cause to fall in our brother's way."

## PLAYMAKERS

Turn on ESPN on most any day, and you are likely to see Chris Mortensen front and center. Chris is known as the "ESPN'S NFL Insider." Some say he is the most respected and accomplished reporter covering the NFL today. He joined ESPN in 1991 and appears on numerous broadcasts, including *Sunday NFL Countdown*, *Monday Night Countdown*, and *SportsCenter*. Chris also contributes to *Outside the Lines*, and he is one of the country's most trusted voices for NFL draft coverage. In 1987 he was honored with the George Polk Award for outstanding reporting, and as of this writing he remains the only sportswriter to receive this award since Red Smith in 1951. Chris has earned eighteen awards in journalism and he has been nominated for two Pulitzer Prizes.

Chris has been married to his wife, Micki, for many years, and during that time he will be the first to admit that he has had an "on again, off again" relationship with Jesus Christ and the church. He attended services on many Sundays, partly because he knew how important it was to his wife and partly because he wanted his son to grow up in the church. Chris openly admits, "Christianity was something I did, not something I was."

Whatever you say about Chris, one thing is clear: you can never say that he is clueless—well, except for one time. At one of the In The Zone events held in Oklahoma, Chris was extremely transparent with the men regarding the important role his wife played in his salvation. Several years ago, Chris had no idea that his wife had been asking all the people in her small groups at church to pray for Chris to receive Jesus Christ as his personal savior. Since they had been attending their church for a long time, she was part of many small study groups. Before long, Chris was on prayer lists throughout the entire church, completely unaware that he was the subject of so much love and concern. Micki was steadfast in her quest, faithfully believing that God would hear the prayers offered on Chris's behalf.

> ## "CHRISTIANITY WAS SOMETHING I DID, NOT SOMETHING I WAS."
> ### —CHRIS MORTENSEN

One Sunday morning Chris readied for church as he had every Sunday that he was not on the road doing TV or speaking. This day, however, was going to be special; he just didn't know it yet. After the moving sermon that day, Chris said, "I had no idea that I was going to accept Christ that day. I jumped up and the next thing I knew I was in my pastor's arms. When I turned around I noticed that the entire church was giving me a standing ovation. It was pretty much the first standing ovation that I had ever had. My pastor smiled, hugged me, and asked me if I had any idea why all these people were standing up and applauding. I told him, 'I have no idea.' He told the story that my wife had been praying for my salvation for years and by now just about everyone in the church has prayed for me at one time or another."[1] How about God's sense of humor? As an award-winning investigative reporter, Chris appeared to be the only person totally unaware of the exhaustive efforts of his wife to engage the body of Christ in a prayer project.

Chris continues to be one of the most popular ESPN commentators of all time. But he is also a God-fearing man and seldom misses an opportunity, if asked, to tell of how his wife prayed for his salvation. Chris has many close friends who are superstars in the world of sports, but he now has a select few who are traveling on the same road with him. Do you think Chris will ever criticize his wife for not telling him of her extensive prayer plan? Probably not! As different as they were when they first married, and as different as they still are today, now the "imperfect Chris" gets to celebrate with the "imperfect Micki" their common love for the "perfect Christ."

## TIME OUT

1. What does your wife do that seems to get under your skin? In your best of moments, how do you look past it?
2. Ask your wife to identify which criticisms of her, made by you, hurt her the most.
3. How can you adjust your attitude so you don't consistently find fault with your wife?

## TODAY'S ASSIGNMENT

Be especially cognizant when you are tempted to criticize your wife today. Look for the good that she does, not her faults, and commend her instead.

## HOME-FIELD ADVANTAGE

*Praises and concerns you want to bring before God*

_____

_____

_____

_____

# DEALING WITH UNEXPECTED BAGGAGE

## LOVING THE FAMILY THAT COMES WITH YOUR WIFE

### THOUGHT OF THE DAY

*You must love your extended family and yet set boundaries to protect your own family.*

### THE COACH'S CORNER

Many of you had no idea that you were marrying a family and not just your wife. Of course, you fell in love with your future wife and met her family. You realize they are not exactly like your parents, but how difficult can this be? You will seldom see them, and you and your wife are one—remember "leave and cleave"?

Shortly after the honeymoon is over, the reality sets in that you have married a whole host of people, some of them you don't even like! Your new wife starts expecting you to act like her father and do the things he did. You immediately expect that she will be similar to your loving mother. When those inevitable arguments come, your wife calls her back-up team for support, and you can instantly feel like the outsider. God calls for your priorities to change once you get married. The new family that you and your wife are creating must have a higher priority than the attachments that both you and your wife have to your old families.

You have often heard it said, "You don't marry a person; you marry a family." You marry their habits, ways of thinking, traditions, personalities, quirks, and rituals. Marriage is the inclusion, and at times the collision, of two completely different cultures. Do you remember the first time you realized that both sets of parents expected you and your wife to be part of their traditional Christmas routine?

### GOD CALLS FOR YOUR PRIORITIES TO CHANGE ONCE YOU GET MARRIED.

You may wonder sometimes how the person you love came out of a family like the one you inherited. Before you married her, she seemed to want all the things you wanted, and now she seems to want all that plus what she grew up with. We each carry our family's traditions within us. Our ongoing connection with our families exerts a subtle, and sometimes not-so-subtle, stress from the outside. Many arguments between you and your wife occur due to issues with extended families. So what do you do when your wife's family is driving you crazy? You may consider the following:

- Try and value each other's family's way of life. You can't successfully discuss these issues without a mutual respect for each other's family. Commit to not critiquing each other's family, though do listen to what each of you appreciates or finds complicated about them.

- Come to the agreement that your new family comes first! This means "My family always did it that way" should not become the rule. Help your spouse understand what you value about your old traditions, and discuss how some of her family's traditions can enrich your family life together.

- Establish your boundaries. Let everyone know that you have established guidelines for the health of your family, and ask that they be supported.

## YOU MAY WONDER SOMETIMES HOW THE PERSON YOU LOVE CAME OUT OF A FAMILY LIKE THE ONE YOU INHERITED.

As the years progress, things do tend to get better, or at least, all sides give up trying to change each other. God wants you to be the head of your home. He expects you to be the spiritual leader, teacher, and example. It is important to be a servant leader and give higher priority to your wife's wishes than your mother's. Sure, some give-and-take is essential, but you (the spiritual leader) will be held accountable for your family, not your in-laws or your parents.

## THE GAME PLAN

The Bible says that God loves family. God also wants you to:

- Value the faith being passed down from one generation to another—1 Timothy 1:5: "Now the purpose of the commandment is love from a pure heart, from a good conscience, and from sincere faith."

- Enjoy the legacy of godly obedience—2 Chronicles 26:4: "And he did what was right in the sight of the LORD, according to all that his father Amaziah had done."
- Beware of a controlling mother-in-law—Matthew 14:8: "So she, having been prompted by her mother, said, 'Give me John the Baptist's head here on a platter.'"
- Beware of a heritage of inappropriate behavior and disobedience to God—1 Kings 22:52: "He did evil in the sight of the LORD, and walked in the way of his father and in the way of his mother and in the way of Jeroboam the son of Nebat, who had made Israel sin."

## PLAYMAKERS

It would be difficult to find a family with more built-in dissention than the one that was created when a future Republican governor married into one of America's most staunch Democratic families. When Arnold Schwarzenegger and Maria Shriver married, Arnold was a strong diehard Republican born in the country of Austria and Maria was a strong-willed Democrat from two of America's most prominent political families, the Kennedys and Shrivers. When the world body-building champion star of *The Terminator* married the famous TV commentator, many media experts suggested the strong probability that this marriage would not last given how different their backgrounds were. Shriver said that in marrying Schwarzenegger she needed to confront expectations, and she is glad she did.

Internationally known broadcaster and investigative journalist Alex Jones quoted Maria as saying, "Everyone assumed that I was going to marry someone like a John Kerry, some preppy that had gone to Harvard or Yale," she said. "I didn't want to marry those boys.

I did not like them. I had been around them my whole life. I interrupted the story line. I wanted out of that suffocation. I wanted someone different. I married my authentic self."[1]

**WHILE WE MAY NOT HAVE MARRIED INTO A FAMILY SUCH AS THE KENNEDYS, NEVERTHELESS, WE HAVE MARRIED INTO A FAMILY THAT IS NOT EXACTLY LIKE WHAT WE EXPECTED OR ANTICIPATED.**

Schwarzenegger told *Vanity Fair* he understood his wife's need to break away from the family, affectionately referring to the Shriver family as "the clones." "Everyone in the family thinks exactly the same," he said. "If her mother says it is green, it is green. If her father says it is black, it is black. When you are in the family, you think this is normal, and then you meet someone from the outside and the lights go on."[2] Here was a guy who was free—if he wanted to be a Republican, he was a Republican. If he wanted to be a movie star, he was a movie star. "I'm not perfect," Schwarzenegger admitted to *Newsweek*, "but I know that out of millions of women, I found the one who understands me and what makes me tick."[3]

Most of us, at one time or another, have experienced issues with our extended families. While we may not have married into a family such as the Kennedys, nevertheless, we have married into a family that is not exactly like what we expected or anticipated. We are forced to spend time with these new family members who sometimes we don't even like . . . family members who may have the potential to hurt our marriages . . . even people who are borderline card-carrying-crazy-people.

The Bible is filled with stories of imperfect families. In biblical times just as today, all families were filled with imperfect people.

And even though Jesus was perfect, His parents and His siblings were certainly not. It is an unrealistic expectation that any family, yours or hers, could ever be perfect. Unrealistic expectations are the cause of much of the problems in our families. The following short fictional letter sent to us from one of our friends was posted on the Internet, and it will provide you with a humorous look at how unloving extended families can be. Be careful—this just may be dead on:

Dear Darling Son and that Person You Married,

Merry Christmas to you, and please don't worry about me. I'm just fine, considering I can hardly breathe or eat. The important thing is that you have a nice holiday with what's her name's family, thousands of miles away from your sick mother. I've sent along my last ten dollars in this card, which I hope you'll spend on my grandchildren. I know the other grandparents will try to outdo me. Thank you so much for the Christmas flowers. I put them in the freezer so they'll stay fresh for my funeral—which is coming soon. It's time for me to crawl off to bed now. Don't even think about sending me any more money because I know you will need it for your expensive family vacation you are forced to take with your in-laws. Give my love to my darling grandbabies and to what's-her-name—the one with the black roots in the Christmas card picture, who seems to have gained quite a bit of weight since last year.

Merry Christmas.

— Love,

Mom

One of the most damaging temptations that many of us face is to compare and contrast our families. Both husbands and wives often have healthy, strong, and valued memories of growing up. We often expect our new family to be simply an extension of our old family, where the customs and traditions are the same. It is imperative that you and your wife create and start your own family traditions to combine with those from both sides of your family. You and your wife can both have unrealistic expectations of each other and the extended families, so the sooner you begin the lifelong progression of negotiating these issues, the better your life will be. So get ahead of the curve because both sets of your parents will have unrealistic expectations of even their own children.

**UNREALISTIC EXPECTATIONS ARE THE CAUSE OF MUCH OF THE PROBLEMS IN OUR FAMILIES.**

We often look at *the Joneses* from a distance and think, *Why can't my wife be like that? Why can't my father-in-law be more like that? Why can't my kids be like that?* We compare our families to others and feel like something is really missing. Unrealistic expectations can frustrate us and cause those around us to feel as though we don't love them because they don't seem to measure up to the culture's standards or our standards . . . our expectations. It is difficult at times like this to remember that God's standard is faithfulness, not perfection.

The best antidote to unrealistic expectations is unconditional love. The more we can communicate to our families that we love them no matter how strange they may be, the better we will be. Loving someone is a choice, not an emotion, and it takes discipline to love unconditionally. The truth is, we are all going to mess up—we are all going to disappoint those closest to us because we are all imperfect people. So what we need to do is let those we love know we will love them no matter what.

## ONE OF THE MOST DAMAGING TEMPTATIONS THAT MANY OF US FACE IS TO COMPARE AND CONTRAST OUR FAMILIES.

One of the best things you can do to ease the tension and conflict in your extended family is let them know you love them just the way they are. That doesn't mean that nobody needs to change or grow, but it means you love them through it all. Your families will never be filled with perfection, but they can be filled with love—the sort of love that accepts people just the way they are . . . the sort of love that gives you the freedom to fail as you seek to become the person God created you to be.

## TIME OUT

1. What is the most frustrating aspect of having in-laws?
2. What boundaries would be most appropriate that you can set with your family to protect your wife?
3. Is there something you can do today that would improve your relationship with your in-laws?

## TODAY'S ASSIGNMENT

Identify the things you most appreciate about your in-laws and call them today to let them know.

## HOME-FIELD ADVANTAGE

*Praises and concerns you want to bring before God*

_____

_____

_____

_____

_____

## DAY 14

# I'VE GOT HER BACK

## LOVING YOUR WIFE— UNCONDITIONALLY

### THOUGHT OF THE DAY

*You are called to love your wife—even on days you may not like her much.*

### THE COACH'S CORNER

Have there been times when you looked at your wife and thought, *Who are you*? You might have even asked God why He thought the two of you getting married was a good decision. The sweet, young, beautiful, smart girl you fell in love with may have changed over time. Chances are, the reasons she has changed just might include the fact that she is tired of being on duty 24/7. She is fed up with babysitting not only the children but you as well. Money is always tight, things are always broken, and there seems no end in sight. You don't look quite the way you did when you were dating, and neither does she, but she wishes you both would look that way again. Homework, science projects, soccer practice, and Bible school make her feel more like a hired helper than a loving wife. There are certainly days when you may not like her very much, but she just may have a very good reason for her unusual behavior—*you*!

## HAVE THERE BEEN TIMES WHEN YOU LOOKED AT YOUR WIFE AND THOUGHT, *WHO ARE YOU?*

Of all the weddings I've attended, I've yet to learn of one where the groom was standing at the altar promising to love his wife while thinking to himself, *I can't stand this woman, and I expect this marriage to make me miserable.* Most men stand there with trust, eagerness, love, respect, and the hope that this is going to be the greatest adventure of their lives.

Sometimes after being married for a while, we find that it seems impossible to love our wives unconditionally—especially day in and day out. If we can be truthful here, sometimes our wives can be difficult to live with, much less love.

What happened to that sweet, agreeable beauty queen you dated? Haven't there been times in your marriage that you simply didn't like her very much? Maybe she overruled you with the kids, made a decision you thought should have been discussed beforehand, prearranged your sacred day off, or gave your favorite pair of *holy* jeans to a charity. There have probably been days that she was a little short with you, treated you like one of the kids, sided with her parents over you, or overstepped her boundaries while helping you solve a problem. God knows that being married can be a challenge. He created different roles for the husband and the wife, and because of these different roles, conflicts should not be a surprise.

You are told that you must love your wife even though she is not perfect. You must love your wife even though she sometimes doesn't show you the respect and love that you need and desire. You must love your wife as Jesus loved the church! So what do you do when she has made you mad? What do you do when she has not shown you respect? What do you do when she just isn't the person you thought you married? You are still called to love her as Christ loved the church.

**GOD CREATED DIFFERENT ROLES FOR THE HUSBAND AND THE WIFE, AND BECAUSE OF THESE DIFFERENT ROLES, CONFLICTS SHOULD NOT BE A SURPRISE.**

Current CBS *College Football Today* analyst Spencer Tillman has had a highly decorated career. He played for the Super Bowl champion San Francisco 49ers, set rushing records at the University of Oklahoma, and penned an insightful book called *Scoring in the Red Zone*. At a recent In The Zone gathering in Nashville, he spoke of a dangerous red zone off the field that challenges every man. "I have to be very careful to avoid situations that can lead to emotional adultery—where no physical contact is made—but you can tell that another woman is beginning to enjoy extended conversations with you. I know I have to 'flee' the situation because of my unconditional love for my wife, Rita."[1] Spencer's example is one practical way to show unconditional love to your wife.

## THE GAME PLAN

The Bible says that God desires you to love your wife unconditionally just as He loves His church. God wants you to know:

- You can love your wife through acts of mercy and service—Ephesians 5:2: "And walk in love, as Christ also has loved us and given Himself for us, an offering and a sacrifice to God for a sweet-smelling aroma."
- Sacrificial love is evidence of Christ in you—Colossians 3:14: "But above all these things put on love, which is the bond of perfection."
- Secular human love at its most passionate is still no match for the love only the Holy Spirit can give—Galatians 5:22–23: "But the fruit of the Spirit is love, joy, peace, longsuffering, kindness, goodness, faithfulness, gentleness, self-control."
- Whenever misunderstandings occur and you sense a division of spirit between you and your wife, both of you should ask Christ for healing—Ephesians 2:14: "For He Himself is our peace, who has made both one, and has broken down the middle wall of separation."

## PLAYMAKERS

Kurt Warner is currently the starting quarterback for the Arizona Cardinals of the National Football League. He first reached celebrity status when he lead the St. Louis Rams from 1998 to 2003. During those years Kurt won two NFL MVP awards and one Super Bowl MVP. He also owns the three biggest single game passing yardage totals in Super Bowl history. Warner is ranked third all-time in career passing with a rating of 93.8.

Kurt was, of course, not always a superstar. While playing football at Northern Iowa University, Kurt met a most intriguing and interesting young woman. He had made little time for anything in his life other than football until he met her. His heart was set on being a star in the NFL, but she seemed to capture something in him that he just couldn't dismiss. But this was not the typical story of "the young hunk quarterback marries the young head cheerleader and lives happily ever after." Kurt was struggling with his dream of playing in the NFL, and she was a former marine and a recently divorced working mother of two. Brenda was a driven woman, and when they met, she was attending college to become a registered nurse so that she would be better able to take care of her physically challenged son.

Kurt might be a guy who makes quick decisions in the middle of big games, but Brenda will be the first to admit it took him a long time to get enough nerve to ask her to marry him. They were with each other for more than five years, and she was ready to either get married and make it work, or go their separate ways. The NFL is certainly full of failed marriages, but Kurt and Brenda's has often been referred to as a great success.

The story goes like this: Brenda lost both of her parents to a severe storm in 1996. After Kurt and Brenda were married, Kurt adopted her two children and grew to embrace her strong Christian beliefs. Kurt's football career turned around about this same time, but the road has continued to be rocky for them both.

While everything appeared to be great on the home front, there have been times when Brenda has been quite outspoken on specific issues that relate to her husband. Kurt has always been known as a loving husband; however, one might wonder if during some of her public comments, there may have been times that he became a little frustrated with her. Brenda came into the media's limelight during Kurt's first Super Bowl appearance. The media was in heaven. They now had a strong-willed female who enjoyed TV time, loved football, and would speak her mind.

As her husband had some struggles with his career after the Super Bowl, Brenda continued to make headlines, appearing on radio and TV talk shows. In late 2002, Brenda insulted Ram's head coach Mike Martz on the radio by saying the idea to have Kurt's hand x-rayed was hers, not the coach's. The following year, Brenda was featured on the radio again for a segment and noted that Kurt would most likely ask to be traded if Mark Bulger was to be the starting quarterback for the Rams instead of him. Some other media attention she has attracted include:

- *The New York Times*: Warner's Family Accepts Bounty and Burden of Football[2]
- *The Arizona Republic*: This time, Warner's wife is ready for the limelight[3]
- ESPN (AP): Warner's wife says trade welcomed[4]
- *Pittsburgh Post-Gazette*: Cook: To be curt, Mrs. Warner should clam up[5]
- FemmeFan.com: The Kurt and Brenda Show[6]
- Fox's MLB commentator Joe Buck suggested that Warner's departure from St. Louis may have had something to do with his wife's proclivity to speak her mind[7]

## NEVERTHELESS, HE LOVED HER UNCONDITIONALLY THROUGHOUT EACH AND EVERY MEDIA ORDEAL.

Ron Cook wrote a column in the *Pittsburgh Post-Gazette* in late 2003, commenting on Brenda's interview style and her ensuing media attention.[8] Her statements caused significant tension in the Rams locker room, and the players began to question Kurt as their leader, according to Cook. When wives become too involved in the public lives of their husbands, Cook argued, they can cause problems for the players' careers. "Shame on Brenda Warner," he wrote. When Kurt signed with the New York Giants in 2004, Joe Buck opined,

"At worst you are going to get a wife's point of view about what's going on with the hot quarterback in town. At best you're going to get some kind of controversy where she may say something that may be considered out of place." He also said, "If I'm a New York radio station, and she is willing to do it . . . I would do anything I could to make a deal happen just hoping Brenda would again stir things up."[9]

While few NFL marriages are as out front and solid as the Warners', there must have been a few times when Kurt might not have appreciated Brenda making a particular comment. Nevertheless, he loved her unconditionally throughout each and every media ordeal.

## TIME OUT

1. What does unconditional love mean to you? Who in your life shows you unconditional love?
2. Ask your wife what unconditional love means to her. How can you show it more?
3. What do you do that makes you difficult to be loved unconditionally?

## TODAY'S ASSIGNMENT

Commit today to write your wife a note with a message of unconditional love and leave it where she can find it tomorrow.

## HOME-FIELD ADVANTAGE

*Praises and concerns you want to bring before God*

_____

_____

_____

_____

_____

# FINDING THE ZONE IN YOUR RELATIONSHIP WITH YOUR CHILDREN

*Train up a child in the way he should go,*
*And when he is old he will not depart from it.*

## —PROVERBS 22:6

# AN IMPORTANT ROLE PLAYED BY TODAY'S MAN

## THE PROTECTOR

### THOUGHT OF THE DAY

*You must guard your children against today's deceptive culture.*

### THE COACH'S CORNER

The American family today is in a cultural war zone. As fathers we must act intentionally to find ways to guard our families. God expects us to act like a military scouts—point men. He calls us to communicate to our families each point of danger that they are getting ready to encounter. Our families and our homes are actually being bombarded by the media to change the way we think and believe. Our homes are being targeted as a source of weakness; therefore, the media is exploiting the home to find cracks as to how to get in and influence what we do and what we purchase. Sometimes it seems it would be best if we could simply build fences around our houses and not allow today's deceptive culture to creep in. But with TV, radio, Internet, text messaging, message boards, chat rooms, and movies we often seem like overreacting dads in our determination to guard our families.

## AS FATHERS WE MUST ACT INTENTIONALLY TO FIND WAYS TO GUARD OUR FAMILIES.

Over the past thirty years, much has been written and discussed about the increased demands placed upon mothers who are balancing career and family. While this is without a doubt true, we don't often hear about the changing roles placed upon the men of today. The roles of men are constantly changing as pressure builds at work, the community, the church, and home. Like our fathers and grandfathers, we share a responsibility to be the primary breadwinners for our families; however, most of us differ from our fathers in that we no longer identify being a successful father solely in terms of our ability to provide economically.

Today, being a godly father also means having a close relationship with our children and being actively involved in their lives. The Gallup Organization studied "over-achieving men," those men who have been super-successful in exceeding their business, financial, and career goals. The organization interviewed hundreds of successful men in business, sports, and politics attempting to identify their keys to personal success. The most essential factor found was the consistent attention they received from their fathers when they were young. As men we sometimes see this as another obligation on our checklist; however, interacting with our families is a privilege that we must cherish. The supreme challenge a man faces is not on the athletic field, not in the boardroom, not in the gym, and not in reviewing his net worth—the greatest challenge a man faces is learning how to be a God-fearing dad for his children.[1]

A young pastor in Pascagoula, Mississippi, once quoted an old story that described a father like this: "When you're small, a father has two huge hands that lift you onto his shoulders and puts worms on your hooks better than any other hands in the world. He is great to be near when there's thunder and lightning or trouble. A father understands when you believe you're too old to be kissed goodnight or have someone hold your hand. He's the one who teaches you how to tie your tie, buys you your first razor, gives you reluctant permission to take the car, and comforts your mom when you aren't home on time. Sometimes he evens helps you fail algebra! A father spends most of his life reaching in his pocket to give you money for something."[2]

**INTERACTING WITH OUR FAMILIES IS A PRIVILEGE THAT WE MUST CHERISH.**

For today's men the challenges are great. We are supposed to provide, protect, encourage, problem-solve, teach, coach, doctor, and discipline—all while the world is watching to see if we can do it. What is different about your approach to this challenge compared to your dad, or your grandfathers?

## THE GAME PLAN

The Bible says that you are expected to protect your family. God wants you to know:

- You must protect your family by providing materially for their needs—1 Timothy 5:8: "But if anyone does not provide for his own, and especially for those of his household, he has denied the faith and is worse than an unbeliever."

- You must protect your family by providing a nurturing and God-fearing style of parenting—Ephesians 6:4: "And you, fathers, do not provoke your children to wrath, but bring them up in the training and admonition of the Lord."

- You must protect your family by telling them of God's love for them—Deuteronomy 6:7: "You shall teach them diligently to your children, and shall talk of them when you sit in your house, when you walk by the way, when you lie down, and when you rise up."

- You must protect your family by setting boundaries of behavior, time, place, and people—Proverbs 2:11: "Discretion will preserve you; understanding will keep you."

## PLAYMAKERS

If you were to ask most sports fans to identify the most important position on an NFL team, many would answer, "The quarterback." He is the team leader, the playmaker, the crunch-time guy. But if you were to ask the quarterback to privately identify the most important guy on the field, his answer just might surprise you. Many pro quarterbacks will identify their offensive tackle who protects their blindside as the most important guy on the field. Yes, that's right. Not one of the highly paid receivers or running backs— the offensive tackles. The reality is, the offensive tackle is the guy whom the quarterback primarily relies on to guard him from potential career-ending injuries more than anyone else. Few positions in professional football are less appreciated by the average fan than the blindside offensive tackle. The fact that the men who play this position are some of the highest paid players on many NFL teams confirms the importance of this position.

On the very same day that it was reported that the Chicago Bears had acquired Jay Cutler as their new quarterback, the Bears also agreed to a multiyear deal with one of the league's premier left tackles, Orlando Pace. Pace has been to the Pro Bowl seven times and is regarded as a potential Hall-of-Famer. Pace is probably most noticeably known as the guy who protected Kurt Warner during the Super Bowl win of 1999 and blocked for three MVP quarterbacks during his career.

### IT HAS BEEN FUSED INTO THE DNA OF ALL MEN TO BE PROTECTORS—WE ARE THE BLINDSIDE TACKLES FOR OUR FAMILIES.

Hall of Fame quarterback Joe Theismann would agree to the importance of the blindside offensive tackle. When Joe was preparing to participate in an In The Zone event in Florida, not surprisingly, he was reminded about the event that changed his life forever. Theismann's NFL career ended abruptly in 1985 when he suffered a horrible compound fracture of his leg while being sacked by the New York Giants linebacker Lawrence Taylor during a live *Monday Night Football* telecast. The injury has been selected by fans as the NFL's "Most Shocking Moment in History" in an ESPN poll. The *Washington Post* dubbed the sack as "The Hit No One Who Saw It Coming Ever Forgot."[3] Taylor sandwiched Theismann into his teammate and inadvertently landed his hip on Theismann's lower right leg, fracturing both the tibia and fibula. The question that was asked most that unforgettable night was simply, "Whose job was it to protect Theismann?" He never saw it coming.

In a sense it has been fused into the DNA of all men to be

protectors—we are the blindside tackles for our families. We are largely defined by the role of provider and protector as men, husbands, and fathers. God is certainly our model, providing for all our essential needs, protecting us from all kinds of dangers, toils, and snares. A father who loves his children will work to provide for their daily, essential, necessary needs . . . and probably a few frivolous wants along the way!

Many fathers have sacrificed their wives and children on the altars they make to their careers. The power and prestige of important jobs can be a tempting alternative to playing the role of protector within our families. Many men today assume all it takes to be a real dad is to be the provider, and oftentimes he's too late in discovering this devious lie. There are only a few children who would prefer more toys over more time with their dad. It is also important for our families that we set suitable boundaries for them. Many times these boundaries appear as unfair limitations to our children and teens who are testing their budding wings. Nevertheless, they are essential to growing in Christ and maintaining discipline, and they are indispensable in raising hearty and vigorous children. Loving dads set time, place, people, and behavior boundaries, and enforce them fairly to make sure their families are adequately protected.

## TIME OUT

1. What has been the easiest behavior boundary to set for your children?
2. What has been the most difficult time boundary to set for your children?
3. Whoever said there are no do-overs in life never held the position of a dad. What do you need to do to make your relationship right with one of your children whom you wronged?

## TODAY'S ASSIGNMENT

Ask your wife, or your children's mother, what she is most concerned about in regard to the current needs for protection for the family. Consider calling and talking with your children today and making sure that each one knows how much you love them.

---

## HOME-FIELD ADVANTAGE

*Praises and concerns you want to bring before God*

_____

_____

_____

_____

---

# DEFINING YOUR LEGACY

## WHAT DO YOU WANT TO LEAVE YOUR CHILDREN?

### THOUGHT OF THE DAY

*Every man leaves a legacy to his children, and it's
your decision what your legacy will be.*

### THE COACH'S CORNER

Sometimes we overhear children talk about what they did over
their summer break. While we know that many dads often spend a
small fortune taking their family on elaborate vacations, most of
their children describe the height of their vacation as hanging out
with their friends or doing something that really was fairly insignificant. We worry, plan, and even go in debt to give them special
experiences, and yet often this is not what they remember. If you
think back regarding what you remember from your childhood, I
think you would agree that we are sometimes on a quest to create

memories that are just not that important. Many times at Christmas you spend large sums of money to purchase the perfect present for your toddler, and what do they play with? Right, the box! So it is time to get real about who you are, what you want to be known for, and how you want to impact your children.

In biblical times the thought of leaving a legacy for your children was extremely important. The value of a legacy is often shown in the genetic lineage of men, as they were connected together across centuries. Jesus, however, seemed to be more interested in a character line more than He was a bloodline. Jesus fulfilled prophecy by being a member of King David's family tree. However, He taught that character was critical. The Bible affirms over and over the value of a man leaving a godly legacy to his family.

IT IS TIME TO GET REAL ABOUT WHO YOU ARE, WHAT YOU WANT TO BE KNOWN FOR, AND HOW YOU WANT TO IMPACT YOUR CHILDREN.

What will your children remember about you? What will your wife remember? What do you want your friends and coworkers to remember about you? Will it be your humor, wealth, career, or compassion? What will be your legacy? Chances are, what they will remember is not at all what you hope they will remember. If you want to leave a solid legacy, start by sitting down alone and compose your desired eulogy—simply using bullet points. What is it that you hope will be said about you? What are the nouns, verbs, and adjectives you want your pastor to use? Write down every last bit—the anecdotes; the nuggets of wisdom you shared with your children; your acts of kindness and generosity; your accomplishments, dreams, and hopes. Then take a hard look at what you've written down. How much of it actually describes your current life, and how much is simply what you wished it looked like? How many of your accomplishments, hopes, and dreams remain unfulfilled? You may realize that much of what you spend time worrying about is inconsequential.

Take time now to reflect on how you would like to be remembered in the future while you still can make changes in the present. Will you be known for your ability to parent a future Super Bowl quarterback? Probably not. We often think about what we will be remembered for; however, most of us haven't invented anything that will change the world, we don't wear a Super Bowl ring, and we are not the president of a large corporation—although these things are impressive, to a degree. Most of us are just regular dads—maybe the owner of a small business or the ex-coach of an awesome T-ball team that went winless. Yet we hope our legacy is something to be proud of. We hope people remember us for turning from the wickedness of our unsaved lives and living out the rest of our days in humble submission to God's will.

## THE GAME PLAN

The Bible says that God wants you to live a life that is pleasing to Him and not the world. God wants you to know:

- You should teach your children that while you are not a perfect dad, you can still have a relationship with the perfect God—Romans 3:23: "For all have sinned and fall short of the glory of God."
- You can leave a legacy of caring financially for your children—2 Corinthians 12:14: "Now for the third time I am ready to come to you. And I will not be burdensome to you; for I do not seek yours, but you. For the children ought not to lay up for the parents, but the parents for the children."

- You can leave a legacy by sharing your faith with each generation—Proverbs 13:22: "A good man leaves an inheritance to his children's children, but the wealth of the sinner is stored up for the righteous."
- You can leave a legacy by showing your love for God and your obedience to Him—Colossians 1:18: "And He is the head of the body, the church, who is the beginning, the firstborn from the dead, that in all things He may have the preeminence."

## PLAYMAKERS

Both the famous and the not-so-famous will all leave a legacy. It doesn't matter if you are rich or poor; it doesn't matter your race or nationality. Most of us believe we have some important things of value that we want to pass down to our children. We have been given a life that is valued by God, and it is our responsibility to pass on to them our beliefs and experiences.

Let's take a look at two prominent celebrity sports figures, and see what legacy each might leave behind. Adam "Pacman" Jones is one of the most talented football players to enter the NFL in recent years. Many NFL experts thought this first-round draft pick out of the University of West Virginia had the talents and skills necessary to be a superstar. Yet by age twenty-five, he had been released from both the Tennessee Titans and the Dallas Cowboys. Talent alone doesn't seem to ever be enough. *USA Today* wrote, "Jones is the poster child for a needed crackdown in the NFL."[1]

**IT IS OUR RESPONSIBILITY TO PASS ON TO OUR CHILDREN OUR BELIEFS AND EXPERIENCES.**

Here is an overview of an extremely sad story. Only days after being drafted in the NFL, Pacman was involved in a serious altercation outside a downtown Atlanta strip club. Police later raided his hotel room and discovered drugs; however, one of his friends took the responsibility for everything. He was later arrested when he got into a brawl at a Nashville club only days prior to signing his first contract with the Tennessee Titans, but charges were dismissed. His Cadillac Escalade was confiscated in a drug bust in 2005, and he was charged with public intoxication only weeks later. It was reported on *Nightline* that he grabbed a Las Vegas stripper, hit her in the face, and then threatened to kill the security guard if he became involved. It's also been reported that a member of his social group then shot at three people outside the same club. Do you wonder what Pacman's legacy will be inside and outside of football? Many of us are still rooting for Pacman to figure it out, and stand up and take charge of his future and legacy. God is also counting on Pacman to find his stride.

On the other hand, most of you know that Archie Manning was a great NFL quarterback. He had an outstanding college career at the University of Mississippi and was the franchise face of the fledgling New Orleans Saints for most of his professional career. Archie was drafted in 1971 by the Saints and played ten full seasons, not one of them a winning season. In 1972 he led the league in pass attempts and completions though the team's record was only 2–11–1. In 1978, he was named the NFC Player of the Year after leading the Saints to a 7–9 overall record. His accomplishments as a starter resulted in only a 26 percent winning percentage, the worst in NFL history among quarterbacks with at least one hundred starts. So why would anyone want to talk about Archie and his legacy?

Archie was known as a player who was tough, smart, and prone to never quit. He was the player who would always show up and give his team 100 percent effort, no matter what the game, the conditions, or the opposing team's record. He was praised by members of the other teams as the guy who was always positive about his situation, his team, his city, and his teammates. He was always seen as the ultimate competitor and the ultimate sportsman. He played before the NFL had free agency, so he never had a choice about who he played for, the city he played in, or the teammates he would play with. Yet amazingly, Archie Manning was consistently faithful even in the midst of his difficult circumstances. We know him as one of the most respected players in NFL history.

## WHILE MOST OF US ARE JUST REGULAR GUYS, WE WILL ALL STILL LEAVE A LEGACY TO OUR CHILDREN.

To some, however, he is known for being the father of two recent MVP Super Bowl quarterbacks—Eli and Peyton Manning. The doors he opened for his two sons, the legacy that preceded each, has made their careers and successes possible—many even say easier to achieve. Archie didn't have the opportunity of playing on a championship team, he wasn't surrounded by Pro Bowl players, and the Saints have never been considered America's Team. Yet his positive name and the legacy he left for his sons have certainly served to be an important foundation in their careers. While most of us are just regular guys, we will all still leave a legacy no less important to our children than Archie's was for his children. Today, football fans remember Archie's toughness, not his won-loss record. What will the world remember about you?

## TIME OUT

1. If you were to be able to listen in on your own funeral, what do you believe you would hear said by those in attendance, especially your kids?
2. What kind of man would your coworkers describe you as being?
3. Would you be happy if you knew that your kids would all grow up with your morals and values? If not, what changes would you like to see them exhibit?

## TODAY'S ASSIGNMENT

Find a quiet time and place and write out what you would like to be said about you at your funeral.

---

## HOME-FIELD ADVANTAGE

*Praises and concerns you want to bring before God*

_____

_____

_____

_____

_____

## Day 17

# Dealing with Daily Stress

### Your Actions Speak Louder than Your Words

## The Coach's Corner

We have all experienced the overzealous dads who seem to get a little too involved in their children's ballgames and activities. They sometimes scream at the officials, bark out specific commands to their children during the game, and act like a card-carrying-crazy-man. Other parents sometime spend more time talking about the these dads than they do watching the players on the floor or field. In some ways, youth games are probably good for society because some of these men just might be at home beating their wives or kicking their dogs if they could not express their anger at youth sports events!

The Bible offers some strict warnings regarding guarding our tongues and monitoring our actions. All of us have some level of emotional expression—and we also have the ability to keep ourselves from saying or doing things that can be embarrassing to us and our families. However, ultimate self-control can come only through the Holy Spirit as identified in the listing of the fruits of the Spirit: love, joy, peace, patience, kindness, goodness, faithfulness, gentleness, and self-control (Galatians 5:22–23). Often the instrument of self-destruction—the tongue—can also be the instrument of great blessing to others. Nevertheless, the old adage "I'd prefer to see a sermon than listen to one" is true for most of us.

## ULTIMATE SELF-CONTROL CAN COME ONLY THROUGH THE HOLY SPIRIT.

J. D. Gibbs is president of Joe Gibbs Racing, a man dealing with the kind of stress that most of us could never imagine. When featured at a recent In The Zone event, J. D. talked about his hopes for the upcoming NASCAR season, and even joked about how his flag football team had finished with a better record than some of his father's NFL teams. He seemed like any other CEO; although he had other things going on that he shared with the men. A short time before speaking in front of hundreds of men, he had been at a Charlotte hospital watching his two-year-old son receive chemotherapy through a port surgically implanted in his chest. With all the talk of winning the Daytona 500 and figuring out the Car of Tomorrow, the toughest opponent J. D. faces right now is far from the racetrack.

The past several years have seen a consistent increase in the number of working mothers, single mothers, supermothers, soccer mothers, and stay-at-home mothers. Yet the title of dad has rarely been linked to a modifier, except for maybe deadbeat dads, workaholic dads, or even overcompetitive dads. It is wrong, however, to assume that the role of fathers has remained the same. Today we are finding the reality of a second shift when we get home for both moms and dads. This is happening along with the pressures affecting men at work, such as layoffs, downsizing, outsourcing, and other aspects of the massive contractions in both the U.S. and global economies. Today men are held hostage by their BlackBerries, iPhones, and wireless laptops twenty-four hours a day, not to mention PTA meetings, basketball practices, church meetings, and homework helpers. There is uncertainty in the role today's man plays at home, and this uncertainty is creating stress.

In trying to find an acceptable balance between life at work and life at home, most men continue to come down decisively on the side of family life, with most (including those who are single) indicating that they would sacrifice advancements at work just to spend more time at home with their family. Despite their best intentions, however, we are not seeing men work fewer hours in the workweek. Nearly all men are working more than forty-five hours a week, and most are working on weekends at least sometimes. The stress is mounting and GDS (Guilty Dad Syndrome) is setting in. GDS is simple.

**THERE IS UNCERTAINTY IN THE ROLE TODAY'S MAN PLAYS AT HOME, AND THIS UNCERTAINTY IS CREATING STRESS.**

When you are at work you feel guilty that you should be home playing and teaching your children how to play ball or ride their bikes. When you take off to do these things at home, you feel guilty that someone is getting ahead of you at work. It's a real double-bind. In addition, your wife often feels left out; therefore, no matter what you do, you feel as though you are never doing the right thing. Oh, by the way, the church needs you on some committees when you can work them in.

## THE GAME PLAN

The Bible says that someone is always watching you to see how you behave in every situation. God wants you to know:

- You can help control stress by avoiding negative people—Proverbs 22:24: "Make no friendship with an angry man, and with a furious man do not go."
- You can help control stress by wisely avoiding a knee-jerk response when aggravated by others—James 3:2: "For we all stumble in many things. If anyone does not stumble in word, he is a perfect man, able also to bridle the whole body."
- You can help control stress by showing self-control in the midst of chaos or an emergency—James 1:26: "If anyone among you thinks he is religious, and does not bridle his tongue but deceives his own heart, this one's religion is useless."
- You can help control stress by begging God to give you peace and understanding—Philippians 4:7: "And the peace of God, which surpasses all understanding, will guard your hearts and minds through Christ Jesus."

## PLAYMAKERS

Most of us never witnessed Bobby Knight coach in person. However, we certainly have seen his great college teams and their highlights on ESPN. And while most don't know Coach Knight personally, it is easy to form an opinion about him by watching the many clips where he has totally lost his composure on the court. Few will forget the time he threw a chair from one side of the court to the other or when he used strong profanity after a loss. We have seen his red face (matching his red Indiana sweater) while screaming at one of his players.

Yes, we all have heard of the infamous coach Bobby Knight. Few coaches are known for losing their temper and showing their temper more than he. He was accused of slapping a player during a timeout while coaching at Texas Tech; however, when questioned, he indicated he was not upset with the player but rather frustrated with what was occurring on the floor. He said he got upset when the young man didn't look him in the eye. Later when questioned, both the player and the player's parents said the incident was no big deal.

That being said, most of us would agree that it is not encouraged for college coaches to slap, choke, hit, or kick their players. It has been said that Coach Knight has done most of these things at various times over his long and successful career. Actually, some in the media have referred to him as a "bully of a man: unable to control himself."[1] His behavior at Indiana University was excused for years by school officials because he did so many positive things for the school. That's the complicated thing about Coach Knight. On many levels, he's the prototype of what a college coach should be. The graduation rate of his players was among the best in the nation, and he has been known for raising considerable dollars for his university. Some say Coach Knight understands the role of sports at a major university better than just about any other coach in America. When Coach John Wooden was asked to name the great coaches of our time, Coach Knight was certainly a name on his list.

Many of the positive aspects that we see in college basketball today are concepts and programs that began with the legendary Coach Knight. Those who attempt to paint him with one large brush will surely miss a complex man. He has a brilliant mind, yet he often loses control. He throws, kicks, curses, and holds grudges. If someone calls him out when his behavior is questionable, if someone even suggests he's out of line, he has been known to go totally ballistic. His stay at Indiana University ended after the school's president said, "Enough, Coach, enough." The sad scenario is that these events may be what Coach Knight is most remembered for. Many won't recall his coaching greatness, the numerous championships his team won, his one-on-one mentoring, and the academic fund-raising he did. Coach Knight will probably be remembered primarily for his lack of personal control.

**IF YOU WANT YOUR CHILDREN TO MODEL SELF-CONTROL IN THEIR LIVES, WHAT EXAMPLE ARE YOU GIVING THEM IN YOURS?**

Most of us have lost our tempers at one time or another and have said things we wish we had not said. We have alleged things to our spouses that we regretted or perhaps treated our children harshly because of what might have happened to us at work. What do others think of us when they see us lose our tempers in public? We have all seen grown men when they just lose it. We have seen men who couldn't control their tempers at work, home, and even at church. Sometimes that man is the man in the mirror!

Do you get angry easily? Do you lose control? A hot temper and uncontrollable anger have been known to tear homes apart, destroy marriages, hurt relationships with children, and end successful business relationships. It has cost men their careers, ruined relationships with relatives, and caused people to leave the church. It often even leads to violence. If you want your children to model self-control in their lives, what example are you giving them in yours?

## TIME OUT

1. What are your hot-buttons that seem to always cause you to lose control?
2. How do your coworkers see you deal with difficulties at work?
3. Would you be happy if you knew that your kids would all grow up with your style of resolving conflicts?

## TODAY'S ASSIGNMENT

When was the last time you really lost your temper and embarrassed yourself? Did you apologize, or is there someone you should call to make things right?

## HOME-FIELD ADVANTAGE
### *Praises and concerns you want to bring before God*

_____

_____

_____

_____

# HOME IMPROVEMENT

## MAKING YOUR HOUSE . . . GOD'S HOME

### THOUGHT OF THE DAY

*You must set the tone so that God will be respected and loved in your home.*

### THE COACH'S CORNER

We all know God is supposed to reside in our churches, right? He attends weddings, church camps, and funerals, and He hangs out at the local seminaries and Bible colleges. He probably really enjoys the stained-glass windows, mega gymnasiums, and the big pipes on the organ. The padded pews are a must, and now some churches even have recliners to relax in. He probably also gets lonesome sometimes because He has visitors only two or three hours a week. Vacation Bible School is surely a real treat to Him because there is nonstop action and He loves children. Meetings probably aren't His deal, as He must get totally bored with all the bureaucracy about how to ensure the lives of the members are well cared for.

Surely you will agree that the church is not where God lives, but sometimes it seems it would be more convenient if it was. The reality is that we must make room for Him in our homes and, therefore, we must create our homes to be a place in which He would enjoy staying for an extended visit.

Few things are more important in creating a home where God is loved than modeling what it means to be a godly man—to represent Him even before we speak. It is not how much we talk about Christ in passing conversations, how many people we bring to church on Sunday, or whether or not we make the sacrifice to send our children to a Christian school—nothing will replace the fact that we must model what it means to be a Christian man if we want to have a Christian home. What do your children see of you when you encounter a difficulty? Do they watch you to see how you handle adversity? How do you approach God? How do you approach others in times of stress? We are modeling what it means to be a disciple of Jesus Christ every day in every situation whether we want to or not. Does your family see you study the Word? Do they hear you pray? Do you pray together with them? What do you model for your kids?

> NOTHING WILL REPLACE THE FACT THAT WE MUST MODEL WHAT IT MEANS TO BE A CHRISTIAN MAN IF WE WANT TO HAVE A CHRISTIAN HOME.

As a young man you probably had the opportunity to visit in the homes of a number of your friends. A few of the homes you visited might have been very large while many were probably rather small. Some homes were simple while others were decorated quite elaborately. You visited homes that belonged to the very wealthy and also those working hard simply to provide. You also may have visited homes where Jesus was always at the center of family activities. Just what was it that made this home different from the others? When your children's friends come to your home, what do they experience? Would these impressionistic young minds assume that God is welcome in your home? What would they notice different about your relationship with your wife and children, your possessions, the tone or your voice, or the spotlight on family? Making our homes the dwelling place for God is hard.

## THE GAME PLAN

The Bible says that God wants you to create a loving, Christ-filled home for your family. God wants you to know:

- Jesus Christ must be the head of your home—Colossians 3:16–17: "Let the word of Christ dwell in you richly in all wisdom, teaching and admonishing one another in psalms and hymns and spiritual songs, singing with grace in your hearts to the Lord. And whatever you do in word or deed, do all in the name of the Lord Jesus, giving thanks to God the Father through Him."
- A husband must love his wife sacrificially, even as Christ loves the church—Colossians 3:18: "Wives, submit to your own husbands, as is fitting in the Lord."
- A husband should not hold a grudge against his wife—Colossians 3:19: "Husbands, love your wives and do not be bitter toward them."
- Children should obey their parents—Colossians 3:20: "Children, obey your parents in all things, for this is well pleasing to the Lord."

## PLAYMAKERS

Have you ever wondered what type of home life some of the greatest athletes of our time must have grown up in? Was God present in the homes of such great sports celebrities as Tom Landry, Lovie Smith, John Madden, Joe Gibbs, Don Shula, or Vince Lombardi? While we don't know what went on in the homes of all of these sports legends, the strong family and spiritual foundation that was part of at least one of these celebrity coaches just might surprise you.

It may be because he was such the ultimate tough guy or the fact that he didn't openly discuss his faith with many people that Coach Vince Lombardi probably doesn't rush to the top of your list of Christian coaches. He was, however, reared in a loving home with a strong spiritual underpinning. One important and widely known fact about Coach Lombardi was his dedication to three things and three things only: family, faith, and football. He would often tell the players he coached that they had time to focus on only three things in their life if they played for him—and three things only. It was up to them to choose what three things they would cherish. He told them that while there would be many distractions for them as players, if they would stay focused on the three main parts of their life, they would be great football players, great men, and happy men.

Vince Lombardi was known by many as one of the most hard-nosed football coaches to have ever coached the game. When he took over the Green Bay Packers in 1959, the team had only won a single game the year before; however, when he departed after nine seasons, he left behind one of the greatest dynasties in NFL history. He led the Packers to five NFL championships, including an unbelievable three in a row. He also led the Packers to wins in Super Bowls I and II and finished his NFL career with an overall 105–35–6 record.

"IF YOU CHEAT ON THE PRACTICE FIELD,
YOU'LL CHEAT IN THE GAME, AND IF YOU
CHEAT IN THE GAME, YOU'LL CHEAT THE REST
OF YOUR LIFE."

—VINCE LOMBARDI

A hard-driving authoritarian, Lombardi was a true man's man and a fireball on the field who did not tolerate mistakes. In practice he often exhibited the passion and drive he had for football and for life. There have been many who have studied his life and accomplishments, and each person writes about his determination and his willingness to sacrifice the small things in life to achieve those things that are great in life. He believed that success in anything depends on 100 percent effort at all times! "If you cheat on the practice field, you'll cheat in the game," he said, "and if you cheat in the game, you'll cheat the rest of your life."[1] What a lesson for us all.

From an early age Vince demonstrated a real curiosity about his faith. He became an altar boy, but he didn't want to be in the background. Soon he worked his way up to being the candle bearer but not just any candle bearer; he wanted to be the one who led the procession holding the golden cross. Sports became very important to Vince, and the more he was around football, the more he loved it. His first opportunity to play contact football changed his life—he simply couldn't get enough. He said years later when asked to summarize football, "Contact, controlled violence, a game where the mission was to hit someone harder, knees up, elbows out, challenge your body, mind and spirit, exhaust yourself and seek redemption through fatigue, such were the rewards an altar boy found in his favorite game."[2]

While attending a prominent Catholic school Vincent continued to play football at every opportunity, against the counsel of his teachers. His school didn't have a football team for him to play on because they were against the violence that the sport represented. The sisters disapproved adamantly of boys participating in brutal sports such as football, and the only thing worse than football was expressing an interest in girls. In the end, Coach Lombardi simply could not give up football for the priesthood. Lombardi said later that he "was not created to be a priest."[3] He noted his strong home life and the prominent Christian influences in his life, but as much as he tried to direct his passions to be a peaceful young man, he could not divert himself from earthly temptations like the thrill of hitting somebody, legally.

If you knew Jesus was coming to stay with you and watch you interact with your family, what would you need to do to get ready? Surely you need to clean the house—but He wouldn't care. The right bread and wine would be a must—but He wouldn't care. Having a place for Him to study and pray would be a priority—but He wouldn't care. Maybe you could replace all the windows with stained-glass windows so that your home would resemble a church—but He wouldn't care. So what would He care about? What would make Jesus feel as though your home was His? What do you need to do to make your house . . . God's home?

## TIME OUT

1. What changes need to be made in your home to make it a dwelling fit for a visit by Christ?
2. Whose home have you visited, either recently or as a child, where you could feel the love of Christ?
3. Would your friends at church be surprised at what goes on in your home?

## TODAY'S ASSIGNMENT

Identify someone from your past whose home made you feel the
love of Christ. With your wife, determine some things you want to
begin to do differently around your house to ensure you are creating the right environment for your children. Be on guard for the
things you are allowing to enter your home that can be damaging
to your family (TV, Internet, magazines, books, and so on).

---

### HOME-FIELD ADVANTAGE

*Praises and concerns you want to bring before God*

_____

_____

_____

_____

_____

---

# DAY 19

# SOMEONE IS ALWAYS WATCHING

## BEING AN EXAMPLE—EVERY DAY!

### THOUGHT OF THE DAY

*Your children pick up many habits, both good and bad, simply by watching you.*

### THE COACH'S CORNER

Most of us hope our children pick up at least some of our good habits, such as working hard, going to church, taking care of the needy, seeking justice for all, paying the bills, loving our wives, and even being a considerate driver. (Well, maybe not the last one.) But we absolutely pray that they don't pick up all of our *terrible* habits, such as taking the Lord's name in vain, being untruthful, skipping church, cheating on taxes, and yelling. Unfortunately, many times our children seem to be more attracted to our bad habits than they are to our good ones. What seems to work best for them is the old slogan "Your actions speak so loudly, I can't hear you talking."

Jesus was respected as a carpenter who learned His craft from His earthly father. We are not told directly that He was a great carpenter; however, one can only assume that He was the best carpenter in the land. We are all created to learn by watching what someone else does. We learn new skills by watching others do them; we teach others to drive a car by letting them first observe us.

> **MANY TIMES OUR CHILDREN SEEM TO BE MORE ATTRACTED TO OUR BAD HABITS THAN THEY ARE TO OUR GOOD ONES.**

When your children become older, it will be shocking to see how many habits they acquire from you and your wife. It has been proven that children learn best, not by being told what to do or even by observing others but by actually doing the activity with someone they desire to learn from. This is the way most people learn to play a musical instrument, participate in a sport, or obtain the skills of studying. What is extremely frustrating is when you realize your children are imitating many of your bad characteristics. What did you try to imitate that your father did? Was it a negative or a positive behavior? What negative behaviors did your father (or grandfather) demonstrate that you intentionally decided you didn't want to hand down to your family?

Most of us have secrets, things about our lives we don't want our children to imitate or even know about. Things like the grades we actually made in school, how many speeding tickets we have, what we did on Friday nights when growing up, and, yes, how honest we were with our parents. Woe to us if, by our examples, our children do not find a relationship with Jesus Christ. Few things are more difficult than walking the talk—but nothing is more important. Many of us have had the experience of doing something we were not very proud of, only to look out the corners of our eyes and see one of our children watching intently.

For many men today, they find that it is true that someone is always watching, no matter what they are doing. Once others find out that Christ is an active part of your life, you often feel under a microscope or as if you live in a glass house. You are watched while at your children's ballgames, solving a crisis at work, shopping at the store, working in the yard, watching TV, reading a book, or even playing a round of golf. People really want to know if there is something different about the man who calls himself a Christian— are you real? Of course, the primary goal of your actions is for them to see something in you that they desire, something they want to learn more about—the Spirit of the living God. There have been more than a few fathers who were surprised when their sons had simply become good citizens with good reputations, instead of spirit-filled vessels for Christ to live through. Do your children see Christ in you, or are you simply trying to be a better, more moral you?

## THE GAME PLAN

The Bible says that if you follow God you will live in a glass house for the world to see. God wants you to know:

- You must set an example in everything you do no matter your age—1 Timothy 4:12: "Let no one despise your youth, but be an example to the believers in word, in conduct, in love, in spirit, in faith, in purity."
- Your word must be the truth—John 17:17: "Sanctify them by your truth. Your word is truth."

- Those around you should see what love is in you—1 John 3:16: "By this we know love, because He laid down His life for us. And we also ought to lay down our lives for the brethren."
- If you see a need, you should act upon it—1 Corinthians 13:1: "Though I speak with the tongues of men and of angels, but have not love, I have become sounding brass or a clanging cymbal."

## PLAYMAKERS

To all but one man, Michael Jordan is the greatest basketball player to ever play the game. The one man who would disagree would be his high school coach, who once cut Michael from the team. After an unbelievable career for the Tar Heels of the University of North Carolina, he was drafted by the NBA's Chicago Bulls in 1984. He quickly emerged as one of the superstars of the NBA, entertaining crowds all over the world with his prolific scoring and leading the NBA with scoring titles multiple times. His vertical jumping ability, illustrated by completing slam dunks from as far away as the free throw line, earned him the nickname "Air Jordan."

In 1991, he won his first NBA championship with the Chicago Bulls and followed that achievement with follow-up titles in 1992 and 1993, securing the term "three-peat." Before his career was over, Jordan's individual accolades and accomplishments included five MVP awards, ten All-NBA First Team designations, fourteen NBA All-Star Game appearances, three All-Star MVPs, ten scoring titles, and six NBA Finals MVP awards. He holds the NBA record for highest career regular season scoring average with thirty points per game, as well as averaging a record thirty-three points per game in the playoffs. In 1999, he was named the greatest North American athlete of the twentieth century by ESPN and was second to Babe Ruth on the Associated Press's list of the top twentieth-century athletes.

Coaches at every level have always told their players that they must practice the way they want to perform. We have heard it said ourselves: "If you don't practice well then you won't perform well." If ever there had been an athlete who didn't have to practice hard, it would've been Michael Jordan. The superstar really had it all going. He had God-given talent and had already proven to the world he was one of the greatest players of all time. Yet he was known as the player who would always give 100 percent in every practice. Jordan also excelled as one of the best defensive players in the NBA. He was known as the master of defense both in practice and in games. According to those who coached him, his practice ethic was unparalleled in the league.

A virtually unknown young player from Arkansas, Scottie Pippen, joined the Bulls in 1987. He played at the University of Central Arkansas, a small state university where he started out as the basketball team's equipment manager and worked his way into a starting position. Once joining the NBA, he lacked the collegiate playing experience Michael had from North Carolina but astonished his peers with his natural athletic offensive skills. Scottie quickly realized that being truly great in the NBA required both an offensive and a defensive game. Every day in practice he had the opportunity to learn from a great teacher. Due to Michael's nonstop focus on defense in practice, the young Pippen began to watch intently, and he spent hours trying to emulate the legend. Every day, he was consistent in his approach to improve, and he tried to work on his total game.

For several years Scottie matured and adopted his mentor's attitude about defense. Soon he became known as a defensive superstar himself. He ended his career with Olympic Gold and NBA championships. In addition, he was selected as one of the greatest fifty players in NBA history. Because Scottie was a successful student of Jordan, he also had the pleasure of being selected to the NBA All-Defensive Team eight times. For this, Michael must be proud. It is hard being an example all the time. It is much easier to turn it on when you know you are being watched. We are always being watched.

## TIME OUT

1. Describe a time your children saw you stumble.
2. If you were to die tomorrow, what would your children remember most about the way you lived your life?
3. When you are at a sporting event, what example do you leave?

## TODAY'S ASSIGNMENT

It is healthy for us to let our children see us worship, not only in church but also at home. How can you model your commitment more intensely at home?

## HOME-FIELD ADVANTAGE

*Praises and concerns you want to bring before God*

_____

_____

_____

_____

# Making Time for What Is Important

## You Must Not Leave Your Children to Themselves

### Thought of the Day

*Spending time with your children just may be your most important daily task.*

### The Coach's Corner

Whether we like it or not, a child's first concept of God is often framed by his relationship with his father. While we can never live up to the perfection of God, that doesn't mean that we can't model a passionate pursuing love for our children in the same way God has expressed His pursuing love for us. We have all heard it said that it is better to spend quality time with your children than to spend quantity time with them. This is also often the line spoken by dads who are spending too little time with their children, and they are looking to feel better about themselves. If you ask young adults, they will tell you that children desire face time with their dads. If it is going to the grocery store, attending a ball game, mowing the yard, or changing the oil—children just want to be with their fathers. If you were privileged enough to have had a dad, when you think back to your childhood you probably remember time that you spent just hanging out with him: a fishing trip where no fish were caught, a camping trip where it rained so hard you never left the tent, or a ballgame when your seats were so far from home plate you couldn't even tell who was playing. You may remember handing him a screwdriver, getting him the garden hose, helping him carry the trash to the curb, or simply sitting on the steps and just throwing rocks.

## CHILDREN JUST WANT TO BE WITH THEIR FATHERS.

Coach Bob Stoops is no doubt one of the manliest men in the country. He is the head coach of the Oklahoma Sooners football team and would be considered a real-man's man in any gathering. His teams have played for the national championship, and in 2000 he was voted the National Coach of the Year. No matter what activities you enjoy doing with your children, one truth every child needs to know is that he is loved. Bob recently participated in an In The Zone event and told of how he and his dad always told each other, "I love you," and hugged each other every time they got together. While some guys might see that as a sign of weakness, he believes that to tell and show your son that you really love him is a true sign of a real man.

God has placed you in a place of high responsibility. Why do some men appear to fail as dads, when others seem to be so successful? Outwardly it often seems they have done the same things raising their children. Is there some mystical, unique combination of characteristics that makes some of us good dads and some of us not? It certainly can't be that our ability to be a good dad rests on our personalities or our socioeconomic status; nor is it contingent on the amount of formal education we have, or our race. It appears to depend on one thing—being there for your children. A godly dad must be there for his children, as a total support system, at all times. Being there is more than just physical presence; it is providing emotional and spiritual support. It means your children know they will never have to face life alone, that you will always share their joy and sorrows, their successes and failures, their sins and their confessions. It means a child knows regardless of how young or old he is or what he has done, that you will never desert him or give up on him.

### A GODLY DAD MUST BE THERE FOR HIS CHILDREN, AS A TOTAL SUPPORT SYSTEM, AT ALL TIMES.

We have heard all the excuses for why some men don't spend time with their children: They are busy making money so their children can go to the finest schools. They are climbing the ladder of success so their families can have more things. They spend time working out to stay in shape so they will live longer. They are hanging out with friends who can help them network in their careers. The list can go on and on, but their prime argument is this: it doesn't matter about the quantity of time you spend with your kids; it is the quality time that matters the most. Many dads want to substitute a trip to Disney World in place of playing pitch in the yard with their sons after work. Many dads want to substitute giving a brand-new car at graduation to make them feel better about not helping their daughters with their homework for the past several years.

We have all heard the argument for quality time over quantity time, but it simply doesn't add up—our children desire time with us. Quality time can be created only from quantity time. It is in this time that they learn what they are going to emulate about us, and they observe our actions in all circumstances. Our children will imitate the adults they look up to and spend the most time with, whether they are good role models or not. Children who grow up without an active man in their lives will often resort to imitating other men, whether he is one of their friends' dads, men on television, men playing sports, or simply guys who are older than they are.

## THE GAME PLAN

The Bible says that God expects us to spend time with our children showing them the way, not simply telling them the way. God wants you to know:

- Don't neglect your greatest earthly gift—Genesis 33:5: "And he lifted his eyes and saw the women and children, and said, 'Who are these with you?' So he said, 'The children whom God has graciously given your servant.'"
- You must make time to teach them biblical truths—2 Timothy 3:15–17: "And that from childhood you have known the Holy Scriptures, which are able to make you wise for salvation through faith which is in Christ Jesus. All Scripture is given by inspiration of God, and is profitable for doctrine, for reproof, for correction, for instruction in righteousness, that the man of God may be complete, thoroughly equipped for every good work."

- You must take time to control them—1 Timothy 3:4: "One who rules his own house well, having his children in submission with all reverence."
- Don't express hate to your children by not disciplining them—Proverbs 13:24: "He who spares his rod hates his son, but he who loves him disciplines him promptly."

## PLAYMAKERS

Clay Dyer is a competitive bass fisherman. He began fishing at the age of five and went on to fish in his first bass tournament at age fifteen. In 1995, Clay became a full-time professional bass fisherman. What might surprise you about Clay Dyer is that he was born without lower limbs or a left arm, and only a partial right arm. Yet he has gone on to finish over two hundred bass tournaments, winning twenty-five. You might wonder how this is possible; can Clay really compete on his own?

To understand the answer to this question, you have to start from the beginning of his journey. In 1978, Clarence and Beverly Dyer eagerly awaited the birth of their new baby. On the day of Clay's birth, Clarence Dyer found himself in the waiting room of the hospital, like millions of nervous and excited fathers-to-be before him. As he waited, the doctor came to inform him that the labor was not progressing as expected. There were complications, and the baby's limbs had not fully developed. Clarence quickly moved to Beverly's side in the delivery room. There was no way for the Dyers to expect what came next, no ultrasounds to prepare them, no warning signs. "When they got him out and held him up, you could have hit me with a baseball bat and it wouldn't have hurt anymore than it did at that moment," says Clarence.[1] The devastated couple spent the next several days in the hospital with their young son before returning home to Hamilton, Alabama.

As parents they were left to wonder and worry how Clay would ever "live a normal life." How were they to prepare their son for the world—and the world for Clay? There was no one to ask, no example to follow. And here the Dyers made a decision that forever shaped the man Clay would become. "We decided to treat him like our other son and see how it worked out," Clarence said.[2] They wouldn't set limits on what he could do or lower expectations for who he could become. Their son, and no one else, would determine what he was capable of. In this way the Dyers gave Clay the most normal life possible. "My family is the reason I am where I am," says Clay. "Never did they look at me and say that maybe I shouldn't try something."[3] So Clay began a lifelong process of "figuring it out." He did it all, learning to do everyday things such as eating on his own. Nothing would hold Clay back; he wanted to try everything, playing youth football, basketball, and T-ball. According to Clay's dad, "He's never had any problems with anything he has ever tried to do."[4]

As you can imagine, it isn't always easy for Clarence and Beverly. They find themselves surprised and excited every day by what their son is able to accomplish, by his relentless spirit. But as a parent, it is hard to see your child struggle. You want to step in and fix things. "I wanted to help so bad . . ." says Clay's mom, "but all I could do was reach out my hand. He'd almost always push it away."[5]

Fishing became a regular activity for Clay, his father, and his grandfather. In fact, his grandfather bought Clay's first rod-and-reel. Clay went on to catch countless fish with that Scooby Doo rod-and-reel. Soon enough this became too easy for young Clay. The single fish that really solidified his excitement for fishing was a twenty-six-pound catfish. It took Clay over forty-five minutes to reel that fish in, a fish bigger than he was. That was it; he was hooked.

From a young age Clay always wanted to compete. He didn't always want to fish, but he always wanted to compete. "I'm a competitor at heart," says Dyer, "I really wanted to play something else, but the NFL wasn't looking for linebackers my size."[6] So at the age of eight, Clay asked his father for a Baitcaster, a delicate reel that only the most experienced fishermen can use. Clarence was taken back. "There have been times when I've thought, *Clay, come on, you can't do that.* But I wouldn't say it. That was one time I did have to say no. Most people don't have the touch to use a Baitcaster even with a full set of fingers."[7] But like most persistent kids, Clay found a way around this, practicing each day while his dad was at work. He perfected his technique of placing the base of the rod under his chin, his face on the reel, releasing the perfect cast. He surprised everyone yet again, finding his own way.

Once when Clay was tying fishing knots with his tongue, as he always does, he caught his mouth. His family offered to help, but he said, "No, thanks. In a tournament I'll need to handle this myself."[8] The Dyers were surprised once again. Tournaments? This would mean riding and driving a boat, competing with professional fishermen. As always, Clay found a way. Clay's next goal is to qualify for the FLW Championship Tournament; we have no doubt that he will.

Clay wanted to do exactly what everyone else does. Many people have offered suggestions and ideas over the years to make fishing a little easier for Clay, but he prefers to remain true to himself. "I thank them and tell them that I'm sure there is someone somewhere who can use it, but I've become comfortable doing it my own way," he said. "I've been fishing like this since I was four or five years old. I don't want to change now."[9]

He refused to allow his disabilities to bring him down or diminish his determination, earning him the respect of fellow fishermen. His motto for life is, "If I can, you can." Jay Yelas, a former Bassmaster Classic winner and friend, sees Dyer as an inspiration: "He never complains about anything. He just looks forward to each new day and each new challenge with eager anticipation. I know of no man who has gotten more out of his potential than Clay Dyer."[10]

It has been a quite a journey for the Dyer family. Clarence Dyer said, "I wish I had known his story would turn out like it has on that day twenty-nine years ago. It would have made that day much easier."[11]

Most people believe Clay is extraordinary. But if you ask Clay, he says, "I tell people that all you really need is a heart, a soul, and a mind. Then you say, 'OK, this is what I've got' and make the best use of it."[12] We believe Clay is an extraordinary person, the result of an extraordinary family who took the time to be there.

## TIME OUT

1. How would your children describe your involvement in their lives?
2. How would your wife describe your involvement in the lives of your children?
3. What is keeping you from spending the time you want with your family?

## TODAY'S ASSIGNMENT

Get out your calendar, call your wife, and get together. Find an active role you can play in supporting one of your kids' passions. Be creative. Be intentional. "Just Do It"!

## HOME-FIELD ADVANTAGE

*Praises and concerns you want to bring before God*

_____

_____

_____

_____

_____

# WHAT YOU SEE IS WHAT YOU GET

## BEING HONEST WITH YOUR FAMILY

### THOUGHT OF THE DAY

*Being open and honest with your family about life's problems teaches them to rely on God for solutions.*

### THE COACH'S CORNER

The Bible teaches us to speak the truth in love. Perhaps there is no place more difficult for men to do this than when we are dealing with our families. Life can be hard, especially today. We all have friends who are struggling to either find a job or hold on to the one they currently have. With all the talk of the bad economy, mergers, and acquisitions, most of us are simply in a holding pattern. For many, it is a scary time in history. However, many of our families are going through life with little thought to such things because of our reluctance to be open and truthful with them. We put on the bold face when we go home, and we act as if we have no problems in the world. After all, it is our nature to protect our families. We don't want them to worry about what may or may not happen. They don't need to worry about how old the cars are getting, that there is no college fund, or about how the paycheck barely pays the bills. When we come home at night, we desire for everyone in the family to be in a great mood, which in turn removes us from the pressures of the world, at least for a little while. Often we keep all of our problems bottled up inside rather than share them with our families.

The Bible says, "A false balance is an abomination to the LORD" (Proverbs 11:1 NASB). We, as caring dads, should present a balanced picture to our children, involving them in the good and bad times, the happiness and the grief, the pleasures and problems, by being honest with them about life's situations. It is hard for most of us to be open and honest with our wives and children when bad things happen. After all, we are the ones who fix problems, not bring them home for others to deal with. Though we are called to be honest with our families about things that involve them, many times we do not fully disclose things to them because we don't want them to worry or be troubled. We hide our feelings and, in doing so, we often teach them to hide theirs.

> OFTEN WE KEEP ALL OF OUR PROBLEMS
> BOTTLED UP INSIDE RATHER THAN SHARE
> THEM WITH OUR FAMILIES.

The FedEx package you were expecting with a check for some completed work didn't come. Your bank account doesn't have enough to cover this month's mortgage, and you've already mailed the check. Rumor has it your employer is considering a layoff. Your third grader runs into the house bouncing off the walls after school and your reply to his cheery greeting is a mumbled "hello." Your family knows by the tone of your voice that something is bothering you. Your wife asks what's wrong and you tell her, "Nothing." Your daughter knows something is wrong and immediately fears that it relates to her, so she asks, "Are you mad at me?" To which you snap, "No, just go and play." We don't need to dump more on our family than they can handle, but we do need to be honest and share our problems.

## THE GAME PLAN

The Bible says that you will have problems in life. God wants you to know:

- You can bless your family by being open and not living in isolation with them—1 Peter 3:8–9: "Finally, all of you be of one mind, having compassion for one another; love as brothers, be tenderhearted, be courteous; not returning evil for evil or reviling for reviling, but on the contrary blessing, knowing that you were called to this, that you may inherit a blessing."

- You can bless your family by thinking consistently about God's truth—Philippians 4:8: "Finally, brethren, whatever things are true, whatever things are noble, whatever things are just, whatever things are pure, whatever things are lovely, whatever things are of good report, if there is any virtue and if there is anything praiseworthy—meditate on these things."

- You can bless your family by dealing with them with a clean heart—Psalm 101:2: "I will behave wisely in a perfect way. Oh, when will you come to me? I will walk within my house with a perfect heart."

- You can bless your family by uniting together through the good and the bad—Zechariah 8:16: "These are the things you shall do: Speak each man the truth to his neighbor; give judgment in your gates for truth, justice, and peace."

## PLAYMAKERS

When corporations fail to take care of those who work for them, the media tends to look for a corporate officer to be the responsible party to blame. In 2001, America witnessed one of the most widespread corporate failures in our country's history. Most of us recall hearing about the collapse of the megacompany Enron, located in Houston, Texas. While some people may have lost everything in that crash, there were others of us who simply followed the news events through the media.

The CEO was a man named Ken Lay. His name became tied with corporate abuse and accounting fraud that brought the corporate giant down. While he may or may not have had direct knowledge of all the events that caused the collapse, he served as chairman and CEO for eight years, ending in 2003. After a long legal procedure Mr. Lay was found guilty and faced up to one hundred years in prison if given the maximum sentence. While waiting for his sentencing, he was vacationing in Colorado with members of his family when he experienced a massive heart attack and died. The news media played him out to be a corrupt businessman with only one thing on his mind—to cheat others out of their money. Stories have been told of employees losing everything as result of the collapse of the company. Understandably, many of his employees and their families wanted to see Mr. Lay get the maximum sentence.

Many of those who knew Ken the best indicate that he simply was a different person at work than when he was at home, in the community, and at church. Members of his family were shocked when the charges against Ken first came out. This was certainly not the husband, father, grandfather, or friend they knew. At his memorial service Ken was remembered by close friends as a kind and generous man who was unfairly characterized after the company's collapse. He was praised for his deep dedication to his family and reverence for all people, whether executives or janitorial staff.

Reverend William Lawson, pastor emeritus of Wheeler Avenue Baptist Church, said, "I am glad to have known Ken Lay and glad that he was willing to reach down and touch people like me. Ken was a rich and powerful man, and he could have limited his association to people who were likewise rich and powerful—but he didn't."[1] Lawson said Lay helped untold numbers of people with college tuition, medical expenses, and other needs. More than one thousand mourners gathered at First United Methodist Church, where Lay had been a member.

Each of Lay's five children spoke, describing a moral and spiritual man who spent endless energy trying to build his family. "He had a lot of loving friends and a lot of loving family," said David Herrold, one of his two stepsons. "He had a strong faith in God, and I know he's in heaven today. I'm glad he's not in a position anymore to be whipped by his enemy."[2] Family friend Mick Seidl defiantly described Ken as a "good, honest, God-fearing friend who did not have a criminal bone in his body."[3] The Reverend Steve Wende, pastor of First United Methodist, cited the last verse of Scripture that Lay wrote in his daily journal—"We live by faith, not by sight"—and praised his family for standing behind him. Late in the service, Lay's twelve grandchildren were brought into the sanctuary. His daughters, Liz Vittor and Robyn Vermeil, read brief comments each grandchild had made about the man they knew as "Papi." It was evident to everyone there; Ken was a different man than most everyone outside his family knew. It seems that only God knew the real Ken Lay.

## TIME OUT

1. What things are you hiding from your family?
2. What can you do to start communicating more effectively with your family?
3. What aspects about your personal life do you keep hidden from your family?

## TODAY'S ASSIGNMENT

Create a file that contains the location of every asset, liability, and important document of your life. Set aside a time to discuss business with your wife.

---

### HOME-FIELD ADVANTAGE

*Praises and concerns you want to bring before God*

_____

_____

_____

---

# FINDING THE ZONE IN YOUR RELATIONSHIPS WITH YOUR FRIENDS

*A man who has friends must himself be friendly,*
*But there is a friend who sticks closer than a brother.*

—PROVERBS 18:24

159

# Making Wise Choices

## Show Me Your Friends; I Will Show You Your Future

## Thought of the Day

*One of the least appreciated skills of a successful man
is how he chooses his closest friends.*

## The Coach's Corner

There are some things we will always remember that our parents taught us when we were growing up: Don't lean back in your chair, or you will fall and break your back. Don't wave your hand out the window of the car, or a passing car will cut it off. Don't leave the house without having on clean underwear, in case you are in a car wreck. Sound familiar? But one we also always heard was, "Watch who you hang out with, because people will judge you by your company." Although this advice (perhaps with different slang words) has been handed down for years, it still applies to us today—children and adults. If we hang around with someone who is ambitious, we are more likely to pursue things that will better us. If we hang out with someone who spends more time with their friends than with their family, we are likely to feel pressure to do so as well.

The quality of our friendships helps determine the value of our lives. We all need friends, but we need people who walk in the door when others seem to walk out. You certainly can't choose your relatives, nor can you choose your neighbors or coworkers, but you can choose those who will be your friends.

Jesus was very meticulous in selecting His friends. He certainly had friends and followers everywhere He traveled, but He also had a handpicked group of friends who some probably referred to as His best friends. He identified twelve men (disciples) whom He trusted with His utmost secrets, His time, and His teachings. He surrounded Himself with like-minded friends, with one common goal.

**THE QUALITY OF OUR FRIENDSHIPS HELPS DETERMINE THE VALUE OF OUR LIVES.**

If you were to take a long, hard look at your friends, would they be men who make you wiser? Are they men who make you a better man, a more godly man, or a better husband? Sometimes our friends are escapes. They are guys to hang out with and help us forget problems in our families, marriages, or careers. They are guys who let us do the things we feel uncomfortable doing around our families. Although they are fun, we know these are not the type of friends who will make us better men. Finding truly godly friends seems as though it shouldn't be so hard. We would welcome someone whom we could be totally confidential with about everything. It would be great to find a man who is going where we are going spiritually. In our best moments, we are looking for an accountability partner. We desire someone who will hold us on line, not allow us to get off track but at the same time not serve as a father figure. He would be a true friend that, if something were to happen to us or our families, we could count on with no reservations. Who we choose as friends will help to determine the men we become.

## THE GAME PLAN

The Bible wants you to be aware that your choice of friends sets a pathway for your life. God wants you to know:

- We need to team up to help one another—2 Corinthians 7:13: "Therefore we have been comforted in your comfort. And we rejoiced exceedingly more for the joy of Titus, because his spirit has been refreshed by you all."
- We need friends who are willing to tell us the truth— even when we don't want to hear it—Proverbs 27:6: "Faithful are the wounds of a friend, but the kisses of an enemy are deceitful."
- Don't make friendships with angry men; the results can be disastrous—Proverbs 22:24–25: "Make no friendship with an angry man, and with a furious man do not go, lest you learn his ways and set a snare for your soul."
- We should be intentional, selective, and wise in selecting friends—Romans 2:13: "For not the hearers of the law are just in the sight of God, but the doers of the law will be justified."

## PLAYMAKERS

Michael Vick has done his time and has been cleared to rejoin the National Football League and play for the Philadelphia Eagles.

When we first heard the story about Michael in 2007, we were all shocked and disappointed as the charges became public. This seemed so unlike the man we had watched on *Monday Night Football*. The tragedy spoke clearly and powerfully to us all: it was certainly about dog fighting, but it was about something more. Michael's story was about the power that our friends have on us and our need for strong accountability by our friends.

Michael was one of the top quarterbacks in the NFL! At age twenty-four, he received a ten-year $100 million contract to play for the struggling Atlanta Falcons. He didn't disappoint his team or his fans as his performance consistently improved until he was one of the best quarterbacks in the NFL. It seemed that everyone in the country knew who he was and that he was possibly destined for the NFL Hall of Fame. His endorsement deals had him in the prime time media consistently. But something went wrong, terribly wrong, and virtually overnight, he found himself out of football and behind bars in a federal prison. In his case, he gambled and lost big when he started running a dog fighting operation with the encouragement and applause of his good friends who did not have his best interests at heart.

Imagine if he had been surrounded by people of greater character—men who would have had the courage to challenge him to take the high road rather than applaud and engage in the illegal activity of dog fighting. If he had strong friends, there could have been a very different outcome to his story and this phase of his life. If Michael had the benefit of true godly friends, his life would no doubt have turned out differently than it has thus far. Michael appears to have underestimated the negative effect that his inner circle of friends exerted on his life. One of Vick's mentors, James "Poo" Johnson, an officer of the Boys and Girls Club back in Vick's hometown, said that Michael had been warned to avoid associating with bad company. Nevertheless, Johnson said, "Michael is loyal to his friends, sometimes to a fault. Sometimes that can create extra baggage that you never anticipated."[1] Michael surrounded himself with men who were not devoted to his best interest.

**IMAGINE IF HE HAD BEEN SURROUNDED BY PEOPLE OF GREATER CHARACTER—MEN WHO WOULD HAVE HAD THE COURAGE TO CHALLENGE HIM TO TAKE THE HIGH ROAD.**

Ignoring the wisdom of his mentors, and unwilling to resist the dark path his friends were taking him down, Vick held on to unhealthy relationships from his past; and it changed his life forever. Consider what it cost him: He lost his freedom for over a year, he lost his reputation maybe forever, and he brought shame to both the game of football and the city that loved him. He lost his considerable financial security. According to some estimates, Michael will forfeit upwards of $142 million, including a salary of $72 million, $20 million in paid bonuses, and $50 million in endorsement income. He gave up his ability to be a positive role model to his fans, and he lost the privilege of doing what he did best—the very thing he was uniquely gifted by God to do—play football.

Michael had a big heart for the guys he grew up with but failed to set boundaries to protect himself from their influences. He failed to surround himself with those who would hold him to a higher personal standard of behavior. How different Michael's life would have been if he had shown wisdom in his choice of friends. It's certainly easy for us to say what he should have done differently. Playing the part of an armchair quarterback is easy where others are concerned. The real challenge for us is to ask, "Who or what guides my decision making?" There's a biblical principle at work here. King Solomon wrote there's "a time to get, and a time to lose;

a time to keep, and a time to cast away" (Ecclesiastes 3:6 KJV). That includes some people who have influence in our lives.

> ## THE REAL CHALLENGE FOR US IS TO ASK, "WHO OR WHAT GUIDES MY DECISION MAKING?"

We would be wise to ask a number of questions about the friendships we have. Are we holding on to friendships that may be personally destructive? Are there those whose advice is clearly not godly or wise? Or do we surround ourselves with those who consistently challenge us to do the right thing? I'm sure there are many lessons we could take away from the story of Michael Vick; surrounding yourself with good counsel and trusted accountability partners would be at the top of that list. For his sake and his future, now that he is back on the NFL turf again, this time with a wise mentor—Tony Dungy—many are rooting for Michael to find a way of utilizing his God-given talents for the kingdom.

## TIME OUT

1. Who do you consider your closest friend, other than your spouse or a family member?
2. Ask your wife if she thinks you need to find a godly best friend.
3. Identify three men who, after deep reflection and prayer, you know you should try to avoid.

## TODAY'S ASSIGNMENT

Write out a plan of action for identifying what you want in a godly friend. Make sure to note individuals who have the specific characteristics you desire.

---

### HOME-FIELD ADVANTAGE
*Praises and concerns you want to bring before God*

_____

_____

_____

_____

---

# CAN YOU KEEP A SECRET?

## WOMEN DON'T HAVE THE EDGE ON GOSSIPING

### THOUGHT OF THE DAY

*One way to honor your friends is to keep their conversations confidential.*

### THE COACH'S CORNER

Few things can be more devastating to a person than when they tell a friend something in confidence and later hear that the gist of the conversation was openly shared with others. Sometimes breaches in confidence like this can permanently damage a friendship and even a life. Knowledge is power, and when we give the information away we give away our power.

The Bible reminds us about the power of the tongue to be both a blessing and a curse. In many ways it performs like a rudder on a large ship. Your tongue can steer you into a safe harbor, and it can also steer you into treacherous waters. One of the most dangerous places it can take you is into the always damaging waters of gossip. A recent national study has shown that men gossip as much as women. Are you kidding? Gossip is for women! Men don't gossip—we simply discuss things. Just like real men don't keep a diary—we keep track of stuff by writing it down. From talking about their weight, wardrobe, shopping lists, and complaining about men, in-laws, and kids, there is no dearth of subjects for women to use to start an interesting chat. But have you ever thought about what men gossip about? Some say that all men ever talk about is sex, women, and sports. But work and money matter to men too. Most men are career-oriented, and they love discussing the same.

**ONE OF THE MOST DANGEROUS PLACES THE TONGUE CAN TAKE YOU IS INTO THE ALWAYS DAMAGING WATERS OF GOSSIP.**

Men often talk about their work and job duties, pay packages, sports teams, or new gadgets. We often discuss everything from local layoffs, to what the national economy is doing, as well as our dreams and frustrations. Work-related talk is often common among men. Men believe in making intelligent choices, and the power to make those decisions won't come from discussing our shopping list, so we'd rather spend time talking about a new job and better business propositions. Besides, we often ponder about the way to deal with our bosses and office politics. Undeniably, it helps when we find others who have gone through the place in life that we are now traveling.

No matter which car or gadget we own, discussing the latest technology and gadgets interests most of us. Be it high-tech phones, iPods, shotguns, music systems, cameras, or digital planners, talking benefits, drawbacks, and pricing is what gets our adrenalin pumping. Watching football, keeping a strict check on the scoreboard, commenting on each and every play being called, and finally discussing the participating teams and the tournament—men find instant gratification talking about sports. However, when our talk turns personal, or we comment on the quality of another person, then we tend to join the destructive world of gossip. Simple discussions turn into destructive actions as we often try to get even and find ways of getting ahead at the expense of others. Gossip is not simply defined as talking about others; rather it seems to be more about planning and desiring harm for another.

## THE GAME PLAN

The Bible wants you to avoid the damage of gossip and embrace the language of encouragement. God wants you to let:

- Your words be withheld when gossip begins—Proverbs 11:13: "A talebearer reveals secrets, but he who is of a faithful spirit conceals a matter."
- Your words bring friends together, not tear them apart—Proverbs 16:28: "A perverse man sows strife, and a whisperer separates the best of friends."
- Your words be righteous, not deceitful—Proverbs 12:17: "He who speaks truth declares righteousness, but a false witness, deceit."
- Your words build people up—Ephesians 4:29: "Let no corrupt word proceed out of your mouth, but what is good for necessary edification, that it may impart grace to the hearers."

## PLAYMAKERS

Why are we so shocked when we hear about cheating in sports? For years we have heard about some level of dishonesty in virtually every sport and unfortunately at almost every level. From T-ball coaches who pad their roster, to cheating in the ranks of NCAA sports, there appears to be a small group of people in every sport who have damaged the reputation of everyone. But it shocks us every time we hear of a new story involving cheating because sports have always been where you teach values, hard work, ethics, and honesty. It's where young boys become men ready for life's challenges. It is where a man's word to another man is a bond and an oath.

What is more American than the NFL? Coaches stomp the sidelines, trying to deal with the egos of high-maintenance megastars. We used to look forward to Coach John Madden grunting on Monday Night Football about the dirt and sweat and the big greasy sausages on the grill. The NFL is testosterone, and testosterone is a man's hormone of choice. You can't have too much of it when you enjoy the timeless game of football.

Even American executives often talk in football terms. "We're going to blitz the opposition." "Let's score a touchdown with this sales pitch." "We are in the red zone, gentlemen." At its heart, football is a powerful force in our culture. Deep down some men truly think that a university isn't worth its salt unless it has a winning football team. But at the heart of this game, football has always been about men having trusted secrets, plays that they only shared with their teammates in the huddle. Football is a team sport, and a sport that relies on holding the confidentiality of the game plan and strategies.

For the most part, NFL coaches and players have always operated with a type of unwritten moral oath, in addition to NFL rules, that teams and coaches will not try to steal or share information that could hurt another team. Then along came Bill Belichick. Coach Belichick has a resume that any NFL coach would envy. In his first seven seasons as head coach of the New England Patriots, Belichick led his team to three Super Bowl championships, three conference titles, and five division crowns. Why then would Coach Belichick and his team steal signals from an opposing team just to get the advantage? It doesn't make sense. NFL commissioner Roger Goodell could have punished Belichick even more harshly (first-round draft choice loss, a $500,000 fine for Belichick, and a $250,000 fine for the Patriots), but the shame the coach now suffers is worse than any penalty. He cheated the game he helped build, tarnishing the one thing he seems to care the most about. His genius and his victories alike will forever be suspect. When he enters a visiting stadium, many chant, "Cheater . . . cheater . . ."

One might ask then, is it ever proper to break the vow of confidentiality between friends? I think the answer may be yes, when the truth is at stake. The entire saga started when the New England Patriots' assistant coach Eric Mangini was offered a new job as head coach for the New York Jets, a position Eric had dreamed of for a long time. Most head coaches who had mentored an assistant like Eric would never stand in the way of helping their friend get a head-coaching job in the NFL, but Coach Belichick acted as if he'd been betrayed. During the Jets' courting of Mangini, Belichick locked down the Patriots' headquarters, and the first time the two teams met after a game Belichick brushed off Mangini's attempt at a post-game handshake as if his ex-assistant had the plague.

**ONE MIGHT ASK, IS IT EVER PROPER TO BREAK THE VOW OF CONFIDENTIALITY BETWEEN FRIENDS?**

When Mangini arrived in New York, he certainly had an insider's knowledge of the Patriots' sign-stealing surveillance tactics, and so he shared the dirty little secret with officials of the NFL. The NFL decided to wait and watch, so it wasn't until the fifth Mangini-Belichick showdown that the NFL was able to determine what the Patriots were doing. Just prior to halftime an NFL security official confiscated a video camera and tape from a Patriots employee on his way to the Patriots' locker room at the Meadowlands. It would seem that he had videotaped hand signals from the Jets' defensive coaches on the sideline, defying an edict from Goodell, who warned teams before the season that he wouldn't tolerate cheating. Several teams have suspected the Patriots of stealing signs. The once-close Belichick-Mangini relationship is now tattered, and this latest chapter in the Border War between the Jets and Patriots has raised the hostility to all-time levels.

By contrast with this modern-day relationship debacle, Pat Forde and Ivan Maisel of ESPN uncovered an example of two high-profile coaches from a generation ago who held the confidence of each other by setting boundaries to their friendship. Former Arkansas head coach Frank Broyles says he used to speak with former University of Texas head coach Darrell Royal about every two weeks; they were friends for over fifty years. At one point, they regularly vacationed together—but they never talked about the specifics of their epic annual series against each other as the coaches at Arkansas and Texas, respectively.

## TIME OUT

1. Would your associates and friends consider you a gossiper?
2. When was the last time you said something you should not have repeated and you found yourself in a bind?

3. Do you want to be seen as someone who can and will keep the confidence of others?

## TODAY'S ASSIGNMENT

If there has been a time recently that you have said more than you should and someone was hurt, ask God to forgive you and give you the strength to control your tongue. Do you have someone you have hurt from whom you need to ask forgiveness?

---

## HOME-FIELD ADVANTAGE

*Praises and concerns you want to bring before God*

_____

_____

_____

_____

_____

---

# BECOMING
# A GREAT FRIEND

## KEEPING EACH OTHER FOCUSED ON
## THE PRIZE

### THOUGHT OF THE DAY

*Holding your friends accountable is the truest sign
of respect for them.*

### THE COACH'S CORNER

Most of us, if we are honest, don't like it when anyone—especially
our wives—tells us that we are wrong. We have heard that our entire
lives, but secretly, we all know it is true. We may find out we are
doing the wrong thing, but when others tell us about our error, well,
we do have an ego, and sometimes we live in denial. The example
many women keep throwing in our faces is our inability to stop and
ask for driving directions. Worse yet is our inability to take directions if we haven't solicited them ourselves. We are not the best at

having accountability partners simply because we don't enjoy someone keeping up with us and telling us what to do. But if you have
ever had a true accountability partner, then you know it is not just
someone telling you what to do. Many of us have had an occasion
when we honestly thought that we should say something to one of
our friends who was allowing his life to get off track. But after careful consideration, we were afraid it might end our friendship, so we
chose to not say anything.

It is common in sports for players and coaches to hold one
another accountable. It is also common in business to hold employees or team members accountable to organizational goals. Yet the
most important use of the concept of accountability just may be in
our Christian relationships with our brothers in Christ. Usually,
accountability focuses on eliminating a certain behavior or encouraging the adoption of a new behavior. Sometimes we have the
privilege to encourage a fellow believer to the high standard of
Scripture, and often we also have the responsibility of holding our
friends accountable to avoid foolish behavior.

While every man seems to have hunting, golf, or sports buddies, we tend not to have close friends we truly listen to. There are
a number of reasons we don't, but one main reason seems to be
that we feel we don't have time for a close relationship other than
with our spouses and children. This void in our lives comes out
when we are asked if we truly desire to have a close friend. Some
men who are fortunate enough to have a close friend refer to him
as an accountability partner because they have found someone
who is truly on the same mission as they are.

**EVERYONE NEEDS A FRIEND WHO HAS THE
SAME PHILOSOPHIES IN LIFE AS HE DOES AND
THE SAME ULTIMATE GOAL—TO HONOR GOD.**

Who keeps you on target? Who keeps you accountable? If you could invent a close friend, what qualities would he have? Would he be rich, talented, successful, or maybe "a ladies' man"? Would he live in the same city, work at the same company, have kids that attend the same school, or work out at the same gym? Would he have attended your alma mater, played the same sport in high school, enjoy the same hobbies, or have similar career interests?

Just like anything else in life, becoming successful at something requires an enormous commitment of energy and time. This is also true with acquiring a great friend. We aren't speaking of passing friends, acquaintances, or neighbors. We aren't just talking about your wife's friends' husbands, your kid's friends' dads, or the guys you spend hours and hours with at work. We are talking about a special kind of friend—we are talking about a real friend. Everyone needs a friend who is after the same decisive prize. Everyone needs a friend who has the same philosophies in life as he does and the same ultimate goal—to honor God.

## THE GAME PLAN

The Bible encourages us to seek out righteous friends for both our good and the glory of God. God wants you to find:

- Men who have a similar heart for God—Psalm 133:1: "Behold, how good and how pleasant it is for brethren to dwell together in unity!"
- Men who love you enough to confront you when you are wrong—Ephesians 4:15: "Speaking the truth in love, may grow up in all things."
- Men who recognize they can fall, or have fallen, and are willing to help you get up when you fall—Galatians 6:1: "Brethren, if a man is overtaken in any trespass, you who

are spiritual restore such a one in a spirit of gentleness, considering yourself lest you also be tempted."

- Men who bring out the best in you—1 Thessalonians 5:14: "Now we exhort you, brethren, warn those who are unruly, comfort the fainthearted, uphold the weak, be patient with all."

## Playmakers

Coach Lou Holtz was one of the first men we contracted to speak at our events when we began In The Zone conferences several years ago. Most of us know the famous Coach Lou Holtz from his days at Notre Dame and the University of South Carolina. But probably one of his more significant moments as a head coach came about thirty years ago when he was the head coach of the Arkansas Razorbacks. His team had finished a terrific season and received an invitation to play in the Orange Bowl to be held in beautiful Miami, Florida. Many Arkansas fans remember this game as if it were yesterday because it is a true testament of how players and coaches should hold each other accountable for results.

Although Arkansas had a terrific season, they had been devastated by post-season injuries and problems, which led them to become twenty-one-point underdogs in their upcoming game against the mighty Oklahoma Sooners. The team's best offensive lineman broke his leg in practice, and something even more devastating happened when three star players were suspended only days before the bowl game for breaking team rules. Two of the men whom Coach Holtz voluntarily chose to suspend had accounted for a combined 78 percent of the teams entire point production that year. Oklahoma was ranked number two in the country coming into the bowl game, and Arkansas players were feeling more and more out-manned.

On the final day of practice in Miami, Coach Holtz brought his team together at the center of the field and told them that he couldn't watch the chaos any longer. He had witnessed the worst days of practice he had ever seen. He told the team that they had already been defeated when they arrived in Miami and listened to all the people talk about how they couldn't win. He told them that the point spread was not twenty-one anymore but had increased. Both he and the team were down.

Coach Holtz took an enormous gamble that day and suggested that the team take just a minute to play a little game that he often played with his family. Coach Holtz decided it was time to remember what got them there and to hold his players accountable for representing their university and state.

The coach explained to the team how his family played a game called "Family Time." The game is based upon when someone in his family does anything that is noteworthy, be it graduating from the eighth grade, becoming president of the PTA, or hitting a home run; the rest of the family makes him feel like king for the night. The honoree not only picks that night's menu but also gets to watch his choice on TV. The best part is at the dinner table, where one by one each of the other members of the family has to look the honoree right in the eye and salute him with a statement that is positive and truthful.

After a moment of extreme discomfort with playing such a childish game, one player offered, "You know, we do have some positive things on this team. If we can get it down there close, our kicker is the best kicker in college football; he's good for three anytime." Soon after, another player laughed as he added, "And all our bad luck has involved our offensive players. Right now our defense is the best in America, and we are all playing. If Oklahoma is going to score, they'll have to beat the best there is!" The team cheered.

Finally and reluctantly, a young inexperienced player spoke up and said, "My name is Roland Sales. This time last year I was pumping gas at a filling station back home, and tomorrow I'm going to start at tailback for the great University of Arkansas. I haven't played much at all this year, but if you guys will help me tomorrow, I'll do everything I can. I've never started in a real game, never in my whole life, but taking the field with you guys tomorrow afternoon will be the biggest thrill I've ever known in my entire life." The team became ecstatic.

**YOU CAN DO JUST ABOUT ANYTHING YOU WANT TO DO IF YOU'LL SIMPLY LEAD WITH A SERVANT'S HEART—AND A TEAM UNITY BUILT ON AFFIRMING EACH OTHER'S STRENGTHS.**

The next day, when thousands of fans packed into the sold-out Orange Bowl, they were joined by over fifty million more fans on the NBC network. The whole country watched with amazement as the Arkansas players—twenty-four-point underdogs without a chance—stormed onto the field. "What on earth did you say to those guys?" the media asked Holtz just before kickoff. He offered back, "I told them the last eleven out had to start!"

You and I know differently—that was anything but the case. He had found a way of holding each man accountable. By the end of the day the inexperienced Roland Sales was the Orange Bowl's MVP. The bigger deal was that Arkansas, the heavy underdog, had trampled the Sooners 31–6 to prove that you can do just about anything you want to do if you'll simply lead with a servant's heart—and a team unity built on affirming each other's strengths.

## TIME OUT

1. Do you find it difficult to hold your friends accountable if they are doing something you know is wrong?
2. Ask your wife to hold you accountable to one thing you want to change about yourself. What will that one thing be?
3. Do you like it when someone holds you accountable, or are you defensive?

## TODAY'S ASSIGNMENT

Identify one thing you want to change about yourself that will strengthen your relationship with Jesus. Set specific goals, and a time frame for the change. Ask God to guide this change.

## HOME-FIELD ADVANTAGE

*Praises and concerns you want to bring before God*

_____

_____

_____

_____

## DAY 25

# SEEK TO UNDERSTAND

## MEN ARE BETTER PROBLEM SOLVERS THAN LISTENERS

### THOUGHT OF THE DAY

*When a friend confides in you, it is better to listen intently than offer a quick solution.*

### THE COACH'S CORNER

Have you ever been asked a question, and before the person speaking was halfway through the question you already knew the answer? When that happens it is hard to continue listening when you already know the best answer, so why not save everyone some time by stopping them and telling them what you think? It seems it would help people to just hurry along through the conversation. But sometimes the person talking is actually not looking for an answer. Sometimes people just need to talk. They really don't want you to help them; they simply want to vent or have someone with whom they can discuss their problems.

On the road to Emmaus Jesus was a good listener. The conversation He had with the two disciples on the road was initially a one-way conversation—them talking and Jesus listening. It would have been easy for Jesus to simply stop them and reveal to them who He was, and the conversation would have been over. But Jesus took the time to listen to everything they said. As men intent on simply providing solutions to others, we rarely display the patience Jesus demonstrated.

There are different kinds of men—some great listeners, some not so great. Most of us would fit into the category of being not-so-great listeners; therefore, friendships can be damaged not only between men and women but also between men. Many of us find ourselves so stressed out over problems in our own lives that we just switch off when someone else has a problem, especially one we quickly identify as one we cannot solve, or at least not solve quickly. We really do listen but only when we want to. If it is a topic we are interested in, we are all ears. For instance, if the discussion is on which Super Bowl commercial was the best this year, then you could probably talk back and forth for hours. Start a discussion about hunting or fishing, and you will get an audience. If you have insight into why the local college coach was terminated, you will hold people speechless. But if the discussion brings up bad vibes or brings focus to problems such as money or relationships, then many times we just check out.

**AS MEN INTENT ON SIMPLY PROVIDING SOLUTIONS TO OTHERS, WE RARELY DISPLAY THE PATIENCE JESUS DEMONSTRATED.**

Sociologists are now realizing that men can be great listeners too. We often pretend not to listen, but in fact, that is sometimes a decoy, a coping mechanism to defer unwanted or frivolous conversations. We are sometimes coolheaded in the thinking process, and we prefer to avoid the small stuff. Instead, we desire to focus on the bigger issues of life since we do not want to make small problems worse. Whether we are good listeners or not, we will probably always live with the stereotype that we are not listening. We can be great listeners—not just selective listeners. One way to affirm a friend is to listen intently and then repeat back to him what we heard him say.

## THE GAME PLAN

The Bible teaches all of us to be ministers of hearing. God wants you to:

- Rejoice with those who rejoice and mourn with those who mourn—Romans 12:15: "Rejoice with those who rejoice, and weep with those who weep."
- Listen to your godly friends carefully and you will create long-lasting memories—Malachi 3:16: "Then those who feared the LORD spoke to one another, and the LORD listened and heard them; so a book of remembrance was written before Him for those who fear the LORD and who meditate on His name."
- Listen to your friends and try to understand exactly what they are asking—Job 2:11, 13: "Now when Job's three friends heard of all this adversity that had come upon him, each one came from his own place—Eliphaz the Temanite, Bildad the Shuhite, and Zophar the Naamathite. For they had made an appointment

together to come and mourn with him, and to comfort him . . . So they sat down with him on the ground seven days and seven nights, and no one spoke a word to him, for they saw that his grief was very great."

- Show respect and be kind to one another—Romans 12:10: "Be kindly affectionate to one another with brotherly love, in honor giving preference to one another."

## PLAYMAKERS

When anybody asks professional fisherman Bill Dance what bait he used to catch the big one, every fisherman in hearing distance will try to listen to his answer intently. When the players in the dugout ask St. Louis Cardinal slugger Albert Pujols what the opposing pitcher is throwing, few will ignore his detailed analysis. They have both a career and economic interest in Pujols's insights. There is no doubt that in dynamic, high-stress settings like athletic coaching, it is easy to stress out and tune out unless you have a *professional* interest. But the reality is that athletes need to be heard in order to be their best. Coaches cannot help them be their best if they do not understand what the players' felt needs are. In coaching, as in every other leadership setting, listening wins. The leaders who do it well have a competitive advantage over those who don't.

According to many men who played for Coach "Bear" Bryant, the secret of the Bear's success was not innovation or cutting-edge *x*'s and *o*'s. He was a master psychologist who applied such concepts as goal setting, repetition, reverse psychology, incentive motivation, and immediate reinforcement long before these terms became popular in the sports world. His uncanny ability to motivate diverse personalities and his unique ability to know just how far to push individual players were what many believe to be his greatest secrets of success.

**THE LEADERS WHO LISTEN WELL HAVE A COMPETITIVE ADVANTAGE OVER THOSE WHO DON'T.**

Many who knew Coach Bryant say that his leadership skills were unique. He could motivate average players into becoming starters on championship teams. Many of his former players have freely admitted that their greatest worry in football was not losing a game but disappointing the legendary Coach Bryant. The Bear was famous for his readiness to heap praise on his players and his staff when Alabama won and to take all the blame when Alabama lost. This served to foster loyalty and love from his coaches and players, and it was always a compelling reason for not letting him down. Some say he was a terrible listener, but those who knew him best indicate that he was a very selective listener. Here are some techniques that have been credited to Coach Bryant that we can all practice:

- Be in the moment: If you don't have the time or energy to listen in the moment, set a time when you can give your player your undivided attention.
- Set the tone: Show your player that you are open to listening by using relaxed words and body language.
- Pay attention: Make a mental decision to listen carefully. Show your interest with eye contact and relaxed body language.
- Withhold judgment: Try to be open to new ideas and constructive criticism. If you feel yourself getting

frustrated, take a breath and suspend judgment until after hearing him through.

- Reflect and clarify: Paraphrase what you heard the player say, and ask clarifying questions to make sure you really understand.
- Share: As you gain a clear understanding of what the player is saying, begin to introduce your thoughts and feelings on the matter. If possible, talk about a time when you or someone you know was in a similar situation.
- Problem-solve: Use your judgment to decide how best to go about solving the issue presented by the player. The best approach will depend on the personality of the player and the overall situation.

The art of listening is an acquired skill, and if you enjoy being married, this may be a worthy skill in which to invest.

## TIME OUT

1. Would you consider yourself a good listener?
2. Would your wife and children say that you are a good listener?
3. Which of Coach Bryant's listening techniques do you most need to implement?

## TODAY'S ASSIGNMENT

Go home tonight and make it a point to listen to your wife and children. Turn off the TV, Internet, or whatever else that would interfere with listening to them. See how they react to your attention. Try to listen without solving their problems.

## HOME-FIELD ADVANTAGE

*Praises and concerns you want to bring before God*

_____

_____

_____

_____

_____

## DAY 26

# IRON SHARPENS IRON

## MEN NEED OTHER MEN AS REAL FRIENDS

### THOUGHT OF THE DAY

*You were not created to fight the battles
of this world alone.*

### THE COACH'S CORNER

It is often lonely being a man. We have few people we trust that we can talk to. Since we are busy and have our own problems, we tend not to burden others with our personal concerns. If we can find a way of opening up to others, we often will discover there are few problems we have that other men haven't also dealt with. The world has become so competitive that we believe we have to face it alone if we want to win. We often compete over who has the smartest kids, who was the best athlete, who has the best job, who drives the nicest car, and who has the most expensive toys. We learn early on that we must have the competitive advantage, and to have this advantage means we must not share our innermost secrets. We were not created to go fight this battle alone; we need friends.

God calls us to connect with men who will encourage our desires to be better men. We are strongly influenced by the character of the people with whom we choose to bond. What will a real friend do for us in times of trouble? Is it true that one man can make another man better? Can simply being around other believers help keep us accountable and help each of us grow in our faith?

Iron sharpening iron is a common phrase among Christian men (Proverbs 27:17). But the physical process of sharpening iron is not widely practiced anymore, and most men haven't seen the process done. At a recent men's conference, an older and wiser pastor talked about the process of how iron actually sharpens iron. He remembered the process from his younger days and decided that maybe it would be helpful if the men really understand what was involved in the process. He asked the men, "Are you guys really prepared to do what you are talking about?" He went on to ask if any of the men present had ever seen iron sharpened. He indicated that when it occurs, large sparks fly all over the place. Rough edges are broken away, sometimes torn away in big pieces. There are long, dangerous metal splinters left all over the floor to be gathered up. There are loud harsh noises made as one piece of iron contacts the other piece of iron. It takes strength, patience, and accuracy to sharpen a tool made out of iron. So this phrase that is easily spoken is actually quite difficult and dangerous to carry out.

> **GOD CALLS US TO CONNECT WITH MEN WHO WILL ENCOURAGE OUR DESIRES TO BE BETTER MEN.**

He went on to say that men say things like, "Use me, Lord" or "Mold me, shape me, make me more like You," but the real truth is that they want to be a better man, but they don't want sparks to fly. They don't want to be broken in any way. They don't want to splinter or be torn apart. They don't like direct confrontation or loud voices of any kind. Many will even sacrifice accuracy and strength to spare them the pain. Do we really want a relationship with someone that can be compared to iron sharpening iron? Are we willing to let ourselves be broken and disfigured? Will we really allow another man to freely speak into our lives to criticize and warn as well as encourage us? The biblical phrase "iron sharpens iron" is a great mental picture of how men can help and assist each other; however, you may lose some of yourself in the process.

## THE GAME PLAN

The Bible teaches us to be "perfectly joined together" (1 Corinthians 1:10). God wants you to:

- Comfort and build your friends up—1 Thessalonians 5:11: "Therefore comfort each other and edify one another, just as you also are doing."
- Bear one another's burdens—Galatians 6:2: "Bear one another's burdens, and so fulfill the law of Christ."
- Be united in mind, compassion, and love to others—1 Peter 3:8–9: "Finally, all of you be of one mind, having compassion for one another; love as brothers, be tenderhearted, be courteous; not returning evil for evil or reviling for reviling, but on the contrary blessing, knowing that you were called to this, that you may inherit a blessing."
- When converted, strengthen the brothers—Luke 22:32:

"But I have prayed for you, that your faith should not
fail; and when you have returned to Me, strengthen
your brethren."

## PLAYMAKERS

There aren't too many rivalries in sports that can match the one
that began over thirty years ago when Magic Johnson and his
Michigan State Spartans played against Larry Bird and his Indiana
State Sycamores for the 1979 NCAA Tournament championship.
In this first matchup between these two great players, few realized
the magnitude of the rivalry and camaraderie that was unfolding
between these two men. Through the years and the intense competition, Magic and Larry became competitors, friends, and men who
were working at sharpening each other.

This rivalry would not end at the college level, but it extended all
the way to the NBA Finals. Once both players were in the NBA, instant
success followed for both of their teams, as five NBA Finals were
won by Magic's Lakers (1980, 1982, 1985, 1987, 1988) and three by
Bird's Celtics (1981, 1984, 1986). In that time, Magic and Bird faced
each other three times—1984, 1985, and 1987—with Magic winning
the rivalry matchup two titles to one.

Magic was born in 1959 in Lansing, Michigan. The son of a
General Motors worker and a school custodian discovered his love
of basketball as a child, claiming to even have slept with his basketball at night. He started playing basketball seriously while a student
at Everett High School in Lansing. It was here that Johnson acquired
his famous nickname when a sportswriter covering a high school
game felt that no other word but *magic* could adequately describe
Johnson's skill with the ball. After being recruited to play locally at
Michigan State, he achieved serious notoriety when the Spartans
took a Big Ten conference title and racked up a 25–5 record!

In his second year on the team, the Spartans took on Indiana State (featuring Larry Bird) in the NCAA Tournament Finals and won. Perhaps more importantly, the beginning of a remarkable friendship between Bird and Magic had begun. Johnson decided to declare his eligibility for the NBA draft in 1979, where he was snapped up by the Lakers. Lakers fans were incredibly excited to see one of the nations' best college players on their team.

Bird's legend was born in the tiny town of French Lick, snuggled in Indiana's corn country, where his family led a modest life. In a state that takes its high school basketball very seriously, most of French Lick's population of 2,059 came out to watch Springs Valley High School's home games. Attendance often reached 1,600—and they were all there to watch the blonde-haired shooting whiz with a funny smile named Larry Joe Bird. Springs Valley went 19–2 and young Larry became a local celebrity. Fans always seemed to be willing to give a ride to Bird's parents, who couldn't afford a car of their own. Bird became the school's all-time scoring champion, and about four thousand people attended his final home game.

Bird found the transition to college life difficult. He started out as an Indiana Hoosier but later left the school and team coached by the legendary Bobby Knight. He attended the local junior college, Northwood Institute, and ultimately enrolled at Indiana State, which had posted 12–14 records in each of the two previous years. The pressure was not quite the same as at Indiana, a perennial Big Ten power and national title contender, but Bird averaged more than thirty points and ten rebounds for the Sycamores during his first campaign. Season-ticket sales tripled, and TV stations showed film clips of Bird instead of commercials. Students skipped class to line up for tickets eight hours before tip-off.

Bird and Magic went on to a professional rivalry that sparked the resurgence of the NBA.

"Back then I disliked Larry," Johnson said. "Then when he ended up with the Celtics I really hated him." But the fierce competitors would eventually become the best of friends. "We've been able to be friends ever since we shot a commercial together and I got to know Larry as a man and as a father and as a husband," Johnson recalled. "We're good friends. We respect each other."[1]

> **AS A CHRISTIAN, YOU HAVE THE OPPORTUNITY TO TAKE CLOSE FRIENDSHIPS TO EVEN DEEPER LEVELS THAN BUSINESS, ATHLETICS, OR SOCIAL RELATIONSHIPS.**

Bird said camaraderie between opposing players was almost nonexistent in their era, but he always felt a special respect for Johnson because of the way he played. They were rivals on the court but have become longtime special friends. Bird is well known for consoling Johnson when the former Lakers star announced in 1991 that he was HIV positive. According to wire reports, Magic called Bird days before making the announcement. "Bird took it tough," Celtics patriarch Red Auerbach said at the time. "You could tell. They were close."[2] Bird spoke two days later about his friend's diagnosis. "These have been the two toughest days for me since my father died," Bird said then. "I've been sort of out of it. I can't believe what happened. He's a friend and a competitor."[3]

For Magic and Larry it was a case of mutual benefits. The more they competed against each other, the better both became. In addition, not only did Bird and Johnson compete athletically, they have borne one another's emotional burdens as friends. As a Christian, you have the opportunity to take close friendships to even deeper levels than business, athletics, or social relationships. You can be a brother in Christ—praying for one another, holding each other accountable—like "iron sharpening iron."

## TIME OUT

1. What groups do you belong to that are targeted at making you a better man?
2. Ask your wife to provide you with a list of men whom she believes could be real accountability partners for you.
3. Do you really desire to have someone who knows your secrets?

## TODAY'S ASSIGNMENT

Identify a small group of men you would like to start meeting with on a regular basis to help you become a stronger Christian man. Set up and schedule your first meeting. The Lord will meet you there.

## HOME-FIELD ADVANTAGE
*Praises and concerns you want to bring before God*

_____

_____

_____

# Day 27

# Calling Men Up

## When Silence Is a Sin

### The Coach's Corner

Close friends often play an important role in a man's life. They encourage us when we are down and out, they stand with us when we are by ourselves, and they are there for us when no one else is. Most of you have known a friend who had made some decisions that were neither in keeping with his personal values nor in line with biblical principles. It may have been a poor decision at work, lying to a friend, or cheating on his wife. We have known guys who were simply engaging in behavior that we knew would ultimately bring disaster for them and their family, and yet we said nothing. We didn't want to meddle or get involved. We didn't want to snoop or have him think we were trying to run his life. But the real reason is we didn't want to directly confront our friend.

A true friend sometimes has to be his brother's keeper. He must be someone who will not allow his friend to throw his life away or sin against God. While it is easier to be passive, God calls us to confront our brother as a means of saving his eternal life. Perhaps you have a friend who is involved in activities right now that you believe he shouldn't be involved in. You may be just the person who can reach him at this time. What is your role? Your role is to show mercy, kindness, and God's love while working to bring him back into God's righteous way of living. There are varieties of friends: coworkers, neighbors, church members, schoolmates, and many more. Each type of friend is helpful in one way or another. But only a real friend will get involved when the time is dismal.

## GOD CALLS US TO CONFRONT OUR BROTHER AS A MEANS OF SAVING HIS ETERNAL LIFE.

Since we don't like to be told what to do, we often assume that our friends are also like that. Some of us have had friends who started going out with a totally new group of friends, which resulted in them going to different places than they once went. Some began to talk differently, and even dress differently. We have had friends who stopped doing family things, in exchange for needing *alone* time. There are certainly danger signs that are visible many times when our friends are getting themselves into trouble. We must not turn our heads and watch them throw away their marriage, their children, their jobs, or their eternity.

## THE GAME PLAN

The Bible wants you to speak up to, not quietly look down on, a friend when he has gone off the path. God wants you to:

- Identify the right way to communicate with your friends—Ephesians 5:19–20: "Speaking to one another in psalms and hymns and spiritual songs, singing and making melody in your heart to the Lord, giving thanks always for all things to God the Father in the name of our Lord Jesus Christ."
- Confess your faults to one another—James 5:16: "Confess your trespasses to one another, and pray for one another, that you may be healed. The effective, fervent prayer of a righteous man avails much."
- When a friend is living his life in sin, tell him and invite him back into God's fold—2 Thessalonians 3:14–15: "And if anyone does not obey our word in this epistle, note that person and do not keep company with him, that he may be ashamed. Yet do not count him as an enemy, but admonish him as a brother."
- Create a community of faith by sharing your story—1 Corinthians 1:10: "Now I plead with you, brethren, by the name of our Lord Jesus Christ, that you all speak the same thing, and that there be no divisions among you, but that you be perfectly joined together in the same mind and in the same judgment."

## PLAYMAKERS

If your friend knew you were in trouble, wouldn't you want him to tell you? Sometimes we choose to be passive and not confront our friends when we know we should. One hero would not let his friends go down the wrong path. He wanted to see them with him in heaven, so he never missed a chance to help them. This football player at the University of Tennessee was huge in both his physical appearance and also in his actions. The Hill, as it is known in Knoxville, has never been the same since Reggie White, a young man from a single mother in Chattanooga, came to campus.

Reggie excelled at football in high school and in time went on to become an All-American at Tennessee. During college he met his wife, Sara, a beautiful, virtuous, and assertive Christian woman who would protect him from the many inevitable hangers-on who wanted a piece of the future NFL star. Reggie stayed in Tennessee after college for his professional debut, joining the Memphis Showboats of the United States Football League in 1984. When the league went out of business the following year, Reggie joined the Philadelphia Eagles of the National Football League.

The game and the NFL were instantly changed. Reggie became the first defensive player to combine three hundred pounds of strength and power with his unprecedented speed. Reggie became the master of the "sack" and became all NFL quarterbacks' worst nightmare. He was the greatest sack artist in the history of the NFL. Opposing teams had to spend precious time reconfiguring their offenses to try to find a way of dealing with him. Because of his strong commitment to his faith and his public status as an ordained Christian minister, Reggie quickly earned the nickname *The Minister of Defense*. His sacks came to be known as *baptisms* all around the league. When he retired after the 2000 season, he had run up a total of 198 sacks, an NFL record at the time. He was selected to the Pro Bowl a record thirteen consecutive times, and was twice named the NFL's Defensive Player of the Year.

Reggie always insisted the most important part of his game was its spiritual dimension. In this, he became that rarest of leaders, one who combined physical and moral courage. A minister since the age of seventeen, Reggie limited his trash-talk to telling opposing players, "Jesus is coming." More important, Reggie was the highest-profile player in a movement started by NFL players to help lead public prayer sessions on the football field. He and a handful of other courageous NFL players commenced the practice, now common, of kneeling in prayer at the fifty-yard line after each game, with players from both teams participating. When Reggie and his friends began these prayers, few pro football players publicly expressed their faith on the field or in the locker room.

Kabeer Gbaja-Biamila, who now holds the Green Bay Packer record for most consecutive seasons with double-digit sacks, remembered Reggie as a "man who tried to follow God's will. He was a man after God's heart. He used his platform to share the gospel. It was an honor to meet him, and to know he experienced some of the same struggles I do."[1]

White shared his faith not only with the community but with his teammates. "I don't go around preaching in the locker room," White said, "But I try to live a certain way, and maybe that will have some kind of effect. I think God has allowed me to have an impact on a few people's lives."[2]

One of those teammates touched by Reggie during his Packer days was Ken Ruettgers, a tackle with the Packers from 1985 to 1996. Reggie baptized both Ken and his wife in the Packers' locker room. Another teammate also related the story of how he and his wife and Mike Arthur, a center with the Packers from 1995 to 1996, had also been baptized by Reggie in the Packers' jacuzzi.

> "I TRY TO LIVE A CERTAIN WAY, AND MAYBE
> THAT WILL HAVE SOME KIND OF EFFECT. I
> THINK GOD HAS ALLOWED ME TO HAVE AN
> IMPACT ON A FEW PEOPLE'S LIVES."
>
> —REGGIE WHITE

Jimmy Sexton and I (Kyle) had the pleasure of representing Reggie as his agents. We both knew he had an eternal impact far beyond his record-breaking football career. The epigraph that appears at the beginning of Reggie's autobiography is a quotation he liked from Paul's second letter to Timothy, perhaps because it is one of the Bible's few references to athletics. As the apostle Paul speaks of his coming death, he summed up his life: "I have fought the good fight, I have finished the race, I have kept the faith" (4:7). When Reggie died tragically and suddenly on December 26, 2004, of pulmonary sarcoidosis, it was obvious to all that he had "kept the faith."

## TIME OUT

1. Do you know a friend who is committing adultery with someone?
2. Do you know a friend who is committing adultery with his job?
3. Would you accept someone who challenged you in confidence because they thought you were sliding in your faith?

## TODAY'S ASSIGNMENT

Identify someone you believe really needs a friend who will tell him the truth. In love—be that man!

# HOME-FIELD ADVANTAGE

*Praises and concerns you want to bring before God*

_____

_____

_____

_____

_____

## FRIENDS WALK IN THE SAME DIRECTION

### IF YOUR FRIENDS FOLLOW YOU, WHERE WILL THEY END UP?

### THOUGHT OF THE DAY

*Don't encourage your friends to be unfaithful;
always travel the high road with them.*

### THE COACH'S CORNER

All throughout your childhood there were people who you just knew would get you in trouble, yet they were still fun to hang out with. They were the friends who always pushed the limits, went *where* they were not allowed to go, went *when* they were not allowed, and often did *what* they knew they were not allowed to do. However, if you remember, they always seemed to have a large following of friends. Every time you went along, there was something that was exciting about the adventure, yet you knew down deep that you were doing something you should not have been doing. It really seemed as though every time you were following these friends, you were going in the wrong direction and praying that your parents would not find out.

Good friends not only enjoy each other's company but also often share similar interests. Have you ever wondered what your life would be like if you really became just like your best friend? Would you be a believer? Would you be faithful to your wife? If your friends in turn were to be just like you, what would their families think? Would they be more loving? Would they be more attentive? True friends may take different paths, but they must have the same ultimate destination. We have all known men who like each other very much but are not on the same track spiritually. They are buddies who hang out together and have many of the same priorities. They seem to click in regard to most things; however, when it comes to their spiritual journey, mission opportunities, church activities, or family responsibilities, they are not on the same page. It seems that they have agreed to simply live a large chunk of their lives separately and independently from each other—and they perceive that to be good and normal.

> **TRUE FRIENDS MAY TAKE DIFFERENT PATHS, BUT THEY MUST HAVE THE SAME ULTIMATE DESTINATION.**

But let's stop and think about why God created the need for men to have good friends. Christian friends should have an intense awareness that they stand to the world as a picture of the relationship between two men who have at their core a love for Jesus Christ! There are men who believe themselves to be Christians who live their lives totally unaware of the presence of Christ except for a brief devotion every now and then, or maybe a church service. But, of course, true Christians realize their reliance upon Christ and their close, cherished relationship with Him at all times—at school, at work, at home, at church, while shopping, while playing, and so on. We long for His companionship; we constantly desire His leadership and His wisdom and His close presence as we live out our lives.

## THE GAME PLAN

The Bible wants you to recognize your privilege and responsibility to influence others. God wants you to:

- Walk the path of life with your friends together—1 Samuel 20:42: "Go in peace, for we have sworn friendship with each other in the name of the LORD, saying, 'The LORD is witness between you and me, and between your descendants and my descendants forever.'" Then David left, and Jonathan went back to the town" (NIV).

- Be like-minded, having the same love, being of one accord and one mind—Philippians 2:1–2: "Therefore if there is any consolation in Christ, if any comfort of love, if any fellowship of the Spirit, if any affection and mercy, fulfill my joy by being like-minded, having the same love, being of one accord, of one mind."

- Be comforted, loved, and wise in the ways of God—Colossians 2:2–3: "That their hearts may be encouraged, being knit together in love, and attaining to all riches of the full assurance of understanding, to the knowledge of the mystery of God, both of the Father and of Christ, in whom are hidden all the treasures of wisdom and knowledge."

- Rejoice in the good works that God will do through you—Hebrews 10:24: "And let us consider one another in order to stir up love and good works."

## PLAYMAKERS

Coach Mike Gottfried is one of the great men of today. He has been one of the enthusiastic motivators and supporters of In The Zone since its conception. He is the founder of Team Focus, an organization for young men without fathers. His organization is currently in twenty-six states in the U.S. with more than one thousand boys involved. Today Mike and Team Focus give boys answers—such as how to be a team leader, how to deal with peer pressure, how to apply for a job, and how to pick out a suit and tie a tie. At summer camps boys are taught to read the Bible and pray. They have a full schedule from 7:00 a.m. to midnight, and the sessions are held in a variety of ways, from small groups to large-group outings to individual mentors. Mike tells boys that every day will get better; it may not be great or good, but it will get better. So why is such a successful college coach and ESPN commentator so committed to boys without fathers? It is a great story that makes him one of our most popular speakers.

Mike understands why young boys need fathers to talk to about guy things because he grew up without one. The middle son of three boys, Mike was brought up in a loving home in Crestline, Ohio, where his father, Fritz, was a great, loving father. He worked as a railroad engineer and was often away for days at a time. When he was home, though, he was involved with his boys—teaching them how to play baseball, basketball, and football, as well as how to bowl. He was one of those men that when he did something all the neighborhood would follow. Mike says his father may have lacked the title, but he was definitely a coach. Fritz loved his boys, and everyone in the small town knew it.

**THERE WAS STILL A STRONG FAMILY; THERE WAS STILL UNCONDITIONAL LOVE; BUT THERE WAS NO DAD.**

When Mike was eleven, he heard his parents talking. His father said he wasn't feeling well and was going to get out of bed. Then there was a loud thump in the bathroom—and that is where the family found their dad lying on the floor. Mike's older brother ran next door for the doctor, while their dad remained on the floor with his head in Mike's lap. He moaned and groaned with his lips turning blue. Feeling totally helpless, Mike talked to his dad and prayed. The doctor arrived and immediately recognized the symptoms of a massive heart attack; at age forty-one, Fritz Gottfried had died, and Mike was without one great father.

Mike's life was shattered into a million pieces. There was still a strong family; there was still unconditional love; but there was no dad. The day after the funeral, his mother told the boys that their dad had no insurance, and the rent was due on their home. She didn't have the money to pay it, so they all went to live with friends for three months until their mother found a job and made enough money to rent a small home for all of them. For months after his father died, Mike would cry himself to sleep.

Mike attended a Catholic school, and a nun at the school, Sister Kathleen, told Mike not to give up. She gave him this verse: "For I know the thoughts that I think toward you, saith the LORD, thoughts of peace, and not of evil, to give you an expected end" (Jeremiah 29:11 KJV). Mike realized the sister had given him a choice to make: he could go on living in bitterness and letting the loss of his father claim him, or he could decide to trust God's plan for good in his life. As an adult, Mike made a total commitment to Jesus Christ.

Mike never forgot that after his dad died he was at a disadvantage to the boy next to him who had a father. Little did Sister Kathleen know that she was placing Mike on the high road that would lead to a world with access to a real hero. The men he coached are fortunate that she set him on the path. But so are the friends he has made, the boys in his program, and the men he mentors, even those he does so unknowingly.

Mike's journey through coaching eventually led him to national prominence as a college football coach where he spent twelve successful seasons as head coach at Murray State, Cincinnati, Kansas, and Pittsburgh. During his four years at Pittsburgh, he won twenty-six games and defeated NCAA powerhouses Notre Dame, Penn State, and West Virginia. He finished his coaching career with seventy-seven victories and parlayed that success into a job as lead college football analyst for ESPN.

## TIME OUT

1. If someone followed you this week, would he be shocked at where you took him?
2. Ask your wife what things you are involved in that she doesn't think are helping you to become a better man.
3. Have you been somewhere in the past month that you hope no one will find out about?

## TODAY'S ASSIGNMENT

We have all done things we are ashamed of. Do you have a secret part of your life that is hidden from everyone but God? Get on your knees right now, wherever you are, and ask God to forgive you and help you turn from your ways.

## HOME-FIELD ADVANTAGE

*Praises and concerns you want to bring before God*

_____

_____

_____

# FINDING THE ZONE IN YOUR RELATIONSHIPS AT WORK

*There is nothing better for a person than that he should eat and drink and find enjoyment in his toil. This also, I saw, is from the hand of God, for apart from him who can eat or who can have enjoyment?*

—ECCLESIASTES 2:24–25 ESV

# Being Real at Work

## Tired of Trying to Be Someone You're Not?

## Thought of the Day

*God placed you in your job. He knows your talents, gifts, and strengths. Allow Him to use them.*

## The Coach's Corner

Wouldn't it be great if you could receive a letter informing you that you had been chosen to receive your ideal job in life? God had been consulted, and knowing your strengths and weaknesses, your talents and skills, your ideal job had been identified and was now available for you—the absolute perfect job. No one wants a job they hate. We all wish we could be in ideal jobs. But what if your current job *is* the ideal job for you? What if God placed you in your current position for a reason? It may be to teach you something that you will need for your next ideal job. Maybe He has someone there you need to influence. Maybe He has someone there who needs you as their friend. Maybe God needs you at your current job, right now, for a very special reason. Believe it or not, He does.

Are you tired of trying to be someone at work you aren't? Do your coworkers really know who you are and who you believe in? When you are living in your sweet spot, are you a blessing to others who need your gifts at work? We want to be who God created us to be! Each man is made for a different purpose. What's yours? We are called to live a life that shows others who Jesus is. The most common reason many men have left the church today is they find church irrelevant to their life. Going to church did not help them to connect with their work, family, world concerns, or their personal spiritual walk. The average Christian man spends less than 2 percent of their waking time at church. Yet the church puts most of its force and resources into preaching about idealistic life in that 2 percent and very little about the real world we live in at work. How many sermons have you heard on work issues? Certainly a few, but unfortunately, the real world we work in and the world that is often preached about is very different. The topic of work has not been high on the agenda of many churches. This may be a natural outcome because many pastors have not worked in the real world of today. As a result, sermons on the meaning, value, and ethical challenges Christian men face in the secular world often miss the mark.

**MAYBE GOD NEEDS YOU AT YOUR CURRENT JOB, RIGHT NOW, FOR A VERY SPECIAL REASON.**

What do your coworkers see in you? Do they see someone who simply goes with the flow, or do they see a man who always stands for truth and justice? For many of us, church on Sunday morning is safe, easy, and a refuge from the real world. Our task is to take Jesus and His actions to work with us Monday through Friday. Many of you have the good fortune of working with and for godly men and women; however, some of you have been placed in a position where nonbelievers get to see how you live and work. How lucky you are to know that every day, God is with you as you show His love to those who don't believe. It is as if you were hand-selected for a mission, given the necessary tools, and encouraged to remember that God is pulling for you to share Him with others.

## THE GAME PLAN

The Bible wants you to be sensitive to others without betraying who you are. God wants you to know:

- Don't be a chameleon—James 1:8: "He is a double-minded man, unstable in all his ways."
- You measure your love of God by how you sacrificially love your fellow worker—1 John 4:20: "If someone says, 'I love God,' and hates his brother, he is a liar; for he who does not love his brother whom he has seen, how can he love God whom he has not seen?"
- You must renounce and confess your internal inconsistencies—2 Corinthians 4:2: "But we have renounced the hidden things of shame, not walking in craftiness nor handling the word of God deceitfully, but by manifestation of the truth commending ourselves to every man's conscience in the sight of God."
- When you sin, admit it, ask forgiveness, and embrace God's mercy—Proverbs 28:13: "He who covers his sins will not prosper, but whoever confesses and forsakes them will have mercy."

## PLAYMAKERS

You have heard the old song "If It Weren't for Bad Luck, I'd Have No Luck at All." That really does describe people sometimes, and not just you. It also applies to many of those we think have it made and have never had to go through any hard times at all.

One of the greatest men in college football today just has to be Mark Richt. You have seen him on television as he always positively represents his school, his family, and his Lord. Mark is an unashamed Christian who has rebuilt a dynasty at the University of Georgia— but all was not perfect for the young Mr. Richt.

Mark was an outstanding high school quarterback in Florida and signed a football scholarship to play at one of the best football programs in the country at that time, the University of Miami. He had a plan. When he set foot on campus his goal was to be the starting quarterback for the Hurricanes his first year. He believed that he could be an All-American after his sophomore year, win the Heisman Trophy his junior year, and leave early for the NFL. It was a great plan for a fine quarterback.

He had been on the Miami campus only a short time when he was introduced to a young man named Jim Kelly. Needless to say, Jim became the starting quarterback as a freshman and Mark suffered his first setback to his plan. After the first season was over, Mark worked hard but the coach announced that Jim would remain the starting quarterback for his sophomore year—another setback for the plan. Mark was extremely frustrated, as nothing seemed to be going right with his lifelong plan.

The summer between his sophomore and junior years at Miami, one of his close friends and a teammate went on a Christian retreat. He came back fired up and told Mark about his experiences and his relationship with Jesus. This was the same guy who had been Mark's partying buddy, so Mark felt what he had to say was worth listening to. Mark noticed a real change in the life of his friend, who began to share the Lord with Mark. He would often read from the Bible and share meaningful scriptures with Mark. And although Mark was drawn to his friend's new faith, it wasn't long before he was back to doing what he had always done. During his senior year, he was still not the starter, but an opportunity arose when Jim Kelly went down with an injury, and Mark was given his first chance to start. However, because he made some poor decisions, he was disciplined, and the opportunity of finishing his career as the starting quarterback for the University of Miami Hurricanes vanished.

After he graduated from Miami he continued to work hard with a dream of playing in the NFL. Mark never got drafted, leading to another busted dream. He did receive a chance to try out for the NFL's Denver Broncos, but soon after arriving in camp, another quarterback by the name of John Elway showed up. Less than a week later, Mark was cut. Very depressed, he moved back to South Florida and worked several odd jobs while trying to figure out what to do. Surprisingly, the next year he received an opportunity to try out with the Miami Dolphins. Soon after Mark arrived at camp, he met another young quarterback by the name of Dan Marino. Less than a week later, Mark was cut.

## HAVE YOU DISCOVERED WHY GOD HAS PLACED YOU IN YOUR CURRENT PLACE?

Mark realized then the plans he had made for his life were gone. After some time had passed, he got a call from Florida State head coach Bobby Bowden. The coach offered him a graduate assistant position working with the quarterbacks, and he jumped at the chance to move to Tallahassee.

At the beginning of Mark's second season at FSU, one of their players was shot and killed while attending a party during an off weekend. The next day Coach Bowden called a team meeting, and no one was allowed in the room but players and Coach Richt. Being a graduate assistant he was only in there to take roll. Coach Bowden addressed the incident, and at the end of his talk he began to speak about spiritual matters. He pointed to the empty chair that was assigned to the fallen player and discussed death and shared his own faith. Coach Bowden explained that God loved them and that He had sent His one and only Son to die for our sins. At the end of the meeting he told the players that if they had any questions or anything on their hearts, to please come and speak to him. The next day Coach Richt went to see Coach Bowden. Bowden took him through the gospel and explained what it meant to be a Christian. Coach Bowden led him in a prayer that day, and Mark received God's mercy, forgiveness, and peace through what Christ had done for him. Mark loves Coach Bowden and is eternally grateful to him for giving him his first job in coaching and most importantly leading him to the Lord.

In December 2000, the president of the University of Georgia and his athletic director came to Tallahassee and interviewed Mark for the position of head coach of the University of Georgia Bulldogs. After many hours of prayer he accepted the position. Throughout all of life Coach Richt has tried to live according to Colossians 3:23: "And whatever you do, do heartily, as to the LORD and not to men." Mark has found out why God has placed him in college sports— have you discovered why God has placed you in your current place?

## TIME OUT

1. Why do you believe God has placed you in your current position?
2. Do you discuss your work struggles with your wife?

3. What would your coworkers know of Jesus if they simply observed you each day?

## TODAY'S ASSIGNMENT

Take an honest assessment of what people think of you at work. Identify something to do today where your actions will speak louder than your words concerning your relationship with Jesus.

---

## HOME-FIELD ADVANTAGE

*Praises and concerns you want to bring before God*

---

---

---

---

# LIVING UP TO YOUR POTENTIAL

## LIFE IS A TERRIBLE THING TO WASTE

### THOUGHT OF THE DAY

*God calls you to be a hard worker,*
*no matter what the job.*

### THE COACH'S CORNER

We are called by God to work. Have you ever met a man who seemed to be just plain lazy, who just always waited around until all the work was done before deciding to show up? In high school many facts were learned and then quickly forgotten. One such lesson was taught in science class—Newton's first law of motion. While it didn't make much sense back then, it now seems like a brilliant concept. It states that an object in motion tends to remain in motion and an object at rest tends to remain at rest. When we think of people, this law just may be more important than we ever realized. Successful men know that to achieve anything of significance, you need to set lofty goals.

There is a story of a man in a nice car from the city who was hopelessly lost along a rural country road. He pulled into a little gas station and asked the attendant for some help. The driver said, "Can you help me? I'm lost. I am trying to find Highway 7." The attendant replied, "Mister, you aren't lost; you just need directions." We are just like the city fellow: unless we know where we are going, we will never arrive where we want to be! Perhaps you have a career change in mind. Determine what your passions are, as well as your God-given talents. You should find out all you can about the vocation you may be considering. Ask God to guide you as you truly seek the ideal position for yourself in keeping with His ultimate plan. Remember Jesus Christ's wonderful promise: "Ask and it will be given to you; seek, and you will find; knock, and it will be opened to you. For everyone who asks receives, and he who seeks finds, and to him who knocks it will be opened" (Matthew 7:7–8).

**UNLESS WE KNOW WHERE WE ARE GOING, WE WILL NEVER ARRIVE WHERE WE WANT TO BE!**

When we consider every job we do—and we remember we are a reflection of Jesus—it seems we will work a little harder and smarter. We don't want Jesus to be seen as approving of a slacker, someone who wants a handout. We don't want Jesus to be seen as approving of laziness. Our desire should be to let others see a man who is proud to have a job, and will do the job to the best of his abilities and in a way that honors almighty God. There is no such thing as a job that is beneath us because we may have been placed there for a very specific reason—perhaps a reason only God knows.

A few years ago at an In The Zone conference in Alabama,

former Alabama head coach Gene Stallings experienced this truth firsthand. Coach Stallings listened with amazement when his former rival—Auburn University's legendary head coach Pat Dye—praised him for the influence he had on Coach Dye's life. He spoke of the tremendous impact Coach Stallings's close relationship with his son, John Mark—born with Down syndrome—had made on his life. John Mark Stallings was the last of five children and the only son born to Gene and Ruth Ann Stallings. John Mark often joined his father on the practice field at coaching stops from Texas A&M to the Dallas Cowboys to the St. Louis/Phoenix Cardinals and back to the University of Alabama. Coach Pat Dye said, "For someone who never played a game or coached a game, I think your son may have touched more college football fans in Alabama than any other person ever did."[1]

## THE GAME PLAN

The Bible wants us to be blessed by our use of the gifts God has given us. God wants you to:

- Live a faithful life and then you will get the prize—Revelation 2:10: "Do not fear any of those things which you are about to suffer. Indeed, the devil is about to throw some of you into prison, that you may be tested, and you will have tribulation ten days. Be faithful until death, and I will give you the crown of life."
- Work in a way that pleases God, as well as your boss—Colossians 3:22: "Bondservants, obey in all things your masters according to the flesh, not with eye service, as men-pleasers, but in sincerity of heart, fearing God."
- Be focused on being faithful and leave the future to God—Psalm 31:23: "Oh, love the LORD, all you His saints!

> For the LORD preserves the faithful, and fully repays the proud person."

- As a member of God's team, realize that while you will be persecuted or harassed, you win at the end—Matthew 10:22: "And you will be hated by all for My name's sake. But he who endures to the end will be saved."

## PLAYMAKERS

Few will disagree that golf's own John Daly has tremendous talent and potential to hit a golf ball. However, he sometimes seems to find ways of painting himself into a position in which he is unable to use his God-given talents. He has been known to stroll down the course drinking beer and smoking cigarettes while saying things that those following him shouldn't have to hear. At other times, it is said that he is one of the most giving men on the tour to children's charities.

Daly seldom runs out of excesses or excuses, and his core fans are hesitant to give up on the blond-haired, self-taught pro from rural Arkansas who captured the nation's attention in 1991 with a surprising storybook win in the PGA Championship. His fans have stuck by him through two PGA Tour suspensions, two trips to alcohol rehab centers, three failed marriages, and countless embarrassing moments. "Why?" Daly asked rhetorically in 2001. "I've been honest with a lot of the problems I've had in life. Everybody has problems. Most people can relate to that."[2]

Over the years, John Daly has become less and less the lovable character and more the guy who gave his God-given talent away. The latest embarrassment may have occurred recently when he admitted to losing between fifty and sixty million dollars gambling in the last twelve years.[3] Many sports writers believe that Daly has wasted more talent than many professional golfers ever have. Here are a few examples:

- John took a camera from a spectator and smashed it against a tree during the Australian Open, later explaining it was just an instinctive move, and he believed the camera was an empty beer can and the tree was his own forehead.[4]
- During a rain delay in a Florida tournament, John went into a beer tent and came out a bit later with ex-NFL coach Jon Gruden as his caddy. As one cynic said humorously, there was no indication either man had been drinking although some people were suspicious on the next tee when Gruden handed Daly a designated driver![5]
- John was captured by a television crew in Missouri, playing golf with some friends while wearing only a tight pair of blue jeans—no shoes, no socks, and no shirt. The video seemed to outrage the PGA Tour leadership executives.[6]
- But the big blow came when he was arrested after a long night in a Hooters restaurant. He spent the night in jail.[7]

"TALENT IS GOD GIVEN—BE HUMBLE. FAME IS MAN GIVEN—BE GRATEFUL. CONCEIT IS SELF GIVEN—BE CAREFUL."

—COACH JOHN WOODEN

Many golf professionals have indicated that they wish they could have seen just how good John could have been. If he had continued to work on his game as he once did, he would be a major force to contend with today. Few have questioned John's talent and instinct in golf. But he leaves us to wonder who John Daly could have become. The famed coach John Wooden once said, "Talent is God given—be humble. Fame is man given—be grateful. Conceit is self given—be careful."[8] John has true God-given talent. Wouldn't it be great to see him get on track and use the talent he has been given? Let's all pray for John to turn it around.

## TIME OUT

1. Is there a part of your life that you feel as though you have wasted?
2. Today is a great day for a fresh start. What change will you make to use a talent God has given you that you have not yet used to the fullest?
3. Do you waste time that you could use for growing the kingdom? What can you eliminate that will free you up to do more for God?

## TODAY'S ASSIGNMENT

If you need to make a change today that would impact your future in a positive way for the kingdom, what would it be? Create a thirty-day plan for improvement. Tell your best friend you want him to hold you accountable.

# HOME-FIELD ADVANTAGE

*Praises and concerns you want to bring before God*

_____

_____

_____

_____

HOME-FIELD ADVANTAGE

Praises and contras you want to bring before God

Day 31

# DETERMINING YOUR PRIORITIES

## THE ETERNAL BALANCING ACT

### THOUGHT OF THE DAY

*You have time to do what is important to you.*

### THE COACH'S CORNER

It has been hard from the very beginning of time for man to understand and appreciate God's timing. Sometimes it seems that things just might work better if we could simply get God on our calendars. Answers to some of our prayers often seem to come too late. There are also times when we just aren't ready for things to happen as quickly as God wants them to. There are days that seem to never end, and there are days that seem not to have enough hours. Surely we have time to do what God feels is important. If you were to take a minute to flip back through your calendar for last month, what would you find? What would your calendar say is the most important thing in your life?

Former Dallas Cowboy tough man Bill Bates addressed this important topic at a recent In The Zone conference in Tennessee. "I have a bunch of kids and a bunch of businesses that I am responsible for. Everyone is counting on me, and I can't let anyone down. I run a business in Texas, one in Florida, help coach a high school football team and work with my two sons. Both are being recruited to play football nationally."[1] Life is stressful!

> **THERE ARE DAYS THAT SEEM TO NEVER END, AND THERE ARE DAYS THAT SEEM NOT TO HAVE ENOUGH HOURS.**

Do you simply react to what life throws at you, or do you proactively plan your life by setting boundaries on your time, your activities, and your expectations? Our lives are structured around our priorities, our jobs, and our families. Every day we make decisions based on our priorities. We are pulled in every direction imaginable. Take a careful look at your calendar and your checkbook; you may have just identified your priorities. You will never do something that you do not see the significance in. Your life choices are value judgments. For example, if you see the value of excellent health, you will find time to work out, knowing that it will provide the fitness and energy your body needs. You might see the value in obtaining a degree, so in order to do that, you give up your leisure time and spend as much time studying as you can in order to pass your exam. If you are not feeling well, as terrible as the idea of taking medicine is, you know you have to take it in order to feel better.

So we can see that in order to obtain something of value, it takes dedication to the right activities, even putting aside things we'd rather do, and doing some things that might make us uncomfortable for a time. Often we get into a disagreement about values when we look only to our own judgments and don't take scriptural models to heart. As children of God, it is important for us to realize that God has a far bigger and more significant purpose for our futures than even we do. In order to pursue God's intention for us and to desire what God desires, the first step is to examine our own wishes to see if they line up with God's.

## THE GAME PLAN

The Bible says that God expects you to make Him your priority. God wants you to know:

- You can help control stress by acknowledging that life is stressful—2 Corinthians 1:8: "We do not want you to be uninformed, brothers, about the hardships we suffered in the province of Asia. We were under great pressure, far beyond our ability to endure, so that we despaired even of life" (NIV).

- You can become a new creation—2 Corinthians 5:17: "Therefore, if anyone is in Christ, he is a new creation; old things have passed away; behold, all things have become new."

- You can avoid stress by rejecting passivity and moving forward with a prayerful decision—1 Kings 18:21: "And Elijah came to all the people, and said, 'How long will you falter between two opinions? If the LORD is God, follow Him; but if Baal, follow him.' But the people answered him not a word."

- He is prepared to give you a new perspective on life—Romans 12:1–2: "I beseech you therefore, brethren, by the mercies of God, that you present your bodies a living sacrifice, holy, acceptable to God, which is your reasonable service. And do not be conformed to this world, but be transformed by the renewing of your mind, that you may prove what is that good and acceptable and perfect will of God."

## PLAYMAKERS

Every man on earth—Bill Gates, Michael Phelps, Donald Trump, and you—has the same amount of time:

- 60 seconds in a minute
- 60 minutes in an hour
- 24 hours in a day
- 168 hours in a week
- 365 days in a year

Time cannot be saved up or stored. It is not how much time we have that matters but rather the way we use the time we have. We have time to do what is important. If you have a choice each day in the tasks you face, a choice between doing what is urgent and doing what is important, which do you choose?

Many of us find we're spinning our wheels, or chasing rabbits, or putting out fires, or whatever your favorite metaphor is for being overextended. We can never seem to get the time to do the things that we know we should or could be doing. No one ever got ahead in life or became successful by simply doing the things that were urgent. It just doesn't happen. The men who get ahead in life, the men who realize their goals and achieve the things they want in their lives, all have one trait in common: every day, they do what is important to God, not what is urgent to others. They do what is important even though it means putting off at least some of the things that seem to be urgent. We must determine what things in our lives, work, and relationships are truly urgent. Then we must identify what the difference is between those things that make a lot of noise and the things we must do. Sometimes those things can be handled by delegating them to a trusted friend or family member or by pairing them with other activities in our daily routines.

> **IT IS NOT HOW MUCH TIME WE HAVE THAT MATTERS BUT RATHER THE WAY WE USE THE TIME WE HAVE.**

One of the most successful and famed NCAA football coaches who has ever coached is Dr. Tom Osborne. That's right—*Dr.* Tom Osborne. He was born in Hastings, Nebraska, near where his grandparents and great-grandparents homesteaded. He was a star athlete, particularly in football, in high school and at Hastings College. After graduating from college, he spent three years in the National Football League as a member of both the San Francisco 49ers and the Washington Redskins. He then went to graduate school at the University of Nebraska, where he received an M.Ed. and Ph.D. in educational psychology. While a student at Nebraska, he became a graduate assistant and then assistant coach for the Nebraska Cornhuskers football team.

During Osborne's tenure as an assistant coach, Nebraska won two national championships. Legendary head coach Bob Devaney retired after the second national championship season and tapped Osborne as his replacement. Over the next twenty-five years, Osborne led the Cornhuskers to a bowl game every season and three national championships (1994, 1995, and 1997). He retired after the 1997 season with a career winning percentage of 84 percent.

> NO ONE EVER GOT AHEAD IN LIFE OR
> BECAME SUCCESSFUL BY SIMPLY DOING THE
> THINGS THAT WERE URGENT. IT JUST
> DOESN'T HAPPEN.

Perhaps it was Coach Osborne's doctorate in educational psychology that enabled him to bond with players and coaches, but Coach Osborne was a head coach that assistant coaches wanted to work for. One of the primary reasons, of course, was his winning ways and his strong dedication to the program, but it was also because of his commitment to family and his faith. Quite ironically, there was another reason coaches wanted to work for the legendary coach—assistants loved the way he organized his time and helped his assistants organize theirs.

As we understand it, all coaches working for Coach Osborne started the day at 7:00 a.m., and for five hours there was protected silence for the coaches to work together—and not be contacted by the outside world. No interruptions were allowed unless it was an extreme emergency, and there were few of those. No calls, no outside meetings, no family, no players, just protected time for the coaches to get their work done. After the initial work time, there were about two hours of "free work time" in which the coaches could return calls, write letters, and do whatever they needed to do for their job. The hour from 2:00 to 3:00 in the afternoon was the regularly scheduled time all coaches were available for their players to meet with them. Another time allocation that set the program apart from others were the two nights all coaches had to be home with their families. The assistant coach's wives and children could count on this specific time and schedule family gatherings, sports practices, school meetings, and other kids-related activities around these nights. Wednesday night was always family night, and all the coaches and their families came to campus to eat together and have some fun.

Now we all know that many head coaches, if not most, operate their program much differently than this with an emphasis on out-working rival teams' coaches with a grinding mentality. Many assistant coaches basically say good-bye to their families in the fall and reintroduce themselves at Christmas. Coach Osborne truly believed that we always have time to do what is important, and family was important.

## TIME OUT

1. What captures more of your time outside of work than anything else?
2. Would your wife say you live a fairly balanced life?
3. What would you do with two extra hours of time each afternoon?

## TODAY'S ASSIGNMENT

We have time to do what is important. Would your children say they are neglected? Would your wife say she is neglected? Would your boss say your work is neglected?

## HOME-FIELD ADVANTAGE

*Praises and concerns you want to bring before God*

_____

_____

_____

_____

# LETTING GO OF YOUR WANTS AND NEEDS

## KNOWING THAT GOD WILL PROVIDE

### THOUGHT OF THE DAY

*God is big enough to meet all of your needs
if you will allow Him.*

### THE COACH'S CORNER

How big is God? Sounds like one of those questions your children would ask, doesn't it? We have all read the stories of successful men who have given their lives and their life's work over to God. Individuals like Truett Cathy, founder of Chick-fil-A; Allen Barnhart, founder of Barnhart Crane; and Norm Miller, founder of Interstate Batteries, to name only a few. All of these men have made millions of dollars, but they have also given millions of dollars away as they have found that God is big enough to continue meeting their needs and those of their company.

**FOR MOST OF US MEN, WE TRY TO FIX WHATEVER IS WRONG BEFORE WE BOTHER GOD WITH IT.**

Do you find it difficult to let go and let God take over? Many of us would surrender our lives totally to Christ if we could have certain conditions built in. We would like to make sure our lives don't change drastically. We usually don't make a complete surrender to Him because we fear the consequences such surrender could involve. Maybe you are afraid that if you surrender to God, you will be on the next flight to Africa with only a suitcase full of polyester shorts for the next five years. Perhaps you have seen people who surrendered everything to Jesus, and their lives seemed to change forever. For most of us men, we try to fix whatever is wrong before we bother God with it. He did provide us with a brain to handle our problems, didn't He? The truth is most of us lack faith to trust that God will totally provide for us. Therefore, we do everything possible to provide for ourselves prior to going to God.

The Bible is clear regarding the fact that we are to provide for our families. Probably the single most important attribute commonly found in all men is our desire to provide for our family. This desire is so inherent in most men that we fail to ask God for our needs. We often feel weak if we can't provide for our family, and therefore we sometimes lack the faith necessary to totally rely upon God to meet all of our needs.

**MOST OF US ARE TOTALLY READY TO GIVE OUR LIVES TO CHRIST AS LONG AS WE HAVE SOME CONTROL OVER ALL DECISIONS.**

Have you ever thought about turning your life, kids, finances, marriage, job, and future over to God unconditionally? The reason the word *unconditionally* is important is most men don't like to give over total control of something they are entrusted with. To give up total control of your kids just might mean they grow up and move away to the foreign mission field. To give up total control of your finances just may mean giving God more of your paycheck. Giving God full control of your job just may mean working for someone you don't like, while doing a job you hate. Most of us are totally ready to give our lives to Christ as long as we have some control over all decisions. Are you willing to let go and let God take over?

## THE GAME PLAN

The Bible says that God expects you to trust Him to provide all the necessities of an abundant life. God wants you to know:

- He will provide your identity—1 John 3:1: "Behold what manner of love the Father has bestowed on us, that we should be called children of God! Therefore the world does not know us, because it did not know Him."
- He will provide your salvation—1 John 4:14: "And we have seen and testify that the Father has sent the Son as Savior of the world."
- He will provide your internal and external gifts—James 1:17: "Every good gift and every perfect gift is from above, and comes down from the Father of lights, with whom there is no variation or shadow of turning."
- He will provide you with children who will walk in the truth—2 John 1:4: "I rejoiced greatly that I have found some of your children walking in truth, as we received commandment from the Father."

# PLAYMAKERS

Hobby Lobby is a one-of-a-kind company. Not because of its unique and extensive product offering but because the company is run by a different set of standards—a higher set of standards, biblical standards. This is evident if you are familiar with the retail chain, but it is also very intentional. Take a look at the Hobby Lobby Statement of Purpose:

In order to effectively serve our owners, employees, and customers, the board of directors is committed to:

- Honoring the Lord in all we do by operating the company in a manner consistent with biblical principles.
- Offering our customers an exceptional selection and value.
- Serving our employees and their families by establishing a work environment and company policies that build character, strengthen individuals, and nurture families.
- Providing a return on the owners' investment, sharing the Lord's blessings with our employees, and investing in our community.
- We believe that it is by God's grace and provision that Hobby Lobby has endured. He has been faithful in the past, we trust Him for our future.[1]

This company is a true success story; its leaders credit that success to complete reliance on God. The Hobby Lobby story began when David Green opened a three-hundred-square-foot frame store in 1972, selling his own manufactured frames. Located in Oklahoma City, the business grew quickly, and over time one small store multiplied into the retail giant Hobby Lobby Creative Centers, with 16,000 employees and 335 retail stores nationwide. Despite the company's countless challenges and the ups and downs of the market, Hobby Lobby is a true success story with annual sales topping one billion dollars. Founder and CEO David Green is quick to attribute this success to faith in Christ and prayer. He built the Hobby Lobby business and culture on biblical principles, with a focus on integrity.

As the leader of this organization, Green finds himself inspired by the ongoing challenge of providing a Christlike example and being a model for business integrity. Like many great leaders, he leads by example because he believes, "You should not expect something from someone that you are not willing to do yourself."[2] He further explained to ChristianNet.com, "All the things we do, all our behavior, should let others know that we are living by, and operating in, biblical principles. Principle and character are the highest quality traits on our list."[3]

One unique and practical way David engineered a Christian culture is the company's customer service policy. We are all familiar with the customer service policies of various businesses such as "the customer is always right" or "satisfaction guaranteed." But Hobby Lobby took a different approach to caring for customers. At Hobby Lobby, every employee views themselves as a servant. Not in a derogatory way but in a Christlike manner. According to Green, "We say that the stores are focused on their customers and should be servants to their customers. Therefore, we at the corporate office see ourselves as servants to the stores."[4] This concept isn't common today. Would this work in your company?

Another unconventional decision was Green's choice to close all retail stores by 8:00 p.m. and electing not to open stores on Sundays. He wanted to affirm the company's commitment to its employees and to the value of family time. The choice to remain closed on Sundays is particularly controversial because it is estimated that the retail giant forfeits millions in Sunday sales each year. But the company has held fast, committed to its employees and biblical principles. Though Hobby Lobby is one of only two billion-dollar organizations choosing to remain closed on Sundays, they are in good company—the other organization is Chick-fil-A.

> "ALL THE THINGS WE DO, ALL OUR BEHAVIOR, SHOULD LET OTHERS KNOW THAT WE ARE LIVING BY, AND OPERATING IN, BIBLICAL PRINCIPLES."
>
> —DAVID GREEN

Green took his commitment several steps farther, providing chaplains and Bible studies for his employees, and enabling them to play Christian music in retail stores. He even incorporated faith into the pay system for his employees, finding a way to "share the blessings." "We are more profitable than other stores within this industry. Because of this, we believe that we should pay above average salaries. We examine each specific position and pay according to that position's responsibility," said the CEO.[5]

When asked about his role in Hobby Lobby's success, Green again turns it over to prayer. "Yes, God did give us some talents, but who do these talents really belong to? They are God's. We are completely dependent on Him."[6] While Hobby Lobby as a business is of course focused on the bottom line, Green knows there is so much more. At the end of the day, profit is not the most important thing. Setting the bar high, David has kept his business accountable to this truth and to biblical principles. According to David Green, "Our organization wants to be remembered as one that knows the difference between temporal and eternal. Our business is only a means to an end and our end is to try to affect lives for eternity. If we haven't done that, then we are just merely a good person."[7]

## TIME OUT

1. Do you worry about bills and money?
2. What is your greatest fear in this life?
3. If you truly believe that God will provide, how much time are you wasting worrying about money?

## TODAY'S ASSIGNMENT

What can you do today that will show others you truly trust that God will provide for you and your family? What behaviors will others notice?

---

## HOME-FIELD ADVANTAGE

*Praises and concerns you want to bring before God*

_____

_____

_____

_____

---

# WHEN IS ENOUGH REALLY ENOUGH?

## IS DAILY BREAD ALL YOU REALLY NEED?

### THOUGHT OF THE DAY

*The pursuit of wealth never creates true satisfaction for you.*

### THE COACH'S CORNER

When is enough really enough? What drives men who have made billions and billions of dollars to continue to want more? For most of us, the true idea of waiting for our daily bread to feed our families is a terrifying concept. Many men believe having lots of money will solve all their problems and amazingly make them happy. A recent study noted that men with higher incomes were reluctant to call themselves rich. Those men in the top percent of incomes—having a net worth of more than four million dollars—described their financial status as "poor" or "just getting along." The study suggested that the desire for money and material belongings often left men feeling deprived. The study noted that "when men focus on money as their measure of achievement in life, they're never going to be satisfied."[1] This study would seem to concur that those who are happiest are the ones who earn their income by devoting themselves to something they love doing. Money is therefore not the focal point; rather it is the by-product.

> **FOR MOST OF US, THE TRUE IDEA OF WAITING FOR OUR DAILY BREAD TO FEED OUR FAMILIES IS A TERRIFYING CONCEPT.**

While it is surprising that the Bible refers to money much more than many realize, it is crystal clear that economic wealth is never enough to live an abundant life. The love of money, not money itself, tends to be the topic of a number of scriptures. It is very easy for us to feel that we never have enough, particularly in today's society. It always seems that the guy down the street works less than we do, yet has more than we have—so we continue on the quest for enough. The pursuit for more and more seems to never end. We hear money will not make us happy, but it sure seems as though it would help. Never to have to worry about money again would be a dream come true for most of us. Jesus, however, wants us to rely on Him to provide for us. Many times men have looked in the mirror when things were going great and said, "Look how smart I am! Look what I have accomplished," only to see what they have built go down the tubes.

Bob Buford authored a terrific book entitled *Halftime*, one of the best and most insightful books for men today. Bob talks about what happens to men after they have fought the battle to make a career, have children, buy a house, and reach a certain level of success in their lives. Once this happens they become restless as they begin to determine what is next for them in their journey with God. The shift from success to significance is the theme of the book and a lesson to us all. He tells of the scores of men he has worked with who pursued their financial dreams only to still find something lacking in their lives. The pursuit of wealth alone never creates true satisfaction.

## THE GAME PLAN

The Bible says that the pursuit of money alone can destroy your life. God wants you to know:

- You must decide what kind of riches you want—Matthew 6:19–21: "Do not lay up for yourselves treasures on earth, where moth and rust destroy and where thieves break in and steal; but lay up for yourselves treasures in heaven, where neither moth nor rust destroys and where thieves do not break in and steal. For where your treasure is, there your heart will be also."
- You must choose your priority: righteousness or revenue—Proverbs 16:8: "Better is a little with righteousness, than vast revenues without justice."
- You must decide if you will balance your life—Proverbs 30:8: "Remove falsehood and lies far from me; give me neither poverty nor riches—Feed me with the food allotted to me."
- You must focus on stewardship—1 Timothy 6:17–19: "Command those who are rich in this present age not to be haughty, nor to trust in uncertain riches but in the living God, who gives us richly all things to enjoy. Let them do good, that they be rich in good works, ready to

> give, willing to share, storing up for themselves a good
> foundation for the time to come, that they may lay hold
> on eternal life."

## PLAYMAKERS

Wayne Huizenga Jr.'s father is undoubtedly one of the most well-known and successful American businessmen of all time. He is one of few people, if not the only person, to develop three Fortune 1000 companies. Wayne followed in his father's footsteps, becoming a very wealthy and influential man as well. He played a crucial role in the history of many noteworthy organizations, including the Miami Dolphins, the Florida Marlins, and Blockbuster Video. This was a man at the top of his game. Wayne Huizenga Jr. achieved the world's definition of success, garnering respect from business and industry leaders around the world. But as he discovered, success—at least the world's version of success—isn't everything.

When he was just five years old, his parents divorced and Wayne moved to a Chicago, Illinois, suburb with his mother. Growing up, he longed to be near his father who lived in Florida. As a kid, Wayne was keenly aware of his father's business success, which began when he founded Waste Management. The young boy idolized his father, a real self-made man. Wayne observed and learned the value of hard work by watching the senior Huizenga. But his father, a workaholic, was busy building a thriving business and had little time for his family. When he did have the opportunity to spend time with his father, Wayne was blown away by his dad's lavish lifestyle. These visits made a lasting impression on the young man, who decided he wanted to join the family business and have private jets and expensive cars too. Who wouldn't?

Years later when his father purchased Blockbuster Video, a new and struggling company, Wayne received his opportunity to join the family business. He didn't start at the top—far from it. Instead, he began as a store clerk, working his way up over time. Eventually Wayne earned the chance to prove himself by participating in several special projects alongside his father and the company's executive team. He became a critical part of the video retailer's success, as Blockbuster soon became the largest video retailer in the world. The senior Huizenga eventually sold the video company to Viacom. But Wayne had proved himself, and his father continued to entrust him with more responsibility, later making him the vice president of Huizenga Holdings.

Wayne Huizenga Jr. paid attention and made some smart investments, buying a significant portion of Blockbuster Video stock. The value of the stock soared, making Wayne and his wife, Fonda, very wealthy. They were living it up. Wayne now enjoyed the lifestyle he had always longed for, one most people could scarcely imagine. Looking back, he admits, "I realized I'd been given these incredible gifts—airplanes, boats, and money—and the ability to do most anything I wanted in life. But I was using it all for me. It was all being used selfishly. In no way did I use any of it to glorify God."[2]

Despite the success, he wasn't satisfied. Wayne had it all, everything he'd always wanted, but still, something was missing. Then he met Brad Fleetwood-McDonald, a nuclear submarine captain. They were on a voyage from South Carolina to Florida and spent a considerable amount of time together. Wayne noticed that Captain Fleetwood-McDonald was different. "He didn't seem to be searching like I was. I saw a calm and a peace in him that I had not seen in anybody else."[3]

The two stayed in contact, with Brad persistently referring Wayne to the Bible for guidance in dealing with issues and concerns. Wayne quickly found himself visiting a church where he ultimately committed his life to Christ. He found what was missing. Suddenly the world looked very different to him. His focus shifted and he discerned the awesome opportunity he had to use his resources to do God's work.

> "SUCCESS IS BEING ABLE TO USE WHAT
> WE'VE BEEN GIVEN TO CHANGE OTHER
> PEOPLE'S LIVES. I HAVE THIS GREAT DESIRE
> TO SHARE WHAT I HAVE WITH OTHER PEOPLE.
> TO ME, THAT'S SUCCESS."
> —WAYNE HUIZENGA JR.

Wayne transformed overnight, drastically altering his lifestyle. His wife, Fonda, who was likely affected most by his change of heart, said, "My immediate response was, have you lost your mind?" Though not opposed to the changes, she was alarmed by her husband's abrupt about face. But she observed her husband in his new changed life and was changed herself. She, too, committed her life to God. "From that point," said Fonda, "it felt like we were in a canoe, and now we were finally paddling together."[4]

Today Wayne and Fonda are working to use their many blessings to impact the world for Christ. Wayne's new-found faith permeated into all aspect of his life, home, finances, and business. The definition of success has changed for Wayne Huizenga Jr., who now says, "Success is being able to use what we've been given to change other people's lives. I have this great desire to share what I have with other people. To me, that's success."[5]

## TIME OUT

1. Is money a major driver for you?
2. Are you and your family in a battle to keep up with the "Joneses"?

3. If you were truly financially sound, what would you do differently each day?

## TODAY'S ASSIGNMENT

God wants us to be responsible and accountable for 100 percent of the money that comes into our hands. Yet, He has also given us a benchmark of 10 percent to consider for our participation in joining with His work here on earth. Decide today how to restructure your financial life to honor God.

## HOME-FIELD ADVANTAGE

*Praises and concerns you want to bring before God*

_____

_____

_____

_____

## DAY 34

# GETTING EVEN
# IS UP TO GOD

### EVERYTHING WILL BE MADE RIGHT

### THE COACH'S CORNER

You have heard it said, or you may have actually said it yourself, "I don't get mad; I get even." For many men this is a statement that whether or not they have said it, they have thought it plenty of times. We want to make sure the score is made even; after all, God wants everything to be fair, doesn't He? If the referee misses a call, he sometimes will make up for it on the other end of the floor. If you are left out of a great business trip at work, you hope you will get to go on the next one. When you buy a house and feel cheated, you think you will make it up on the sale of the house. We instinctively want to be assured that everything is made even, and sometimes we even take it upon ourselves to make sure it actually happens.

If you have ever been mistreated or observed your children being mistreated, you probably have felt an irresistible desire to get even with the one who wronged you or your family. It may be you were passed over for a promotion at work, or you purchased a lemon for a car, or you were cheated on a big deal. It takes a great deal of faith to be harmed by someone and then step back, trusting God will work it all out (in His way and in His timeframe). We sometimes think that He needs us to do His judging, so we gladly step up for the challenge. However, the Bible makes it clear our job is not to get even, get back at someone, or settle the score. For many of us, this is a very hard lesson. We just want to make everything right—even the score for everyone. But we don't need to worry because God is in charge of that, not us.

> **IT TAKES A GREAT DEAL OF FAITH TO BE HARMED BY SOMEONE AND THEN STEP BACK, TRUSTING GOD WILL WORK IT ALL OUT.**

We love being the judge and jury. If you don't believe that, just look at many of the most popular shows on television today. We have *American Idol*, *Dancing with the Stars*, the Miss America pageant, *America's Next Top Model*, *America's Got Talent*, *Star Search*, and don't forget about *Divorce Court*, *The People's Court*, *Judge Hatchet*, *Judge Karen*, *Judge Mathis*, and of course *Judge Judy*, just to name a few. Being a judge is certainly a good thing; in fact it is necessary to maintain a lawful society. However, this is not the type of judging Jesus seems to be talking about. To judge means to come to a conclusion about someone and condemn them. You have heard sayings such as, "Don't judge a book by its cover." This happens when we form a negative conclusion about someone without knowing all the details or facts.

## THE GAME PLAN

The Bible wants you to follow certain principles and procedures when you have a dispute. God wants you to know:

- There is no need to be the avenger because He has that role—Romans 12:17–19: "Repay no one evil for evil. Have regard for good things in the sight of all men. If it is possible, as much as depends on you, live peaceably with all men. Beloved, do not avenge yourselves, but rather give place to wrath; for it is written, 'Vengeance is Mine, I will repay,' says the Lord."

- You shouldn't consider suing a fellow believer without first following God's mediation plan—Matthew 18:15–17: "Moreover if your brother sins against you, go and tell him his fault between you and him alone. If he hears you, you have gained your brother. But if he will not hear, take with you one or two more, that 'by the mouth of two or three witnesses every word may be established.' And if he refuses to hear them, tell it to the church. But if he refuses even to hear the church, let him be to you like a heathen and a tax collector."

- You are to be a blessing, not a curse—1 Peter 3:9: "Not returning evil for evil or reviling for reviling, but on the contrary blessing, knowing that you were called to this, that you may inherit a blessing."

- You should pray for those who despise you—Matthew 5:38–43: "You have heard that it was said, 'An eye for an eye and a tooth for a tooth.' But I tell you not to resist an

evil person. But whoever slaps you on your right cheek,
turn the other to him also. If anyone wants to sue you
and take away your tunic, let him have your cloak also.
And whoever compels you to go one mile, go with him
two. Give to him who asks you, and from him who wants
to borrow from you do not turn away."

## PLAYMAKERS

Where were you during the chase of O. J. Simpson down the Los
Angeles freeway in his white Ford Bronco? Most of us remember
seeing the chase live on television or at least remember the numerous times it was shown on program after program over the next
several weeks. His murder trial was the most publicized trial
America had ever seen. And after the longest jury trial in California
history, O. J. Simpson was a free man. To this day there are many
people who believe that a guilty O. J. got off scot-free, and that
angers them. Some blame a faulty judicial system and high-paid
lawyers while some believe he was freed simply because he was a
famous celebrity and football star. For the people who are concerned that a murderer got off free of charges in this Simpson trial,
be assured that Judge Lance Ito is not O. J.'s final judge, but God
will be—just as He is for us.

More recently, the famous NFL standout got into some more
trouble, and this time O. J. was sent to prison. He was charged
with breaking into a hotel room and committing an armed robbery along with several other men. A jury heard the case in Las
Vegas, Nevada, and found him guilty of all charges; however, following O. J.'s conviction on all twelve charges, his lawyer, Yale
Galanter, said, "This was just payback."[1] Galanter believes jurors
remembered the first O. J. trial and felt as though the star had
gotten off free and clear, and they wanted to settle the score. He

was sentenced to prison for what may end up being the rest of his life. "A lynching from the first second to the end," agreed Thomas Scotto, a close Simpson friend who testified and was overcome by emotion in the courtroom after the verdicts were read. "It's a total injustice."[2]

The case against Simpson was won the moment the jury was chosen, according to the consultant who helped prosecutors pick the panel. "That was the best possible jury prosecutors could ever have," said Howard Varinsky, who drafted a questionnaire for the prosecution that formed the basis of a survey.[3] While the members of the jury were told to ignore what they had heard or read about Mr. Simpson's past, many of those present thought the thread connecting the two incidents were very clear. Ronald Goldman, who was killed alongside Nicole Simpson, has a father who just would not give up in his quest to see O. J. behind bars. Ron's father has been credited with hounding Simpson so much to collect the $33.5 million wrongful death civil judgment that he may have pushed him to a desperate gambit to recover personal items he lost. "We drove him into that room to grab the sports memorabilia before we could seize the stuff," said David Cook, who represents Goldman's father, Fred. "Going to jail for beating Fred Goldman out of footballs and family mementos. Is this closure for Fred Goldman? No. Is this closure for America? No."[4]

**IS IT OUR JOB TO GET EVEN WITH ALL THOSE WHO HAVE WRONGED US? OR SHOULD WE LEAVE THAT UP TO THE ETERNAL JUDGE?**

You have to ask: Did O. J. Simpson really get a fair trial? Most of the world thinks he was guilty and should have gone to prison for a perceived injustice in his first trial. Many didn't want him to go to prison for his latest convictions for armed robbery and kidnapping since it appears to them that it was all about what he did in 1994 when Nicole Brown Simpson and Ron Goldman were slain. Even though the second set of jurors say it has nothing to do with the murders, no one can seem to forget about it. Many will always judge him to be guilty no matter what he does. So we ask ourselves the question, is it our job to get even with all those who have wronged us? Or should we leave that up to the eternal judge?

## TIME OUT

1. Do you ever get the urge to get even when you have been wronged?
2. Would your wife say you forgive and forget, or remember and seek revenge?
3. Can you give "a wrong doing" up to God and move on?

## TODAY'S ASSIGNMENT

When was the last time you were really mistreated or cheated? If you still carry the memory with you, why not today give it to God and forget about it? It is not up to you to get even.

# HOME-FIELD ADVANTAGE

*Praises and concerns you want to bring before God*

_____

_____

_____

_____

_____

# CLIMBING THE LADDER OF SUCCESS

## WHILE KEEPING YOUR FEET ON THE GROUND

## THOUGHT OF THE DAY

*Pride is the key ingredient to your personal disaster.*

## THE COACH'S CORNER

Isn't a little bit of pride a good thing? Don't we want our men to have healthy self-esteem in today's competitive world? The question just may be, how much pride is too much? We have all been around those men who have an inflated view of themselves—men who seem to see themselves differently than the world sees them. Men who think they are smarter, better looking, richer, and more successful than all the rest of us. If we are honest, we have often wanted to see these men tumble, for them to get what they truly deserve. Now I know that is not very God-like, but we usually dislike prideful men.

One definition of pride is having an excessively high opinion of oneself. Pride can also be defined as feeling that you are better than others, even to the point of regarding others with dislike, as if they were not worthy of a relationship or interaction with you. Pride shows the basic thinking "I am better than you are!" Other synonyms for being proud are arrogant, boastful, stiff-necked and haughty. Pride keeps us away from Jesus as it restricts the flow of His character in our lives. We have seen this in sports many times. When a player gets to the point in his athletic development that he truly believes he is the best, he is usually done. He is the player who catches the pass for a touchdown and beats his chest, never acknowledging the guy who threw the pass, the guys who blocked for the quarterback, the guy who called the play . . . anyone. In his mind, the entire play revolved around his self-made outstanding personal talents.

## PRIDE IS TAKING THE GLORY THAT BELONGS TO GOD ALONE AND KEEPING IT FOR OURSELVES.

Throughout Scripture we are told about the consequences of pride. Proverbs 16:18–19 (NIV) tells us, "Pride goes before destruction, a haughty spirit before a fall. Better to be lowly in spirit and among the oppressed than to share plunder with the proud." The Bible tells us Satan was cast out of heaven because of pride. He had the selfish audacity to attempt to replace God Himself as the rightful ruler of the universe. For those who rise up in defiance against God, there is nothing ahead but disaster. Pride is giving yourself the credit for something God has accomplished. Pride is taking the glory that belongs to God alone and keeping it for ourselves. Pride is essentially self-worship.

# THE GAME PLAN

The Bible warns us about the tempting lure of toxic pride. God wants you to know:

- Don't compare yourself to others—2 Corinthians 10:12: "For we dare not class ourselves or compare ourselves with those who commend themselves. But they, measuring themselves by themselves, and comparing themselves among themselves, are not wise."
- Don't limit yourself to front-row seats, even if you can always afford them—Luke 14:8–9. "When you are invited by anyone to a wedding feast, do not sit down in the best place, lest one more honorable than you be invited by him; and he who invited you and him come and say to you, 'Give place to this man,' and then you begin with shame to take the lowest place."
- Being sober isn't just being alcohol free—Romans 12:3: "For I say, through the grace given to me, to everyone who is among you, not to think of himself more highly than he ought to think, but to think soberly, as God has dealt to each one a measure of faith."
- There is only one way to rejoice with pride—Jeremiah 9:23–24: "Let not the wise man glory in his wisdom, let not the mighty man glory in his might, nor let the rich man glory in his riches; but let him glory in this, that he understands and knows Me."

# PLAYMAKERS

We have all heard the player who talks only of himself after the game, not recognizing any of his teammates or coaches. Also, we have experienced leaders at work who claim all the credit for a project, knowing they would never have been able to complete the project without many others. Here are some direct quotes that exemplify this prideful attitude that seems to be so prevalent in America today:

- Keith Bulluck, professional football player: "I want it all, and I want it as quickly as I can get it."[1]
- Dennis Rodman, professional basketball player: "As long as I play ball, I can get any woman I want."[2]
- Muhammad Ali, professional boxer: "It's hard to be humble when you're as great as I am."[3]
- Terrell Owens, professional football player: "Get your popcorn ready, 'cause I'm gonna put on a show."[4]

About pride, someone has said that it is a disease that makes everyone else sick except the one who has it. It is certainly not enjoyable to be with prideful or arrogant people. Many of today's professional athletes seem to be a most unique breed of individuals. It is agreed that in our current culture having a healthy ego in order to excel against the world's most intense competition is a must. Along with an often cult-like following and the tremendous fortunes that come with being a superstar athlete, they are also always in the public eye. The paparazzi, fans, and members of the news media are jammed in their faces daily, and they're required to answer a series of ridiculous questions from members of the media who act as if they know more about the sport than the athlete does. While high-profile athletes usually are unable to go out to dinner without people hounding them for autographs, there is a fine line between humility and boastfulness, between knowing you're talented and making sure everyone else knows you are.

### PRIDE IS A DISEASE THAT MAKES EVERYONE ELSE SICK EXCEPT THE ONE WHO HAS IT.

Even though there are countless athletes who crave public attention, there is also a large group of megastars who are simply modest and act with class. NBA celebrities Tim Duncan, Allan Houston, and Shane Battier are often mentioned as true "good guys" who seem to survive the NBA with their egos in check. A few years ago Tim Duncan scored fifty points in a single game, and he credited his teammates, the fans, and the coaching staff for his performance. There are others, however, who take their egos to a different level. They perform and give interviews as if it were all about them. It seems they cannot get enough media time, and when they aren't in the spotlight, they create controversies to make sure the attention stays on them. Many have become standoffish with their fans and arrogant with the media, and they do more to turn potential new fans away than gain new fans. Owners of NBA teams are often frustrated as their pride-driven players' outward behavior often comes at the expense of the entire team. Rather than be grateful and respectful of their celebrity status, their super-talented teammates, and the sport itself, their attitude is emblematic of what's wrong with professional sports.

### THERE IS A FINE LINE BETWEEN HUMILITY AND BOASTFULNESS, BETWEEN KNOWING YOU'RE TALENTED AND MAKING SURE EVERYONE ELSE KNOWS YOU ARE.

Terrell Owens, known to the world of sports as simply T.O., just may get the nod for being this era's most self-absorbed NFL player with a reputation for being a player who many feel is self-centered and self-serving. Just ask many of his teammates in San Francisco, Philadelphia, and Dallas. Only Owens could coin and copyright the expression "I love me some me." The media circus follows him everywhere and feeds his ego even further. Although few people really know the real T.O., he often seems to be the very essence of pride. Owens has been known to hold press conferences in his front driveway while doing sit-ups.

Pro athletes can either be a positive influence for their team or they can be a negative influence. There does seem to be a trend emerging with athletes who are taking all the credit for wins and quickly placing all the blame for losses on their teammates and coaching staff. With so many young boys and girls watching these superstars, this self-destructive attitude must be having an effect on kids playing youth sports who want to act just like their heroes. While today's professional athletes without a doubt all have very different personalities, thankfully most of them still have a positive and friendly relationship with their teammates and fans.

It is a proven fact that overblown egos are not desirable in the locker room of professional sports. Players don't like other players who want to take all the credit, and coaches certainly don't like them either. It seems to create real division among the team, and often these players are seen as outcasts. Nothing seems to destroy a team faster than a player blaming his teammates for the team's lack of success.

We all know men who seem to have a problem with keeping their ego in check. When in elementary school, boys who go around acting very confident seem to serve as magnets for other boys. But as we get older, instead of attracting men, it often repels them. Few men really enjoy being around people who brag on themselves all the time.

## TIME OUT

1. Is pride something you have to deal with in your life?
2. Would your wife characterize you as prideful or humble in your dealings with her?
3. How important is image to you?

## TODAY'S ASSIGNMENT

There are many ways that our pride can get into our way. Think of a way your pride continues to come between you and God. Are you prideful about your kids, your house, your cars, or your financial status?

## HOME-FIELD ADVANTAGE

*Praises and concerns you want to bring before God*

_____

_____

_____

_____

_____

# FINDING THE ZONE AS YOU LOOK TO THE FUTURE

*Do not boast about tomorrow,*
*For you do not know what a day may bring forth.*

**—PROVERBS 27:1**

## DAY 36

# FIGHTING THE BATTLE

## DELIVERING THE MESSAGE

### THOUGHT OF THE DAY

*You were created to carry the message for God—you must not drop the ball.*

### THE COACH'S CORNER

Hopefully the last thirty-five days have challenged you to tell someone about your relationship with Jesus Christ. Maybe you recently heard a sermon on the Great Commission and you feel compelled to share the Word. Maybe you have always known that you need to tell others about your walk and your relationship with God. It doesn't matter why you are contemplating your role in carrying the message for God—the important thing is that you are ready.

IF WE REALLY LOVE A PERSON, WE WILL LOVE
THEM ENOUGH TO TELL THEM ABOUT JESUS!

Les Steckel, former NFL head coach and current president of the Fellowship of Christian Athletes, challenged the men attending an In The Zone conference near Memphis, Tennessee, "to be disciplined in every part of your life—physically, spiritually, and emotionally."[1] These efforts cause others to respect and admire you, but more importantly, those disciplines often are the catalyst to get people to ask about the hope that is within you—Jesus Christ.

And although real men don't get scared (right?), you are probably nervous about being so open. You realize you don't know everything about the Bible; you didn't sign on to be a full-time pastor; you know you still make mistakes; and you are not a perfect Christian. Well, my friend, you're right. There's no way that you could be perfect, no way to know everything in the Bible; so don't let that you stop you! Today we attempt to reach all kinds of men using a variety of approaches. Many of us would like to share the gospel with our family members and our friends, but it can be difficult. Ultimately, we are afraid we will be rejected or made fun of. We must remember that those we share with are not rejecting us; they are rejecting Jesus. How can we claim to love a person and not want to share our good news with them? If we really love a person, we will love them enough to tell them about Jesus!

## PEOPLE WANT TO SEE JESUS LIVING IN YOU PRIOR TO YOU TELLING THEM THEY SHOULD ALLOW HIM TO LIVE IN THEM.

You may be a regular guy at church, attending Sunday school each Sunday and singing in the choir. You may be on the administrative board at your church, coach a church baseball team, or take up the offering. But have you ever told anyone about Jesus? This is truly difficult for many men, and they have decided to leave that up to the pastor or the members of the church staff. What is our role in bringing other men to Christ? Are you ready to get started?

More men are brought to Christ through an example than they are through a sermon. Whether it is your children, your friends, your coworkers, or your extended family, people want to see Jesus living in you prior to you telling them they should allow Him to live in them. Some people will even set traps for us to see how we will respond. While this is scary, it can also be enjoyable. God is preparing you to tell others about Him. He will not let you down. He will be with you as you share the good news. He will be with you during every conversation. Put your complete trust in Him and start sharing.

## THE GAME PLAN

The Bible wants every believer to have a ministry. God wants you to know:

- Every believer is a minister—1 Peter 2:6–8: "Therefore it is also contained in the Scripture, 'Behold, I lay in Zion a chief cornerstone, elect, precious, and he who believes on Him will by no means be put to shame.' Therefore, to you who believe, He is precious; but to those who are disobedient, 'The stone which the builders rejected has become the chief cornerstone,' and 'A stone of stumbling and a rock of offense.' They stumble, being disobedient to the word, to which they also were appointed."
- God wants us to be bold and not ashamed of the gospel—2 Timothy 1:7: "For God has not given us a spirit of fear, but of power and of love and of a sound mind."
- You should seek the Holy Spirit to get all the help you need—Acts 1:8: "But you shall receive power when the

Holy Spirit has come upon you; and you shall be witnesses to Me in Jerusalem, and in all Judea and Samaria,
and to the end of the earth."

- You should persevere when you are ignored—Matthew
10:14–15: "And whoever will not receive you nor hear
your words, when you depart from that house or city,
shake off the dust from your feet. Assuredly, I say to you,
it will be more tolerable for the land of Sodom and
Gomorrah in the day of judgment than for that city!"

## PLAYMAKERS

Truett Cathy established one of the most beloved and successful
businesses in the world, and he did it by bringing his faith to work.

Truett grew up during the Depression, developing a strong
work ethic. He opened his first business in his front yard at the age
of eight, selling Coca-Cola. His father was a successful farmer who
fell on hard times and relocated his family to Atlanta, Georgia.
There Truett Cathy obtained a paper route, delivering the *Atlanta
Journal*, to help support his struggling family. Around this time, a
man named Mr. Abbey entered the young man's world and made a
lasting impact. Cathy did not have a close relationship with his
father, and Mr. Abbey, his Sunday school teacher, became his mentor and teacher. Abbey shared the Bible with Cathy, providing an
example of what it meant to be a loving man of God. Most importantly, Mr. Abbey believed in Truett, supplying him with the faith
and confidence to succeed. To this day, Cathy attributes much of
his success to Mr. Abbey.

Almost everyone in America knows about and loves Chick-
fil-A, the restaurant chain that brought us the chicken sandwich
and the lovable cows urging us to "Eat Mor Chikin." But before it
became a nationwide success, the Chick-fil-A story began over

sixty years ago in the small town of Hapeville, Georgia, with Truett Cathy's first restaurant, the Dwarf Grill.

Truett Cathy's trademark was the boneless breast of chicken sandwich, a new concept at the time. With this sandwich he founded Chick-fil-A, Inc. in the 1960s. He went on to revolutionize the restaurant business when he decided to place his restaurants in shopping malls, opening his first in a suburban Atlanta mall in 1967.

But what makes Chick-fil-A's success really interesting is not just the innovative concepts, clever advertising, or delicious food but the unique leadership of Truett Cathy. From the beginning, he was out to do more than turn a profit and feed people. Cathy wanted to make a difference in the lives of others: his customers, his employees, and young people. One example of this is his decision to close his restaurants on Sundays. This decision was and is a controversial one since 20 percent of all fast-food revenue comes in on Sundays. Many people may say, "That's crazy! Close your business on a weekend? You'll lose millions!"

The company received a lot of pressure to keep their stores open, particularly from malls, even incurring financial penalties. But for Cathy this wasn't just a practical decision but a faith-based decision. He believes Chick-fil-A team members should "have an opportunity to rest, spend time with family and friends, and worship if they choose to do so." Cathy says, "I think the most important decision I ever made was to stay closed on Sundays. We all need a day off. We feel we've created the caliber of people who understand that."[2] To the surprise of many people, this decision has not adversely affected the chain. In fact, the family-owned company has experienced forty-one consecutive years of positive sales growth. Truett Cathy views his Sunday stance as an edge, now explaining, "People get tired of eating at the same restaurant every day. We give them the privilege of eating somewhere else on Sunday."[3]

Faith isn't just for Sundays. Cathy remains committed to

combining his faith and business. He provides a consistent model to his employees, his customers, and the business world of what it means to bring your faith to work. Today, Chick-fil-A is the country's second-largest quick-serve chicken restaurant chain. It is one of the largest privately owned restaurant chains in the country, with over 1,430 locations in thirty-eight states and Washington, DC. Cathy's tremendous success enables him to pursue one of his passions of helping young people and making a difference in the lives of people who enter his restaurants. He sets an example for us all.

## FAITH ISN'T JUST FOR SUNDAYS. CATHY REMAINS COMMITTED TO COMBINING HIS FAITH AND BUSINESS.

In his words, "We must motivate ourselves to do our very best, and by our example lead others to their best as well."[4] Perhaps Jimmy Carter described him best when he said, "I hope that people will learn from Truett Cathy the virtues that have brought him remarkable success in life. He has dedicated himself to service in the broadest sense, following Christian principles, not only in his personal life but in his relations with his customers and employees."[5]

## TIME OUT

1. Is it hard for you to tell others about your relationship with Jesus?
2. Have you ever had the opportunity of sharing Jesus with people and having them accept Christ?
3. What person do you know who is seeking a relationship with Christ, yet you have felt uncomfortable discussing it with him?

## TODAY'S ASSIGNMENT

Ask God to put someone in your path this week with whom you may share your relationship with Jesus. God has promised He will supply the words.

---

## HOME-FIELD ADVANTAGE

*Praises and concerns you want to bring before God*

_____

_____

_____

---

# BECOMING THE NEW YOU

## WHO DO YOU REALLY WANT TO BE?

### THOUGHT OF THE DAY

*God may never give you enough to be what you want yourself to be, but He always gives you enough to be what He wants you to be.*

### THE COACH'S CORNER

"If I only had . . ." That is the story for the centuries. We are constantly looking for the golden ship to arrive bringing us our rightfully deserved earthly treasures. If we only had enough money, we would feed all the hungry children in America. If we only had the time, we could visit people who are unable to get out of their homes or the many confined to the beds. If we only had a larger car, we could get more involved with the youth of our church or the Meals on Wheels program in our city. If we only had the energy, we could help people who simply need a helping hand with their small children or small businesses. If we only had . . . The truth is, we do have—because we have God. God has all the money we need, all the time we need, and all the energy we need to do His will. He is waiting on us to utilize His gifts for His kingdom.

Most of us have heard the slogan "Be all that you can be" on TV and radio for what seems like forever. For over twenty years it has been the marketing tagline used by the United States Army. Essentially the advertisement challenges individuals to mull over becoming the person he or she has the potential to be. Some believe this slogan would be a fitting slogan for Christian men today. God's precise challenge for us is to become the full man we are capable of being through Jesus Christ. God states as fact that evil will never allow you to be all that you are capable of being. While most of us want to "be all that we can be," we don't necessarily believe the army creates that opportunity. The same problem exists regarding our faith. Many who profess to be Christians are convinced that following God can often be a liability.

> **GOD HAS ALL THE MONEY WE NEED, ALL THE TIME WE NEED, AND ALL THE ENERGY WE NEED TO DO HIS WILL.**

What kind of man do you want to become? Do you desire to be the best man you can be? If you do, honestly answer two questions: 1) Knowing your God-given strengths and weaknesses, personality and intellect, internal and external resources, do you believe at this moment that you are the best man you are capable of being? 2) Are you making the best use of what God has given you?

## THE GAME PLAN

The Bible tells us we will be perfectly sanctified at Christ's return, but how are we to be holy in the meantime? God wants you to:

- Put His Word into your heart for your inheritance— Acts 20:32: "So now, brethren, I commend you to God and to the word of His grace, which is able to build you up and give you an inheritance among all those who are sanctified."
- Act as if you are dead to sin—Romans 6:1–6: "What shall we say then? Shall we continue in sin that grace may abound? Certainly not! How shall we who died to sin live any longer in it? Or do you not know that as many of us as were baptized into Christ Jesus were baptized into His death? Therefore we were buried with Him through baptism into death, that just as Christ was raised from the dead by the glory of the Father, even so we also should walk in newness of life. For if we have been united together in the likeness of His death, certainly we also shall be in the likeness of His resurrection, knowing this, that our old man was crucified with Him, that the body of sin might be done away with, that we should no longer be slaves of sin."
- Exercise your privilege to get His forgiveness when you sin—1 John 1:9: "If we confess our sins, He is faithful and just to forgive us our sins and to cleanse us from all unrighteousness."
- Rejoice and embrace the fact that Jesus, who died for you, also lives in you—Galatians 2:20: "I have been crucified with Christ; it is no longer I who live, but Christ

lives in me; and the life which I now live in the flesh I
live by faith in the Son of God, who loved me and gave
Himself for me."

## PLAYMAKERS

Coach Tom Landry was the founding coach of the Dallas Cowboys
who brought the team from a winless initial season into a powerful
dominance in the NFL. Under his leadership that lasted for almost
thirty seasons, the Cowboys had twenty consecutive winning seasons, nineteen NFL playoff appearances, thirteen division titles,
five Super Bowl appearances, and two Super Bowl victories. "From
the late 1960s through the 1970s and into the 1980s," contended
*Washington Post* staff writer Bart Barnes, "the Cowboys under
Landry were a perennial power in the NFL, with a mystique that
transcended the sports community and Texas."[1]

Tom was born and raised in the small town of Mission, Texas.
His father worked as an auto mechanic, served as the town's fire
chief, and supervised Sunday school at First Methodist Church. At
Mission High School, Tom was an A student and excelled on the
football field, playing all-regional fullback on a team that outscored
its opponents 322–0 during his senior year. Landry felt that being
a star in high school football would be all he desired, so he worked
harder than his teammates.

Landry was called after high school to serve in the air force in
World War II. After he was discharged as a first lieutenant, he
immediately enrolled in the University of Texas, where he resumed
playing fullback for the Longhorns football team. In 1948, Texas
won the Sugar Bowl, and in 1949 his team won the Orange Bowl.
He graduated from the University of Texas with a degree in business
administration and later earned a degree in mechanical engineering
from the University of Houston. He was confident that if he could

be a star in college football that would be all he needed, so again he worked harder than his teammates.

Landry was drafted and began his professional football career playing cornerback for the New York Giants where he was selected to the All-Pro defensive team in 1954. When Jim Lee Howell became head coach of the Giants, he chose Landry to become his player-coach for the season. He left the field permanently as a player the next year when he took a position as the team's defensive coordinator. From 1956 to 1959, he worked as assistant coach alongside offensive coordinator Vince Lombardi, who later rose to fame as coach of the Green Bay Packers. Coach Landry just knew if he could be a success as a professional football coach that would be all he would need, so he developed into one of the hardest-working coaches of his era.

In 1956, the Giants played the Chicago Bears in the World Championship and won 48–6. It was the most significant win of his young career. Immediately after the game he said that winning the game was the worst experience of his life because there were no more mountains to climb, nothing greater than what he had already accomplished to do. There was still an awesome void in his personal life. He finally asked Christ into his life and realized that this relationship was the fulfillment that had been missing. He realized this void couldn't be filled with football or winning. He recognized the spiritual peace that neither being a successful coach, being a standout pilot, nor being an outstanding player had ever given him.

**HE FINALLY ASKED CHRIST INTO HIS LIFE AND REALIZED THAT THIS RELATIONSHIP WAS THE FULFILLMENT THAT HAD BEEN MISSING.**

A few years later, Landry accepted the position as the new head coach of the Dallas Cowboys expansion team. A group of Dallas businessmen headed by owner Clint Murchison Jr. and general manager Tex Schramm sought out Coach Landry for the top job, contracting with him for five years at $34,000 a season. Landry continued to run an insurance business in Dallas during the off-season just in case it didn't work out. The coaching position gave him a chance to move closer to home and to his family. In his first season as head coach, Landry failed to win a single game, as the Cowboys posted a 0–11–1 record. However, those in the NFL just knew he would be successful. "He was renowned in the NFL for his ability to think ahead," noted *Washington Post* staff writer Bart Barnes. "Not just for the next down but to the next series of downs."[2]

Despite a sub-par inaugural season, Coach Landry had won the respect and confidence of the Cowboys owner Clint Murchison. In 1964, Murchison signed Landry for an additional ten years to be the head coach of the Dallas Cowboys. This sent shock waves through the NFL and marked an unprecedented show of support for a coach who had only put together a 13–38–3 record. The gamble paid off for Mr. Murchison because by 1965 the team had won as many games as they had lost. In 1966, the Cowboys made the playoffs for the first time after posting a 10–3–1 season, and they were off building the Dallas Cowboy dynasty. That year Coach Landry was selected as the NFL Coach of the Year. The following year the team won the Eastern Division title, and after the 1970 season, the Dallas Cowboys advanced to the Super Bowl for the first time in franchise history. They lost the championship game to the Baltimore Colts, but Landry and the Cowboys eventually made it to the Super Bowl five times, winning in 1972 and 1978 and losing in 1971, 1976, and 1979. Throughout his career, Coach Landry earned a record of 250–162–6 in the regular season and 20–16 in the playoffs.

Tom knew he would be happy if he could just be a great high school football player—but he wasn't happy. He knew if he could be a successful fighter pilot in the war, he would be happy—but he wasn't. He knew if he could be a college standout that he would be happy—but he still wasn't happy. Tom knew if he could be a great NFL player he would be happy—but he wasn't. Finally, Coach Landry knew he would be happy if he became a successful NFL coach—but he still wasn't at peace. The famous coach finally figured out that only God could fill the void for him, and only God will fill the void for us too.

## TIME OUT

1. If you could change your profession, what would you want to be?
2. Are you currently in a profession that lets you use your God-given talents and gifts?
3. What would God say to you regarding what you have done with your life thus far?

## TODAY'S ASSIGNMENT

Maybe it is time for a change. Ask God to lead you in determining if you are in the right vocation, doing the right thing. Identify your desires and lift them up to God. Be open to what He has to say about your future.

## HOME-FIELD ADVANTAGE

*Praises and concerns you want to bring before God*

_____

_____

_____

_____

_____

## DAY 38

# NO WORRIES

## DOING THE RIGHT THING IS
## SOMETIMES DIFFICULT

### THOUGHT OF THE DAY

*There is no right way for you to do the wrong thing—*
*there is no wrong way for you to do the right thing.*

### THE COACH'S CORNER

In our hearts, we may want to do the right thing, but our sinful nature often takes over. Sometimes the right thing seems to be less fun or boring and even outdated. It is even sometimes difficult to know the difference between right and wrong if we take our cues from today's culture. Although there may appear to be circumstances when it doesn't seem there is a clear line between right and wrong, our internal compass seems always to lead the way. What is this internal compass? It's the bad feeling we get when we know we are not doing the right thing. God made a promise to us when we accepted Him into our lives, and that promise was this: "I will never leave you or forsake you." That feeling deep inside is the Holy Spirit helping to guide your steps. Yes, there is a right and wrong, and we usually do know the difference.

We certainly don't like to admit it, but many of us are worriers. We spend enormous amounts of time dealing with worry and guilt about our children, our spouse, our finances, and our work. So just how do we pursue the "peace that passes all understanding"? No one has to teach a young child how to lie. Children learn at a very early age to hide if they are caught in an act of being dishonest. Many times a boy's instinct is to hit others if he doesn't get his way. We seem to know how to act bad at an early age, but we have to be taught what is right. This continues to be true as we get older as well. While most of us are not pathological liars, we sometimes tell only part of the story when we are asked a question or simply don't convey the whole truth out of jealousy or just spite.

**THERE IS A RIGHT AND WRONG, AND WE USUALLY DO KNOW THE DIFFERENCE.**

Adam's unwillingness to come clean with his sin when God first confronted him in the Garden of Eden seemed to set the standard for sometimes choosing wrong over right. If you remember, his son Cain soon went even further, lying to God directly and maliciously. From the beginning of time, man has grappled with right versus wrong. Most of us have experienced a time when we decided to do the wrong thing, only to discover later how easy it would have been to do the right thing.

One of the greatest sports celebrities of this century is Lee Corso. The sometimes outrageous but always engaging main man on ESPN *College GameDay* is one of the most entertaining speakers in America. At an In The Zone conference, Lee said, "Your integrity is your most important possession. You must guard it. If someone asks you to violate what you believe, then you should quit. Never sell your integrity."[1]

In the world today the line between right and wrong seems to be getting blurred. Is being clearly dishonest on your taxes cheating, or simply using your head to keep as much of your hard-earned money as possible? Is watching an inappropriate movie while in a hotel room on business wrong, or is it much better visiting the bar and finding live women to talk to? Is it all right to tell a lie at work that may get you promoted? After all, your kids are the ones who will benefit from the extra money and time you will have. We all have a moral compass. It lets us know when we are moving from the right way of living to the wrong way. Have you looked at your compass lately to see if you are still sure about right and wrong? Someone truly is watching.

## THE GAME PLAN

The Bible wants you to be active, not passive, when it comes to obedience to God. God wants you to:

- Choose life and blessings, not death and cursing—Deuteronomy 30:19: "I call heaven and earth as witnesses today against you, that I have set before you life and death, blessing and cursing; therefore choose life, that both you and your descendants may live."
- Confess your primary loyalty upfront—Matthew 10:32: "Therefore whoever confesses me before men, him I will also confess before My Father who is in heaven."
- Be honest, just, pure, good, and virtuous—Colossians 3:23: "And whatever you do, do it heartily, as to the Lord and not to men."

- Follow His road map to few regrets—1 Timothy 6:11–12: "But you, O man of God, flee these things and pursue righteousness, godliness, faith, love, patience, gentleness. Fight the good fight of faith, lay hold on eternal life, to which you were also called and have confessed the good confession in the presence of many witnesses."

## PLAYMAKERS

Before Tiger Woods . . . before Arnold Palmer, Jack Nicklaus, and Phil Mickelson; before professional golf soared into the major sports industry that it is today; one unbelievable man stood as one of the most ethical athletes the world has ever known. His remarkable skills and strong competitive spirit accompanied by his God-given talent earned him the Grand Slam of Golf and international respect as one of the greatest golfers in history. An honest guy, his poise and charm made him one of the sports heroes of his day. His name was Bobby Jones.

The 1925 U.S. Open Championship was one of the most attended golf events of the decade, but the story of what happened on the final round is still told all over the world to show golf is a game of honesty and integrity. Bobby was a young budding star of the game and an up-and-coming professional who was playing in one of the biggest events of his career. In the final round of the Championship he was looking at his ball in the tall rough, when he accidentally touched his ball, moving it only slightly. When he looked around he saw that there were no officials to call a foul, no golf authorities to hand down a penalty. His playing partner for the final round was the world-famous Walter Hagen, who didn't see Bobby's ball move either, nor did his caddie or any member of the gallery. It appeared to everyone but Bobby that he had won the U.S. Open Championship by one stoke. However, when Bobby turned in his score card at the official's tent, everyone soon became aware that he had assessed himself a one-stroke penalty, resulting in a tie.

Bobby explained that when he accidentally moved his ball, he didn't improve his line to the hole, nor was it considered by many to be a great violation. Although what happened . . . happened; Bobby indicated that the rules were the rules and he had agreed to play by the rules when he signed on, so he thought little about it. Although he was aware that his one-stroke penalty cost him the outright championship, that changed nothing for him. The following day he went on to compete in a nine-hole playoff, which he lost to Willie MacFarlane. In the press conference that followed, the famed sports-writer O. B. Keller met with Jones and asked him about why he would self-impose a penalty that cost him the U.S. Championship. Bobby requested that he not write about the incident. "You might as well praise me for not robbing banks," Jones said.[2]

## THERE IS ALWAYS SOMEONE WATCHING, ALWAYS. GOD HIMSELF IS AN AUDIENCE OF ONE!

In golf, the ethics of the game are sacred even when some of the rules don't seem to make much sense. What makes the sport of golf all the more impressive is that golfers are usually left to police themselves. This could be why many high-paid executives decide to play golf with a potential senior executive prior to employing him. According to Larry Papasan, former CEO of Smith and Nephew, "If a guy will cheat on the golf course, then you can count on it—he will cheat at the office as well."[3]

In PGA events today a player is not around an official at all times, so it becomes the player's job to enforce the rules on himself, many times at his own expense. There's that old saying in some sports that if you're not cheating, you're not trying. However, this statement does not apply to life; nor did it apply to Bobby Jones or to golfers today. In life, just as in golf, you learn there is always someone watching, always. God Himself is an audience of One!

## TIME OUT

1. Are you a worrier?
2. What is your greatest worry at this time? Write it down.
3. Do most of your worries come true?

## TODAY'S ASSIGNMENT

We can often become paralyzed by worry. Identify your greatest worry and give it to God.

---

# HOME-FIELD ADVANTAGE

*Praises and concerns you want to bring before God*

_____

_____

_____

_____

---

# AN AUDIENCE OF ONE

## WHO WILL YOU PLEASE TODAY?

## THOUGHT OF THE DAY

*While many people want you to do what they need done, there is only one person you ultimately have to please.*

## THE COACH'S CORNER

A young writer for a college Christian magazine kept a sign above her desk: "Only one life, 'twill soon be past, only what's done for Christ will last." There are so many people in line for us to please: the world, the neighbors, the family, the church, the boss ... the list goes on and on. And while we are busy pleasing, we never seem to find a stopping place. Who is it that you will please today? What will you do today to please God? What are you doing today that is pleasing to the world but not God?

"Take a number" or "Stand in line" are the two comments that we want to say to the world. Enough is enough; we simply can't please everyone, no matter how hard we try. It seems that someone is always disappointed that he didn't get enough time. Oftentimes, men, when so overburdened, run and hide. They may not officially run away; however, we see them as they draw back from things that they were once significantly involved in. Many choose to leave their family when they can't seem to please them. Southwest Airlines is running creative ads on TV today with the theme "Wanna Get Away?" The reality is, men often think about getting away, and that is often the easy way out. Saying we only have to please God is one thing, but making that our life mission is another.

## WHAT ARE YOU DOING TODAY THAT IS PLEASING TO THE WORLD BUT NOT GOD?

The pressures to act spiritual among other Christians can be very extreme at times—especially if you are in any type of leadership role within the church. For we all know that leaders don't have problems; they don't have any down times; and they are always *on fire* for God, right? They're invincible! That's why we made them our leaders. Modern-day gladiators! OK, so we're going over the top now. Nevertheless, it is sad but true that the extra pressures leaders face in being spiritual does lead to performances devoid of the right heart condition. But it's certainly not just the leaders who feel the pressure. Let me ask you a couple of questions. When was the last time you sat in a small group setting and felt you had to pray because everyone else was and if you didn't, people would think you were "unspiritual"? What about worship in church? When was the last time you clapped your hands in worship to God while all the time you were just thinking about lunch or maybe even who was looking at you? Let's try to remember the words of King David: "I know, my God, that you test the heart and are pleased with integrity" (1 Chronicles 29:17 NIV).

**SAYING WE ONLY HAVE TO PLEASE GOD IS ONE THING, BUT MAKING THAT OUR LIFE MISSION IS ANOTHER.**

The Holy Spirit doesn't work in your life while you are still just putting on a show for your friends and family. But He does delight in those who are honest about the condition of their own hearts and in humility look to Him for the reality of the Christian life. Life is meant to be about pleasing Him and no one else!

## THE GAME PLAN

The Bible tells us that God knows us intimately and forever. God wants you to:

- Work hard in all your activities—Colossians 3:23: "And whatever you do, do it heartily, as to the Lord and not to men."
- Let everything you do be pleasing to Him, not man—1 Thessalonians 2:4: "But as we have been approved by God to be entrusted with the gospel, even so we speak, not as pleasing men, but God who tests our hearts."
- Don't get distracted or off course; there is only one Finisher to your faith—Hebrews 12:1–2: "Therefore we also, since we are surrounded by so great a cloud of witnesses, let us lay aside every weight, and the sin which so

easily ensnares us, and let us run with endurance the race that is set before us, looking unto Jesus, the author and finisher of our faith, who for the joy that was set before Him endured the cross, despising the shame, and has sat down at the right hand of the throne of God."

- Submit to one another as an act of obedience to God—Ephesians 5:21: "Submitting to one another in the fear of God."

## PLAYMAKERS

Pat Tillman had it made. He was a budding star in the NFL, with a solid family and great friends. Many of his friends say Pat was a man on a mission, a man with a purpose. Pat played four seasons with the Arizona Cardinals, winning league-wide respect as a smart and hard-hitting, if somewhat small, defensive safety before he and his younger brother Kevin enlisted into the United States Army shortly after 9/11. Pat turned down a multiyear $3.6 million contract with the Cardinals to enlist in the army in 2002 in the wake of the September 11, 2001, terrorist attacks. Pat was sent to Fort Lewis, Washington, where he joined the 75th Ranger Regiment. He was deployed to Afghanistan and was involved in Operation Mountain Storm somewhere in the southeast part of the country. His battalion was in the area to fight Al-Qaeda and the former Taliban government close to the border of Pakistan. At the age of twenty-seven, with dreams unfulfilled, Pat was killed by friendly fire.

Dave McGinnis was Pat's coach with the Arizona Cardinals prior to his enlistment in the army. According to Dave, "Pat knew his purpose in life. He proudly walked away from a career in professional football to a greater calling."[1] Tillman told *NBC News* in an interview the day after severe attacks on his battalion, "My great-grandfather was at Pearl Harbor, and a lot of my family fought in wars, and I really haven't done a thing as far as laying myself on the line like that."[2]

There have been numerous other professional athletes who have answered the call to serve their country, and although most, unlike Pat, returned alive, our next athlete's life was changed forever—because only half of his body came home. His name is Bob Weiland, *Mr. Inspiration*. Bob grew up in Milwaukee, Wisconsin, and was a standout high school baseball player and was in negotiations with the Philadelphia Phillies when he received a call he was not expecting. Bob received an invitation from the U.S. Government calling him into full-time service in the army. He put his professional baseball career on hold, and after basic training he was stationed at Cu Chi base as a combat medic in Vietnam.

Being around constant injuries and deaths was very unnerving for the young potential baseball standout. He was depended on by his men because he was a medic, but he longed to return to the states and pursue his baseball career. After a short time in Vietnam, Bob's squadron was out on patrol when they walked up on a field full of mines and buried mortar rounds. The sound was unlike anything Bob had every encountered. The loud explosions and the crying of grown men traumatized Bob, but he had a job to do. As his friends called his name, he ran and tried to help as many as he could. While running to assist one of his friends, Bob stepped on a land mine himself. The result was a major explosion as he was hit with a buried eighty-two millimeter mortar, a round that was designed to destroy tanks. After the reinforcements finally arrived, Bob was pronounced dead, but another medic kept forcing oxygen down into Bob's lungs. Once the helicopter evacuated him to the field hospital, it was discovered that Bob was still alive but only barely.

After fighting for weeks to live, Bob began to improve, and when he felt better he wrote the following short letter to his parents.

June 14, 1969

Dear Mom and Dad,

I'm in the hospital. Everything is going to be O.K. The people here are taking good care of me.

Love,

— Bob

P. S. I think I lost my

legs.

Bob often says, "My legs went one direction, my life another." His future in Major League Baseball was over. Many of the things he loved such as dancing, hiking, climbing, and walking were also over. Most of us would have become depressed and looked for a way to give up. But not Bob—he chose to face this challenge with hope, faith, and courage. Bob says, "Life is a gift, and we should not waste any of it worrying over what might have been but instead focus on what can be . . . I survived. If that's not a miracle, what is?"[3] Bob is a miracle. While lying in his hospital bed, he decided to lift weights. At that point he couldn't even lift five pounds, but he persisted. Every day he trained, and every day he got stronger. The athlete in him took over, and he eventually shattered the world record in his weight division in the bench press on four occasions, lifting 507 pounds. The ironic thing is that he was disqualified all four times—for not wearing shoes!! He was finally banned from the sport. So much for sportsmanship!

> "LIFE IS A GIFT, AND WE SHOULD NOT WASTE ANY OF IT WORRYING OVER WHAT MIGHT HAVE BEEN BUT INSTEAD FOCUS ON WHAT CAN BE."
> —BOB WEILAND

Yet even that didn't make Bob bitter. He just turned to another sport—the marathon! Bob has competed in dozens of marathons, including the New York, Los Angeles, and Marine Corp Marathons and is the only double amputee ever to compete in the grueling Ironman Triathlon in Kona, Hawaii—without a wheelchair! Bob also completed the most exciting marathon of all—a walk across America . . . on his hands. It took him three years, eight months, and six days—and he did it as a fund-raiser for his fellow Vietnam Vets. The NFL Players Association presented Bob with the National Award for Courage. Bob also served for a period of time as the strength coach for the Green Bay Packers. Bob wakes every day with one person to please, and only one person—God.

## TIME OUT

1. What tasks do you have to do that you are dreading?
2. Does your wife ever have any idea when you are stressed to the max?
3. What do you feel God calling you to do for Him today?

## TODAY'S ASSIGNMENT

If you have only one job today, and that is to please God, what will you do differently?

## HOME-FIELD ADVANTAGE

*Praises and concerns you want to bring before God*

---

---

---

---

---

## DAY 40

# THE DAY
# HAS FINALLY COME

## I WILL NOW BE A BETTER MAN

### THOUGHT OF THE DAY

*You can be the man God intended you to be.*
*However, you must start being that man today.*

### THE COACH'S CORNER

OK, now what? Hopefully in the past forty days you have made some serious decisions that will influence your daily walk with Jesus. Hopefully, with God's help, you have also changed some of your behaviors as you endeavor to be more like Christ. The reality is simple: you are the exact same guy you were forty days ago, but by now you are looking to live more consistently In The Zone—God's Zone! Will the world see you differently? What is there for you to do now? Do you keep studying God's Word and His desires for you, or do you simply go back to the way you were forty days ago? This is only the beginning; it is up to you to write your ending.

God's secret is revealed in the gospel, which tells us that He sent Jesus Christ to earth. Jesus desires for every man and woman to repent in order to live an abundant life. In the Bible Jesus says, "I have come that they may have life, and that they may have it more abundantly" (John 10:10). This means a changed life, one that is holy, and one that is committed. We must be altered from men who are caught up in living a life "full of sin" to men who want and seek righteousness. When we are living the life of the Spirit instead of the desires of the world, abundant life begins.

## YOUR HOPE IS IN CHRIST—NOT IN A BETTER, MORE MORAL YOU.

The things Jesus offers cannot be given to us without our being trustworthy and seeking and knowing Him. Jesus says, "But seek first the kingdom of God and His righteousness, and all these things shall be added to you" (Matthew 6:33). Why? Because it is in Jesus "in whom are hidden all the treasures of wisdom and knowledge" (Colossians 2:3). But it is still kept a secret from those who deny God's way and offer people another way.

If you could create the ideal godly man, what would distinguish him? Would it be his elevated outward morality as an upstanding citizen, or would it be a man humbled by God's grace who struggles internally with the daily challenge of dethroning his own ego while simultaneously begging the Holy Spirit to take over? Now is the time for you to see just how much you can live with an exchanged life. Your hope is in Christ—not in a better, more moral you.

Why do you need to keep going? You can change the world. Yes, you can! Just remember the impact that such a small number of ordinary men had about two thousand years ago. They thought they were just regular guys, and God taught us that regular guys are who He uses most often to change the world.

## THE GAME PLAN

The Bible wants you to be a new creation in Christ, not simply a modification of the old you. God wants you to:

- Be ready with an answer when people see change in you—1 Peter 3:15: "But sanctify the Lord God in your hearts, and always be ready to give a defense to everyone who asks you a reason for the hope that is in you, with meekness and fear."
- Train yourself spiritually—1 Timothy 4:7–8: "But reject profane and old wives' fables, and exercise yourself toward godliness. For bodily exercise profits a little, but godliness is profitable for all things, having promise of the life that now is and of that which is to come."
- Get together with the guys on a regular basis; it's not only fun, it is biblical—Hebrews 10:25: "Not forsaking the assembling of ourselves together, as is the manner of some, but exhorting one another, and so much the more as you see the Day approaching."
- Make a prayer list and pray to God constantly—Philippians 4:6: "Be anxious for nothing, but in everything by prayer and supplication, with thanksgiving, let your requests be made known to God."

## PLAYMAKERS

Most of us have been up late at night watching television and clicked upon one of the channels selling products. Over the past few years, this way of purchasing has taken over the country, and now there are many stations that sell products by using the television. Many of you have probably either purchased something from them, or someone in your family has.

While most people have heard of the Home Shopping Network, the genius behind it is much lesser known. Bud Paxson is known as a direct-marketing guru, and many give him credit for reshaping the way America shops. Today, the Home Shopping Network is alive and well and counts millions of people as their customers.

Bud traveled a great deal when he was running this international business, sometimes even being gone for weeks at a time. In a single year, he traveled for over 250 days. While many men are forced to make these difficult choices, it certainly can't be recommended for improving relationship within our families. As one might expect, the constant traveling took a toll on both Bud and his wife. Knowing that he had been gone too much, Bud made a special effort one year to be home in time for the family to celebrate a great Christmas. During the festive holiday, Bud's wife announced to him that she was leaving him for another man. Bud was devastated, and so was the family.

Prior to Christmas that year, the family had made plans to spend the New Year's holiday in Las Vegas. As expected, Bud was in no mood to go on a vacation, but his children insisted. So he decided to go as it might get his mind off of his life for a few days. They flew to Nevada to enjoy the New Year and some needed family bonding and healing time. The children could see how broken he was and were insistent in finding something funny to do while in Vegas that would brighten the day and possibly help their dad deal with his loss. Bud remembers being present for the activities but not really being there.

After the activities on the first night, all the kids went to their own rooms and Bud found himself all alone for the first time. "I was absolutely and completely bankrupt," he says. "Yes, I was a millionaire, but my success was worthless."[1] He walked the floor, stared out the window, and continually played back the conversation a hundred times that his wife had with him at Christmas. It was over, and although he had almost everything in the world he needed, he was alone.

Like many men before him, as he was sitting in his quiet lonely room he thought about God and wondered if He could help. He looked around the room, and in the nightstand he found a Bible left there by the Gideon organization. He was unsure where to begin, so he searched the book looking for something to read that just might help him in his darkest moment. As he read, searched, and prayed, Bud started feeling some peace, so he closed the Bible and called it a night.

Adjusting to a life without his wife, a life of being alone, was consuming for him. However, he turned his life over to Christ, and although it didn't happen overnight, he finally found happiness again. He remarried, sold Home Shopping Network, and started PAX-TV, one of America's most watched family entertainment networks. His decision to give his life over to God in that hotel room in Las Vegas turned his life around.

Bud once said, "A business principle God has taught me is if you ask Him to lead you in serving Him with your business, job, or career, you'll be successful beyond your wildest dreams. But to do this, you must devote your capital, your profits, your resources, and your time to a cause that has been given to you by God. Then look out because God will help you so you can devote even more of your capital, profit, and time to His purposes."[2]

It often sounds so simple for someone to turn his life over to God, and everything goes his way. Frankly, there are also many stories of men who turned their lives over to God and then began to have problems they never had before. But someone else besides Jesus becomes more active in our lives when we give our hearts to Him. Satan hates it when we turn our lives over to God, and often he comes after us with vengeance. Be prepared. If you aren't doing anything for the Lord, Satan has no need to trouble with you.

## TIME OUT

1. What man on earth do you admire the most?
2. What do you want people to notice that is different about you?
3. Are you really ready to change your life?

## TODAY'S ASSIGNMENT

Enjoy your fresh start. Find something to carry with you that will remind you of the commitments you have made these past few weeks. May God bless your journey, and may you live life In The Zone because every man matters!

## HOME-FIELD ADVANTAGE

*Praises and concerns you want to bring before God*

_____

_____

_____

_____

_____

# DISCUSSION QUESTIONS BY WEEK

## WEEK ONE

### DAY 1

1. What problem are you grappling with today that you need to turn over to God?
2. Ask your wife who she sees as your first responder when you are in trouble.
3. Describe a time in your life when your relationship with God has been more about Him pursuing you than you pursuing Him.

### DAY 2

1. What time each day could you commit to consistently spend with the Lord?
2. How can you help protect your spouse's quiet time from the day-to-day grind of life?
3. Where is your favorite place to meet God?

## DAY 3

1. What impresses you most about the respect Coach Wooden shows for his wife?
2. What are some ways you can show honor to your wife?
3. Of all the numbers attached to Coach Wooden's life, what impresses you the most?

## DAY 4

1. If you were a pro athlete, what one lifestyle temptation would be most difficult for you?
2. What would your spouse say is your most obvious disconnect between your walk and your talk as it applies to your children?
3. What occasion do you most regret when you failed to walk the talk?

## DAY 5

1. Outside your family, who would be your closest friends?
2. Who would your wife say is the friend who helps you become more faithful to God?
3. Which friend of yours is the best role model for your children? Why?

## DAY 6

1. Would most people you work with know that you are a Christian?
2. Which, if any, of your coworkers would your wife suggest as potential partners in ministry for you?
3. What is the most difficult part of your job in regard to living out who you are as a man of God?

## DAY 7

1. What gifts do you believe God will use in your future to honor Him?
2. What is your spouse's biggest concern regarding your family and the future?
3. Is it difficult to believe that God truly has a plan for your life?

## IF YOU DESIRE ADDITIONAL QUESTIONS FOR WEEK ONE

1. What was the most difficult part of starting a daily study?
2. Which of the concepts that you read and studied about this week do you consider most difficult in living life In The Zone?
3. Which day this week did you find the reading to be most directly related to you?
4. As you consider your future, what do you feel God is calling you to change?
5. Describe a time in your life when you truly felt as though you were living life In The Zone.
6. Which friend may you engage as a prayer partner through the remainder of this study?
7. Who do you know at work that appears to be spiritually strong, who you can seek wisdom from as you study God's Word?

## WEEK TWO

## DAY 8

1. Have you had a time when you felt tempted to cheat on your wife and family?

2. Are there places you visit, shows you watch, or Internet sites you visit that tempt you?

3. Is something going on in your life right now that you know is wrong but you are having a hard time dealing with?

## Day 9

1. Remember the last time you truly worked hard at making your marriage more interesting and fun. What did you do?

2. What would your wife identify as the single thing most missing from your marriage?

3. Identify a couple you know who seems to have a marriage that is alive and well, with aspects you would like to replicate. What do you admire most about them?

## Day 10

1. On a scale of 1 to 10, how would you classify your sex life with your spouse?

2. Ask your wife the same question as well.

3. Is there anything you can do that could strengthen your sex life with your spouse? If so, what?

## Day 11

1. What tasks do you know that your wife hates that you can take off of her plate?

2. Ask your wife to help you identify how you can best create a real dream team at home.

3. Identify things you both dislike to do in your home, and then determine how to share the responsibilities to still get the job done.

## DAY 12

1. What does your wife do that seems to get under your skin? In your best of moments, how do you look past it?
2. Ask your wife to identify which criticisms of her, made by you, hurt her the most.
3. How can you adjust your attitude so you don't consistently find fault with your wife?

## DAY 13

1. What is the most frustrating aspect of having in-laws?
2. What boundaries would be most appropriate that you can set with your family to protect your wife?
3. Is there something you can do today that would improve your relationship with your in-laws?

## DAY 14

1. What does unconditional love mean to you? Who in your life shows you unconditional love?
2. Ask your wife what unconditional love means to her. How can you show it more?
3. What do you do that makes you difficult to be loved unconditionally?

## IF YOU DESIRE ADDITIONAL QUESTIONS
## FOR WEEK TWO

1. What makes most men have affairs today?
2. What things do you and your wife do to try and keep your marriage alive?
3. Has having children negatively affected your sex life? How?
4. What ways have you heard other men use to build up their wives?

5. What is the one thing your wife does that drives you crazy?
6. Do you have a friend today that you know is being unfaithful to his wife? Why?
7. What can you do to help your wife grow in Christ?

# WEEK THREE

## DAY 15

1. What has been the easiest behavior boundary to set for your children?
2. What has been the most difficult time boundary to set for your children?
3. Whoever said there are no do-overs in life never held the position of a dad. What do you need to do to make your relationship right with one of your children whom you have wronged?

## DAY 16

1. If you were to be able to listen in on your own funeral, what do you believe you would hear said by those in attendance, especially your kids?
2. What kind of man would your coworkers describe you as being?
3. Would you be happy if you knew that your kids would all grow up with your morals and values? If not, what changes would you like to see them exhibit?

## DAY 17

1. What are your "hot buttons" that seem to always cause you to lose control?
2. How do your coworkers see you deal with difficulties at work?

3. Would you be happy if you knew that your kids would all grow up with your style of resolving conflicts?

## DAY 18

1. What changes need to be made in your home to make it a dwelling fit for a visit by Christ?
2. Whose home have you visited, either recently or as a child, where you could feel the love of Christ?
3. Would your friends at church be surprised at what goes on in your home?

## DAY 19

1. Describe a time your children saw you stumble.
2. If you were to die tomorrow, what would your children remember most about the way you lived your life?
3. When you are at a sporting event, what example do you leave?

## DAY 20

1. How would your children describe your involvement in their lives?
2. How would your wife describe your involvement in the lives of your children?
3. What is keeping you from spending the time you want with your family?

## DAY 21

1. What things are you hiding from your family?
2. What can you do to start communicating more effectively with your family?
3. What aspects about your personal life do you keep hidden from your family?

## IF YOU DESIRE ADDITIONAL QUESTIONS FOR WEEK THREE

1. What is the number one thing you feel that you must protect your family from?
2. How would your children describe you to their friends?
3. Do you often bring home problems from work that make you hard to live with?
4. Would Jesus feel comfortable visiting your home? What would trouble Him?
5. What have your kids seen you do that was embarrassing for you?
6. If tomorrow you found you had a free day off, how would you spend it?
7. Do you find it hard to be honest with your family about money?

## WEEK FOUR

### DAY 22

1. Who do you consider your closest friend, other than your spouse or a family member?
2. Ask your wife if she thinks you need to find a godly best friend.
3. Identify three men who, after deep reflection and prayer, you know you should try to avoid.

### DAY 23

1. Would your associates and friends consider you a gossiper?
2. When was the last time you said something you should not have repeated and you found yourself in a bind?

3. Do you want to be seen as someone who can and will keep the confidence of others?

## DAY 24

1. Do you find it difficult to hold your friends accountable if they are doing something you know is wrong?
2. Ask your wife to hold you accountable to one thing you want to change about yourself. What will that one thing be?
3. Do you like it when someone holds you accountable, or are you defensive?

## DAY 25

1. Would you consider yourself a good listener?
2. Would your wife and children say that you are a good listener?
3. Which of Coach Bryant's listening techniques do you most need to implement?

## DAY 26

1. What groups do you belong to that are targeted at making you a better man?
2. Ask your wife to provide you with a list of men whom she believes would be real accountability partners for you.
3. Do you really desire to have someone who knows your secrets?

## DAY 27

1. Do you know a friend who is committing adultery with someone?
2. Do you know a friend who is committing adultery with his job?

3. Would you accept someone who challenged you in confidence because they thought you were sliding in your faith?

## DAY 28

1. If someone followed you this week, would he be shocked at where you took him?
2. Ask your wife what things you are involved in that she doesn't think are helping you to become a better man.
3. Have you been somewhere in the past month that you hope no one will find out about?

## IF YOU DESIRE ADDITIONAL QUESTIONS FOR WEEK FOUR

1. How would you describe your best friend to God?
2. Has there been a time you had a friend divulge the confidence you placed in him?
3. Do you have friends you study the Bible with? If not, would you enjoy doing so?
4. What is the most difficult thing for you to do when someone wants you to listen?
5. Describe what your ideal friend would be like.
6. Do you have a close friend? What things do you do together?
7. What can you do to bring men closer to God that your friends would find intriguing?

## WEEK FIVE

## DAY 29

1. Why do you believe God has placed you in your current position?

2. Do you discuss your work struggles with your wife?
3. What would your coworkers know of Jesus if they simply observed you each day?

## DAY 30

1. Is there a part of your life that you feel as though you have wasted?
2. Today is a great day for a fresh start. What change will you make to use a talent God has given you that you have not yet used to the fullest?
3. Do you waste time that you could use for growing the kingdom? What can you eliminate that will free you up to do more for God?

## DAY 31

1. What captures more of your time outside of work than anything else?
2. Would your wife say you live a fairly balanced life?
3. What would you do with two extra hours of time each afternoon?

## DAY 32

1. Do you worry about bills and money?
2. What is your greatest fear in this life?
3. If you truly believe that God will provide, how much time are you wasting worrying about money?

## DAY 33

1. Is money a major driver for you?
2. Are you and your family in a battle to keep up with the "Joneses"?

3. If you were truly financially sound, what would you do differently each day?

## Day 34

1. Do you ever get the urge to get even when you have been wronged?
2. Would your wife say you forgive and forget, or remember and seek revenge?
3. Can you give "a wrong doing" up to God and move on?

## Day 35

1. Is pride something you have to deal with in your life?
2. Would your wife characterize you as prideful or humble in your dealings with her?
3. How important is image to you?

## If you desire additional questions for Week Five

1. How would you describe your coworkers at your current job?
2. Are you in your "perfect job"? If not, what would that job look like?
3. What is your top priority at work? Is your current job open to you sharing your faith?
4. How would your life change if you truly lived as though God would provide for you and your family?
5. How much money would it take for you and your family to be happy?
6. How do you feel when you have been personally wronged? Do you want to make it right?

7. Does your job embrace your desire to be a true family man? What have you found that works to help the balance between work and family?

# WEEK SIX

## DAY 36

1. Is it hard for you to tell others about your relationship with Jesus?
2. Have you ever had the opportunity of sharing Jesus with someone and having them accept Christ?
3. What person do you know who is seeking a relationship with Christ, yet you have felt uncomfortable discussing it with them?

## DAY 37

1. If you could change your profession, what would you want to be?
2. Are you currently in a profession that lets you use your God-given talents and gifts?
3. What would God say to you regarding what you have done with your life thus far?

## DAY 38

1. Are you a worrier?
2. What is your greatest worry at this time? Write it down.
3. Do most of your worries come true?

## DAY 39

1. What tasks do you have to do that you are dreading?
2. Does your wife ever have any idea when you are stressed to the max?

3. What do you feel God calling you to do for Him today?

## Day 40

1. What man on earth do you admire the most?
2. What do you want people to notice that is different about you?
3. Are you really ready to change your life?

## If you desire additional questions for Week Six

1. What is the most difficult thing for you, in regard to telling others about Jesus?
2. What things would you most like to change about yourself?
3. We all have things we have done in our past that we are not proud of. Is there someone in particular you need to ask forgiveness from, or give forgiveness to?
4. When you die, what would you most like to have Jesus say to you about your life?
5. What is different about you today versus forty days ago?
6. What type of small group do you want to be a part of as you move forward?
7. What has God done in your life over the past forty days?

# IN THE ZONE MINISTRIES

I n The Zone is a cutting-edge new national event for Christian men. This is a place for men to be men, where you will hear from peers on life, work, leadership, relationships, faith, and understanding women. Connecting with today's man is not easy. Who better to tackle these issues than a core group of regular guys who will invite thousands of men into a giant conversation about the challenges they face, including balancing family and work, leading spiritually, relationships, integrity, and more? This fast-paced, engaging format will give you the opportunity to learn from the experience of men like yourself while laughing and interacting with the core speakers. There will be special celebrity interviews, music, videos, Q & A, and more. You are invited to come and hang with the guys while discussing the things today's men deal with, all in the context of a fun and motivating environment.

In The Zone focuses on the four topics central to the life of today's man:

- Balance, Making It All Fit
- Life at Work

- Differences between Men and Women
- Fatherhood

Just come as you are and be ready to laugh and learn from the experiences of men like yourself. Bring your men's group, your buddies, your next-door neighbor, your father, or yourself. Just don't miss it! Notebooks not required. Just come as you are and be ready to laugh and learn.

The thrill of victory, the agony of defeat . . . this drama is lived out daily in sporting arenas all across the U.S.—and in the everyday lives of America's men. In The Zone, a groundbreaking live event is coming to arenas across the nation in 2010, meeting men at the intersection of faith and sports—the common language that most men speak.

Taking a cue from popular talk shows such as *Pardon the Interruption*, *NFL Primetime*, *College Football GameDay*, and *NBA Halftime*, In The Zone produces a forum for anything-goes conversation—a peppery mix of sports talk, strong opinions, and fast-paced media mixed with ESPN-style music. Creating an atmosphere much like a locker room with coaches laying out the big game plan, In The Zone engages men in a spiritual discussion of life and faith. It's real guys discussing real issues, such as: How do you climb the ladder of success while staying connected to your wife, kids, and faith?

"Our years of research have identified a generation of men that are living in the most stress-infused culture in history," says Dr. Joe Pettigrew, a highly distinguished leadership consultant and leading authority on the issues affecting the world's senior executives. Pettigrew founded In The Zone with Kyle Rote Jr., the first American-born player ever to win a major professional soccer league scoring championship, three-time ABC-TV *SuperStars* champion, and founder of Athletic Resource Management, Inc., a successful sports agency that represents over fifty pro athletes and several dozen coaches.

"Men are being pulled apart by their desire to succeed in their career, provide for their family, meet the needs of their spouse, and be a 'Super Dad' for their kids," continues Pettigrew. "When they add faith to their already packed schedules, church tends to seem more of an obligation than a possible solution to their unbalanced life. At our events, participants will hear how well-known sports personalities and some of the world's most successful businessmen struggle on a daily basis with the same issues that regular guys do. These speakers will also share with participants the ways they have found to live according to their personal calling."

You'll connect with new ideas for finding balance in your life, working hard for your employer without checking your spiritual convictions at the door, making your marriage work against all odds, and becoming the father you want to be. In The Zone is a fast-paced Saturday morning or Friday evening event combining live teaching with top speakers, honest guy-talk about life's challenges, outrageous sports clips, multimedia scrambles, and some serious belly laughs. Created by men who are stoked about life and pumped about getting together with a few thousand like-minded men of faith, it's anything but a business-as-usual men's conference.

Each In The Zone event welcomes a live visit from a top Fortune 500 business executive, as well as well-known sports celebrities such as Gene Stallings, Pat Dye, ESPN's Chris Mortensen, the NBA's Allan Houston, Oklahoma's Bob Stoops, ESPN's Lee Corso, ESPN's Mike Gottfried, CBS's Spencer Tillman, and Dallas Cowboy Bill Bates, among many others.

"When I first heard about In The Zone, I wasn't sure I wanted to hear more—commitments scare me," says Mortensen, ESPN NFL senior analyst featured on *Sunday NFL Countdown*, *Monday Night Countdown*, and *SportsCenter*. "I'm glad I got over the fear—there's no question God quickened my heart and opened my eyes to a great opportunity. We get to talk about our real Christian life in a sports-like setting? That's too good to be true for a guy like me. Sign me up."

"Having your priorities in the right order is key to living a successful life," notes T. Michael Glenn, executive vice president, Market Development and Corporate Communications, FedEx Corporation. "In The Zone is designed to help you deal with the challenges we face on a daily basis while not compromising those priorities."

"In the Zone is a relevant, fast-paced, life-changing forum that I am proud to be a part of," says Gottfried, ESPN college football analyst, former NCAA football coach, and Team Focus founder. "Being a college football coach and an ESPN analyst, I love talking sports. However, one of the most important things in my life is my Christian walk. In the Zone allows me to talk both!"

The four-hour In The Zone events take a four-quarter approach and utilize the connecting thread of sports, hunting, fishing, and cars to transition to the more weighty issues that most men face today—work, women, fatherhood, and how to balance it all. The events aim to help redefine men's perceptions of success, manhood, and what it means to live out their faith in today's society. In The Zone is about uncovering the best practices, not perfect practices, in regards to finding solutions to the most common struggles of manhood—an opportunity for men of all walks of life to identify and discuss the challenges and difficulties they all face, with humorous video segments tying everything together.

With its unique approach, In The Zone is already gaining the attention and support of respected organizations such as the Fellowship of Christian Athletes, Promise Keepers, and Men's Fraternity. "Men's Fraternity is thrilled to partner with In the Zone, a revolutionary concept in men's events designed to meet the needs of real guys," says Men's Fraternity president Rick Caldwell. "We're so excited that In the Zone not only provides a quality one-day experience but also has a strategic plan of action for guys after the event."

For more information about this revolutionary new men's event or to find a location near you, visit www.inthezone.org. For information on bringing this event to your city, contact info@inthezone.org or call 901-831-1101.

# FEATURED PLAYMAKERS

| | | |
|---|---|---|
| Charles Barkley | TNT Basketball Commentator | 28 |
| Bill Bates | Former Player, Dallas Cowboys | 225 |
| Coach Bill Belichick | Coach, New England Patriots | 171 |
| Larry Bird | Former Player, Boston Celtics | 191 |
| Coach Bobby Bowden | Head Coach, Florida State University | 64 |
| James Brown | CBS Sports Featured Analyst | 13 |
| Coach Bear Bryant | Former Coach, University of Alabama | 184 |
| Truett Cathy | Chairman, Chick-fil-A Corporation | 265 |
| Lee Corso | ESPN *College GameDay* | 278 |
| John Daly | PGA Professional Golfer | 220 |
| Coach Tony Dungy | NBC Sports NFL Analyst | 4 |
| Clay Dyer | Professional Bass Fisherman | 148 |
| J. D. Gibbs | President, Gibbs Racing | 125 |
| Mike Glenn | President, Federal Express Services | 41 |
| Coach Mike Gottfried | ESPN Football Analyst | 205 |
| A. C. Green | Former Player, Los Angeles Lakers | 74 |
| David Green | President, Hobby Lobby | 235 |
| Orel Hershiser | ESPN Baseball Analyst | 42 |
| Coach Mike Holmgren | Head Coach, Seattle Seahawks | 79 |
| Coach Lou Holtz | ESPN Featured Football Analyst | 177 |

| | | |
|---|---|---|
| Allan Houston | Former Player, New York Knicks | 30 |
| Wayne Huizenga Jr. | President, Huizenga Corporation | 242 |
| Magic Johnson | Former Player, Los Angeles Lakers | 191 |
| Bobby Jones | PGA Professional Golfer | 280 |
| Michael Jordan | Former Player, Chicago Bulls | 141 |
| Coach Bobby Knight | ESPN Basketball Analyst | 127 |
| Coach Tom Landry | Dallas Cowboys Legendary Coach | 272 |
| Ken Lay | Former CEO, Enron | 156 |
| Coach Vince Lombardi | Former Coach, Green Bay Packers | 134 |
| Archie Manning | Former Player, New Orleans Saints | 121 |
| Chris Mortensen | ESPN NFL Insider | 87 |
| Joe Namath | Former Player, New York Jets | 73 |
| Coach Tom Osborne | Former Coach, University of Nebraska | 228 |
| Terrell Owens | Player, Buffalo Bills | 257 |
| Bud Paxson | President, ION-TV | 294 |
| Scottie Pippen | Former Player, Chicago Bulls | 142 |
| Coach Mark Richt | Head Coach, University of Georgia | 213 |
| Mark Sanford | Governor of South Carolina | 57 |
| Arnold Schwarzenegger | Governor of California | 94 |
| O. J. Simpson | Former Player, Buffalo Bills | 249 |
| Ron Springs | Former Player, Dallas Cowboys | 36 |
| Coach Gene Stallings | Former NFL and NCAA Head Coach | 219 |
| Roger Staubach | Former Player, Dallas Cowboys | 49, 72 |
| Les Steckel | President, Fellowship of Christian Athletes | 263 |
| Bob Stoops | Head Coach, University of Oklahoma | 145 |
| Joe Theismann | Former Player, Washington Redskins | 114 |
| Michael Vick | Player, NFL | 162 |
| Everson Walls | Former Player, Dallas Cowboys | 36 |
| Kurt Warner | Player, Arizona Cardinals | 103 |
| Bob Weiland | Mr. Inspiration (Vietnam Veteran) | 287 |
| Reggie White | Former Player, Green Bay Packers | 198 |
| Coach John Wooden | Former Coach, UCLA | 21 |

# NOTES

## How Do You Know when You Are "Living Life in the Zone"?

### DAY 1: WITH GOD

1. Rick Stroud and Tony Dungy, "I got to live a dream," *St. Petersburg Times*, January 2009.
2. Super Bowl Breakfast, Detroit Marriott Renaissance Center, February 2006.
3. Ibid.

### DAY 2: WITH YOURSELF

1. Andrew Knox and David Sisson, "James Brown: What It Means to Have Success," *The 700 Club*.
2. Jbjamesbrown.com/news, "James Brown: The Sporting Life," 2009.
3. Andrew Knox and David Sisson, "James Brown: What It Means to Have Success," *The 700 Club*.

### DAY 3: WITH YOUR WIFE

1. James Dobson, *Straight Talk to Men* (Nashville: Thomas Nelson, 2000).

2. Joseph Pettigrew, private meeting with Coach Wooden, Los Angeles, California, October 2007.

## DAY 4: WITH YOUR CHILDREN

1. J. Oswald Sanders, *Spiritual Leadership (Commitment to Spiritual Growth)* (Chicago: Moody Publishers, 1994).
2. Leigh Montville, "He's Everywhere," *Sports Illustrated*, May 1993.
3. Les Payne, Les Payne blog, "Charles Barkley Is Forced to Model a Different Role," March 2009.
4. Gary Sailes, "Cultural Icons or Social Anomalies?" *USA Today*, September 2001.

## DAY 6: AT WORK

1. Mike Glenn, live interview with In The Zone, Desoto Civic Center, Southaven, Mississippi, August 2007.
2. Orel Hershiser, *All I Ever Wanted* (Wheaton, IL: Good News Publishers, 2002).

## DAY 7: REGARDING YOUR FUTURE

1. Janis Kelly, "Pain Compounds Depressions' Impact for Retired NFL Players," *NeuroPsychiatry Reviews*, June 2007.
2. Heisman Trophy, ESPN Heisman Show, 1981.
3. Ken Biggs, Lone Star Internet, Inc., "Famous Texans, Roger Staubach," 1989.
4. *Retail Traffic*, "Pass Completed, Question and Answers with Roger Staubach," July 2007.
5. Les Steckel, live interview with In The Zone, Desoto Civic Center, Southaven, Mississippi, August 2007.

# FINDING THE ZONE IN YOUR RELATIONSHIP WITH YOUR WIFE

## DAY 8: GOING AGAINST THE TREND

1. Billy Graham, funeral of his wife, North Carolina, June 2007.
2. Mary Ann Chastain, "S.C. governor says he 'crossed lines' with

handful of women," *USA Today*, June 30, 2009.

## DAY 9: LOVING AN IMPERFECT WOMAN

1. Charlie Barnes, "Ann Bowden—The first lady of football," *Florida State Times*, 1996.
2. Ibid.
3. Bobby Bowden, speech given at Bellevue Baptist Church, Memphis, Tennessee, 2002.
4. Cal Fussman, "What I've Learned: Bobby Bowden," *Esquire* magazine, September 2001.
5. ESPN College Football Awards, NCFAA Contributions to College Football Award, May 2009.
6. Ibid.
7. Ibid.

## DAY 10: IMPROVING YOUR SEX LIFE

1. "Making Marriage Last," American Academy of Matrimonial Lawyers, 2009.
2. Neil Best, "In '75, Roger Staubach liked sex as much as Joe Namath," *Newsday*, July 2009.
3. Allen Salkin, "The Quarterbacks' Sideline Play," *The New York Times*, January 2008.

## DAY 11: BUILDING UP YOUR SPOUSE

1. Rick Starr, "Seahawks notebook: Silence is golden," *Tribune-Review*, February 2006.
2. Sheri and Bob Stritof, "Mike and Kathy Holmgren Quotes about Marriage," *Decision* magazine, October 1997.
3. Alice Maggin, *World News Tonight*, "Super Bowl Family Worlds Apart on Big Day," February 2006.
4. Sheri and Bob Stritof, "Mike and Kathy Holmgren Quotes about Marriage," *Decision* magazine, October 1997.
5. Packer Plus Online, Mike and Kathy Holmgren Marriage Profile, December 1997.

## DAY 12: DON'T LOOK FOR TROUBLE

1. Chris Mortensen, live interview with In The Zone, Mabee Center, Tulsa, Oklahoma, August 2007.

## DAY 13: DEALING WITH UNEXPECTED BAGGAGE

1. Reuters.com, "Maria Shriver: Schwarzenegger Won't Be President," November 2004.
2. Ibid.
3. Michelle Tauber, "Arnold: He's Back," *People* magazine, Vol. 60, July 2003.

## DAY 14: I'VE GOT HER BACK

1. Spencer Tillman, live interview with In The Zone, 700 Studios, Nashville, Tennessee, June 2007.
2. Karen Crouse, "Warner's Family Accepts Bounty and Burden of Football," *The New York Times*, January 2009.
3. Craig Harris, "This time, Warner's wife is ready for the limelight," *The Arizona Republic*, January 2009.
4. ESPN.com, "Warner's wife says trade welcomed," September 2003.
5. Ron Cook, "To be curt, Mrs. Warner should clam up," *Pittsburg Post-Gazette*, October 2003.
6. Ivette Ricco, "The Kurt and Brenda Show," FemmeFan.com, July 2009.
7. Joe Buck, Fox MLB, "Warner Leaving St. Louis," live TV Show, St. Louis, Missouri, 2005.
8. Ron Cook, "To be curt, Mrs. Warner should clam up," *Pittsburg Post-Gazette*, October 2003.
9. Ivette Ricco, "The Kurt and Brenda Show," FemmeFan.com, July 2009.

# FINDING THE ZONE IN YOUR RELATIONSHIP WITH YOUR CHILDREN

## DAY 15: AN IMPORTANT ROLE PLAYED BY TODAY'S MAN

1. Fatherhood: The Changing Family Photo, The Gallup Poll, April 9, 2002.

2. Minnie Lagrone, "Mr. Henderson's Wife Halts Sign Plan," *Deadwood News*, Panola Watchman. August 1957.

3. Leonard Shapiro, "The Hit That Changed a Career," *The Washington Post*, November 2005.

## DAY 16: DEFINING YOUR LEGACY

1. Jon Saraceno, "Tennessee's Pacman Jones is the poster child for a needed crackdown in the NFL," *USA Today*, February 2007.

## DAY 17: DEALING WITH DAILY STRESS

1. Richard Justice, "Bob Knight Misbehaves. Watch Texas Tech pretend it didn't happen," SportsJustice blog, November 2006.

## DAY 18: HOME IMPROVEMENT

1. David Maraniss, *When Pride Still Mattered: A Life of Vince Lombardi* (New York: Touchstone Books, 2000).

2. Vince Lombardi, sign in his restaurant in Appleton, Wisconsin, 2009.

3. Ibid.

## DAY 20: MAKING TIME FOR WHAT IS IMPORTANT

1. Robert Stephens, "Miracle Worker," *Boating Life*, 2009.

2. Mike Bolton, "Pro Bass Angler has no legs and just one arm, but he has 'a heart, a soul and a mind,'" *The Birmingham News*, April 2008.

3. Ibid.

4. Clarence Dyer, personal interview, Memphis, August 2009.

5. Ibid.

6. Clay Dyer, speech in Memphis, Tennessee, August 2009.

7. Clay Dyer, promotional video for use with In The Zone, August 2007.

8. Robert Stephens, "Miracle Worker," *Boating Life*, 2009.

9. Mike Bolton, "Pro Bass Angler has no legs and just one arm, but he has 'a heart, a soul and a mind,'" *The Birmingham News*, April 2008.

10. Clarence Dyer, personal interview, Memphis, August 2009.

11. Clay Dyer, speech in Memphis, Tennessee, August 2009.

12. Clay Dyer, promotional video for use with In The Zone, August 2007.

## DAY 21: WHAT YOU SEE IS WHAT YOU GET

1. Mike Tolson, "Ken Lay praised and defended by family and friends," *Houston Chronicle*, July 2006.
2. Ibid.
3. Ibid.

# FINDING THE ZONE IN YOUR RELATIONSHIPS WITH YOUR FRIENDS

## DAY 22: MAKING WISE CHOICES

1. Jim Daly, "Friends in Low Places," Focus on the Family online, May 2009.

## DAY 26: IRON SHARPENS IRON

1. KDKA Channel 2, Pittsburgh, "Bird and Magic: A Rivalry Born at March Madness," March 2009.
2. Baxter Holmes, "Bird, Magic still linked," Boston.com. June 2008.
3. Ibid.

## DAY 27: CALLING MEN UP

1. Maxwell Quinn, "Larger than Life: Remembrance of Reggie White," TheGoal.com, 2004.
2. Ibid.

# FINDING THE ZONE IN YOUR RELATIONSHIPS AT WORK

## DAY 30: LIVING UP TO YOUR POTENTIAL

1. Pat Dye, live interview with In The Zone, Birmingham, Alabama, August 2007.
2. Press conference in Memphis, Tennessee, St. Jude Classic, 2009.
3. "A Life Out of Control," FoxSports.com, May 2006.
4. Rich Tosches, "What does Daly do for an encore?" YahooSports. com, December 2008.
5. Ibid.

6. Mulligan Stu, "John Daly: 'Shoeless and Shirtless with a Cigarette in His Mouth,'" WaggleRoom.com, April 2008.
7. Jason Cohen, "John Daly Provides 4000th Use of 'Fat, Drunk, and Stupid,'" Cantstopthebleeding.com, October 2008.
8. John Wooden, private interview in Los Angeles, California, April 2006.

## DAY 31: DETERMINING YOUR PRIORITIES

1. Bill Bates, live interview with In The Zone, Knoxville, Tennessee, August 2007.

## DAY 32: LETTING GO OF YOUR WANTS AND NEEDS

1. Hobby Lobby Board of Directors Commitment Statement, Oklahoma City, Oklahoma, 2009.
2. Jennifer Palmer, "Families come first at Hobby Lobby," NewsOK.com.
3. Ibid.
4. Don Wildmon, American Family Association, Hobby Lobby CEO, David Green, 2009.
5. Randy Ellis, "Hobby Lobby hikes pay rate," NewsOK.com, April 2009.
6. Oklahoma Baptist University online, "Hobby Lobby Exec Shares Story of Legacy, Ministry," November 2008.
7. "David Green: Hobby Lobby Stores. (Entrepreneur of the Year)," *Dallas Business Journal*, June 27, 1997.

## DAY 33: WHEN IS ENOUGH REALLY ENOUGH?

1. Leaderpoint Consulting Services, Memphis, Tennessee, January 2004.
2. Kevin Miller, "Success in the Ownership of Professional Sports Teams," SecretsOfSuccess.com, 2009.
3. Kevin Miller, "An Underwater Insight," SecretsOfSuccess.com, 2009.
4. Paul Kingsbury, "Call of the Wild Blue Marlin," *Vanderbilt University Alumni News*, 2006.
5. Interview of Wayne Huizenga Jr. by Paul Seebeck, FaithInTheWorkplace.com.

### Day 34: Getting Even Is Up to God

1. Fox News, "Attorney: O. J. Simpson Verdict Was 'Just Payback,'" October 2008.
2. KCAL, Las Vegas, Entertainment News, "This Was Just Payback Simpson Lawyer Says," October 2008.
3. Ken Ritter, Associated Press, "Reaction to O. J. Simpson verdict," October 2008.
4. Ken Ritter, ABC News, "Emotions Connect Old OJ Acquittal, New Conviction," October 2008.

### Day 35: Climbing the Ladder of Success

1. Keith Bulluck, KeithBulluck.com, 2009.
2. Dennis Rodman, *Bad as I Wanna Be* (New York: Dell Publishing, 1997).
3. www.mahalo.com/muhammad-ali.
4. Terrell Owens, *Catch This! Going Deep with the NFL's Sharpest Weapon* (New York: Simon and Schuster, 2004).

## Finding the Zone as You Look to the Future

### Day 36: Fighting the Battle

1. Les Steckel, live interview with In The Zone, Southhaven, Mississippi, August 2007.
2. Truett Cathy, TruettCathy.com, "Chick-fil-A's Closed-on-Sunday Policy," 2009.
3. Lori Arnold, "When it comes to biblical business values, Truett Cathey is no chicken," Christian Examiner Online, January 2007.
4. Truett Cathy, TruettCathy.com, "Chick-fil-A's Closed-on-Sunday Policy," 2009.
5. TruettCathy.com.

### Day 37: Becoming the New You

1. Bart Barnes, "Tom Landry," *The Washington Post*, 1999.
2. Ibid.

## Day 38: No Worries

1. Lee Corso, live interview with In The Zone, Southaven, Mississippi, August 2007.
2. Bob Harig, "Several PGA Tour Players leery of accidental positives with new doping policy," ESPN.com, June 2008.
3. Leaderpoint Consulting, interview with Larry Papasan, August 2005.

## Day 39: An Audience of One

1. Donna Miles, "Former Football Star Pat Tillman Killed in Afghanistan," MilitaryConnection.com, April 2004.
2. Fox News, "On Independence Day, Honor Heroes Who Fought for Freedom," June 30, 2006.
3. Bob Weiland, live interview with In The Zone, Memphis, Tennessee, April 2006.

## Day 40: The Day Has Finally Come

1. Kevin Miller, "The Shocking Cost of Success," SecretsOfSuccess.com, 1986.
2. Dan Stuecher, "No Brief Candle," Christianstandard.com.